STRIDING OUT

*Aspects of Contemporary
and New Dance in Britain*

Stephanie Jordan

DANCE BOOKS
Cecil Court   London

First published in 1992 by Dance Books Ltd, 9 Cecil Court,
London WC2N 4EZ.

© 1992 Stephanie Jordan

A CIP catalogue record for this book is available from the British Library.

ISBN 1 85273 033 1 (cloth)
ISBN 1 85273 032 3 (paper)

Designed by Sanjoy Roy.
Printed in Great Britain by The Bath Press

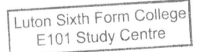

Contents

Illustrations

Acknowledgements

Without the cooperation of many choreographers and of their colleagues in dance, this book would not have been possible. To all of them, first, my thanks, for their patience in interview, their generosity in lending me personal archive material and their most helpful comments on draft chapters.

I am also grateful to the staff who helped me with my archive searches at Chisenhale Dance Space, the Laban Centre, The Place and Rambert Dance Company, and especially to Judith Chapman and Kate King at the National Resource Centre for Dance, University of Surrey.

My thanks to Angela Kane for working on an expanded version of her Richard Alston chronology, which first appeared in *Dance Research* (1989), also to Peter Brinson, Theresa Buckland, Susan Davies and Jane Nicholas for offering expert advice on sections of the text. Special appreciation to my friend and colleague at the University of Surrey, Joan White, for finding time to read the full text. Her knowledge, clear perceptions and encouragement were invaluable.

Finally, my thanks to my husband Howard Friend for sustaining me throughout the lengthy research and writing process and for his astuteness as a colleague in the art of watching and writing about dance.

Some of the ideas developed here first appeared in articles and reviews in the following publications: *Ballet Review*, *Dance and Dancers*, *Dance Research*, *Dance Theatre Journal*, *The Dancing Times*, *The Listener* and *The New Statesman*.

Stephanie Jordan
Autumn 1990

*For my
mother and father*

Introduction

In the mid-1960s, expressionist contemporary dance, derived from the model of Martha Graham and subscribing to the notion of dance as an expression of emotional condition, became the first established alternative to ballet in Britain. The turning point was the transformation of Ballet Rambert from a classical into a contemporary dance company in 1966 and the founding of the London School of Contemporary Dance (LSCD) and London Contemporary Dance Theatre (LCDT) in 1966 and 1967 respectively. In certain respects, the two companies created a movement: for the first time, there was a professionalism in contemporary dance that stood comparison with that of ballet, with wide public and critical recognition of a new genre of dance. The importance of this development cannot be overstated. However, looked at another way, the two companies provided a stronghold for an aesthetic that had existed, though quietly, in Britain for many years. Expressionist American and Central European modern dance traditions had reached Britain not long after their inception. (The original term 'modern dance' was changed to 'contemporary dance' in Britain in the mid-1960s[1]). There had been teachers working here from both these traditions of modern dance, and Kurt Jooss had based his company in Britain from 1934 to 1947. By the 1960s, numerous modern dance groups existed, albeit short-term and of an amateur or semi-professional nature. Perhaps ironically, the arrival at last of a strong professional representation also prompted an immediate reaction against the expressionist aesthetic, and the seeds, through the LSCD, of an alternative movement. It is this alternative movement that is the subject of this book.

In fact, the aesthetic embraced by Graham and her contemporaries was, even before the foundation of LCDT, being challenged in American modern dance, and, indeed, in the other arts internationally. So too were the physical training techniques that supported American modern dance, which, unlike those of ballet, had been devised specifically to support the style of an individual modern dance pioneer. The new generation of American choreographers no longer thought of dance as a statement about emotional and psychological conditions. There was a tendency towards ridding dance of emotional content, towards abstraction or a new political content, away from theatrical illusion and towards more informal presentations of the human body.

In Britain, clear indications of these American developments in dance were given with the visits of the Merce Cunningham Dance Company in 1964 and 1966. Post-Cunningham developments in dance were also glimpsed. In 1965, Yvonne Rainer appeared in a concert of pedestrian solos at the Commonwealth Institute, and in 1967 Twyla Tharp performed her *Re-moves* (1966) with Sara Rudner and Margaret Jenkins at the Royal College of Music, bouncing balls and smashing eggs; this was before Tharp became a proscenium choreographer.[2]

In our own dance tradition, there were no corresponding moves of note, in the absence of any form of modern dance having taken firm root. Then, in the early days of the LSCD, students emerged who were well-informed artistically (several already trained in another art form), and determined to explore the new aesthetic and political areas in dance terms. For these students, whatever they thought of their fundamental training in the Graham technique – one student, Diana Davies, a former fine arts lecturer, described it as excellent, but in spirit like 'a commando course for nuns'[3] – any hopes that they entertained of LCDT as a showcase for their artistic interests were dashed as soon as the regular company seasons began in 1969. Richard Alston, who joined the school in 1967 and became a major independent force there, recalls the disappointment as students realized the extent of the artistic divide: there were people

> individual enough to have searched out this rather smelly cat-ridden alley [Berners Place, the School's first home], and they all had a very clear idea of what they wanted. Because there was no company in existence ... everyone began to use their imaginations, and they all thought that something was going to be there which in the end wasn't. It was something else, it was what Bob [Robert Cohan, Artistic Director of LCDT] made, and the more concrete that became the more problems there were.[4]

Fergus Early, whose interests also lay in experimental dance forms and who, in 1976, became a founder of the X6 Dance Collective, has perceived that the problem lay in the company policy, its primary concern to 'create a dance style, an audience and indeed a respectability to rival those of ballet'.[5] Diana Davies noted the lack of 'alignment' between the 'underlying concepts' of choreography in general at this time and those of the other arts.[6]

This book does not attempt to be an overview or history of the alternative movement. It is a series of essays on selected organizations and choreographers. I admit to having been led by my interests in planning this book, but there is reason, too, behind my eventual strategy. It seemed important to start with a focus on what I call the first generation of alternative choreographers, whose creative careers began during the late 1960s and 1970s, and the institutions that supported their careers, before this period fades from memory. It also seemed important to make a detailed study of selected topics, rather than to fall into the trap of making false generalizations that can arise when overview histories are written before thorough groundwork has been carried out. Hence, several notable choreographers have not been given more than cursory mention.[7] Other contributions cry out for more discussion than I was able to give them.[8] The focus throughout the book, too, is on the dance itself; context is included, primarily as it informs our understanding of the dance that it allowed to happen. There is much more to be written about this period.

The 1970s was the decade in which British contemporary dance gradually established its own identity (or identities), independent of the American tradition. None too early, this was recognized by some New York critics when they saw Second Stride performing there in 1982. Deborah Jowitt, for instance, in *The Village Voice*, wrote 'What I've seen on visits to England and now here ... convinces me that youngish contemporary British choreographers are finally developing their own style – or styles – of "modern dance".'[9] It seems too that Britain nurtured some of the most vital contemporary dance activity in Europe during this period. However, in some quarters, strong links with American tradition were retained through this period. In the 1980s, a link with the continent of Europe became much more pronounced. A further point about the late 1960s and 1970s: more than we perhaps realize today, this period sowed the seeds of ideas about dance that were taken further in the 1980s.

Two main branches of work emerged during the late 1960s and 1970s as alternatives to work of an expressionist kind: a second more formalist phase of contemporary dance, and New Dance/post-modern dance. (Distinctions and overlaps between the meanings of the terms 'New Dance' and 'post-modern' dance are discussed in Chapter 3.) This book is concerned with both branches, because they have interconnected in many interesting ways, as well as maintaining separate identities. Indeed, a number of the choreographers discussed in this book have overlapped categories at some point in their careers.

It has been a fascinating task to clarify the connections and differences between these two threads of dance activity. In doing so, I have drawn upon the theory that has arisen from the continuing debate on post-modernism in relation to modernism. An outline of this debate is given here.

The term 'post-modernism' has acquired various meanings, different for different art forms. The question of what post-modernism means for dance, and consequently what and how much work can be covered by this term, remains open to debate. The question is complicated by the fact that the

3

theory of what constitutes modernism in dance has not yet been fully developed.[10] However, discussions of post-modernism in dance have tended to refer to modernism in terms of its meaning in architecture and the visual arts. Modernism here means a concern with abstraction. A movement that began in the latter half of the nineteenth century, it is about a gradually sharpening focus on the essential qualities of the art medium. Eventually, content arises only from the terms of the medium itself, external reference eliminated, or, as idealized by the American modernist art critic Clement Greenberg, 'content is to be dissolved so completely into form that the work of art or literature cannot be reduced in whole or in part to anything not itself'.[11] There is a parallel in British contemporary dance with the move away from expressionism to 'dance about dancing', to cooler, more abstract styles of choreography with increased emphasis on the languages and structures particular to dance. This is what I call 'second phase' contemporary dance. Even when exponents of this kind of work have embraced meaning and emotion, the formalist, medium-specific interest remains strong. The term 'modernist' is applied to this kind of work in this book.

The most widely held view is that the Judson Dance Theater in New York in the early 1960s was the beginning of a post-modern movement in dance. Yvonne Rainer started to use this term for dance at the time, and in a chronological sense, implying that, as a Judson member, she was of the generation after modern dance.[12] Sally Banes, author of the seminal book on post-modern dance in the USA, *Terpsichore in Sneakers* (1980 – a second edition with a new introduction came out in 1987),[13] confirmed that this Judson work was post-modern dance, a movement in opposition to modern dance. She has also explained her use of the term 'post-modern' as the one used by the dance practitioners themselves.[14]

The work in question, and its legacy extending into the 1970s, rigorously avoided conventional theatricality. It asked spectators to be aware of the context in which they perceive art, and of their attitudes adopted in seeing it; to look at any movement as dance, including pedestrian and found movement – there was a body of minimalist work; to be conscious of real space, real time, the workings or structures of a piece. Sometimes an idea was as important, or more so, than its physical manifestation. Many post-modern choreographers sought the detached stance of their spectator: analytical rather than drawn into the 'world' of the dance through kinaesthetic empathy, or through identifying with the passions of a character, as in much previous modern dance. Traditional hierarchical, climax/release structures, flowing or developmental progressions, gave way to structures with repetition and bold interruption, or the radical juxtaposition of diverse elements sparking against each other. After what she terms 'breakaway' post-modern dance, a period of broad experiment in the 1960s, Banes identifies a dominant phase of 'analytic' post-modern dance during the 1970s.[15]

Roger Copeland[16] puts the beginnings of post-modernism in dance earlier, to include Cunningham (who, for Banes, is somewhere between modern and post-modern dance[17]). Copeland's reason is that Cunningham was the first to take the crucial step of encouraging the spectator to be more detached and aware of making choices in the perception of work. Cunningham achieved this by rejecting the 'wholeness' of previous modern dance for a post-modern fragmentation. Following the principle that anything can follow, or happen next to anything else, he introduced radical dissociations within the dance, and between the dance, its music and design, some juxtapositions aleatorically determined. He also provided a multiplicity of possible centres of attention.

Both Banes and Copeland are aware of the problem of assembling the huge range of work that spans out from Judson into the 1980s under only one label. They recognize the difficulty that some of the early dance corresponds with what has often been seen as late modernist work in the other arts.[18] But they see that other work, and increasingly the dance of the 1980s, conforms to today's most broadly agreed notions of post-modernism across the arts.[19] Banes, for instance, characterizes analytic post-modern dance as essentially modernist in nature. But it is modernist not simply in the sense of displaying movement designs for their own sake; rather, it has a reflexive stress: 'that the work not merely be itself but that it be about being the kind of thing it is'.[20] In other words, the structures of a work and the spectator's self-conscious awareness of the process of perceiving these structures are thrust into the foreground. Banes then identifies the 1980s as the period of a 'rebirth of content'.[21] Yet she finds a coherence between the different phases, common processes and use of the technique of radical juxtaposition[22] and, returning to the practitioners' view, she maintains that the artists of the 1980s saw themselves sharing as well as extending the post-modern heritage of the previous generation.[23] The dance philosopher David Michael Levin, while agreeing with this notion of aesthetic coherence across the three decades, the 1960s to the 1980s, has proposed terminology to highlight the shift between two phases of post-modernism. The first phase is 'modernist' – concerned with 'a disclosure of the essence of the modern'; the second 'post-modernist' – concerned with 'a critical deconstruction of the essence still at work in the modernist'.[24]

Some writers now prefer to restrict the use of the term post-modern dance to work of the second phase. This deals with signs/symbols and their deconstruction, in other words, their use in such a way as to reveal their operation and to stress a fluid, open relationship between symbol and meaning. The influence of semiology and post-structuralism from the 1970s onwards contributed to this shift: the belief that there is no such thing as the essence of a work – all is cultural and conventional – and that the individual spectator/reader, not the author, holds the key to determining meanings from a 'text'. Thus, Susan Foster prefers to see post-modern dance statements as growing out of, and largely subsequent to, the Judson experimentation (her examples are the Grand Union, Meredith Monk and Twyla Tharp) and extending beyond Cunningham's liberation of the signifier (movement) from domination by the signified (meaning). Whereas Cunningham chose, with his aleatoric methods, to suppress this relationship between movement and meaning, post-modernists examine this relationship anew, taking the step of 'unmask[ing] human movement as a signifying practice' and, by corollary, unmasking the human body as a signifying presence.[25]

Foster's view bears a relation to characterizations of post-modernism by Umberto Eco[26] and Charles Jencks[27] for literature, the visual arts and architecture. Jencks, for instance, contrasts the 'semantic' focus of post-modernists, their renewed concern with symbolism and allusion, with what he calls the 'aesthetic' focus of modernists.[28] Both Jencks and Eco acknowledge at the same time the post-modernists' particular ironic or double-coded use of symbols. This double-coding draws attention to itself reflexively, to the very operation of symbol, in other words, to the 'unmasking' of the 'signifying practice', the process by which meaning is made.

Susan Manning sees post-modern dance as emerging around 1979–80, as a kind of dance that fails to fulfil either or both of her two conditions of modernism: the 'reflexive rationalization of movement', and the separate practices of modern dance and twentieth century ballet.[29] The problem of defining the borderline between modernism and post-modernism is further complicated by the fact that, according to some notions of post-modernism, examples of a post-modern attitude can be found earlier this century, for instance in the Dada movement.

This book does not attempt to continue the definitions debate, but it will relate British work to the ideas that have emerged and been theorized internationally since the 1960s. In terms of dance, the American debate is far too useful and important to be ignored, whether or not British artists have been consciously aware of it (many have not). But I have deliberately kept an open relationship to this debate. Sometimes I have found revealing a choreographer's volunteered self-assessment in relation to these categories, and the reasons for this assessment. In that case, it seemed important to record and discuss the choreographer's own viewpoint. Being a series of essays rather than an overview, the book does not attempt to establish what is essentially British about the dance that is discussed.

The book is organized in two parts. The first part is devoted to the organizations that were most influential to the development of alternative movements in dance in the late 1960s and 1970s: the Contemporary Dance Trust as an umbrella for the LSCD and a variety of professional dance activity at The Place (Chapter 1); Strider, the first alternative dance group to emerge from the LSCD (Chapter 2); X6 Dance Space, a major force behind the movement called New Dance as it was labelled in the late 1970s (Chapter 3); three festivals – ADMA, Dance at Dartington and Dance Umbrella – which, in their different ways, celebrated and supported the dance activity that had sprung up by the end of the 1970s (Chapter 4). Chapters 3 and 4 chart developments through into 1980, the year of the closure of the X6 Dance Space.

The second part is devoted to four choreographers whose careers began during this period: Richard Alston (Chapter 5), Siobhan Davies (Chapter 6), Rosemary Butcher (Chapter 7) and Ian Spink (Chapter 8). All four emerged from a background in expressionist contemporary dance (in the case of Spink, ballet as well), and remained key figures in dance through the 1980s. The careers of these four first-generation choreographers are followed through from their beginnings into the present, since it seemed logical to examine the full span of their work, following it through into their maturity.

Organizations and choreographers obviously call for different approaches. All the chapters contain history as well as analysis of work, but there is more detailed analysis of choreographers' works in Part 2. Different kinds of work have suggested different analytical approaches, according to whether they are abstract or narrative, contemporary or New Dance, modernist or post-modernist, in bias. The analytical discussions are intended to establish and illustrate the main stylistic characteristics of these four choreographers. Needless to say, much more can be said about individual works than there is space for here. Furthermore, in order to reach my level of generalization, I undertook a close examination of every work by these choreographers that I could find on record, and uncovered far more information than could be documented here. Nor is every work that these choreographers made necessarily discussed. Works are referred to insomuch as they illustrate a characteristic point about a choreographer's style, and it seemed sensible to concentrate on the works that I have found most interesting.

Appendices include supplementary lists of artists and groups, those involved in the institutions discussed in Part 1, and chronologies of works by Alston (researched by Angela Kane), Davies, Butcher and Spink. There is also a list of the full Strider repertory, and a sample of its touring schedule.

The lack of adequate documentation of the dances made in Britain during the 1970s has been a serious problem and has often determined the degree of detail in which work can be discussed. Dances made for LCDT and Ballet Rambert (re-named Rambert Dance Company in 1987) have fared reasonably well. Since the early 1970s, these dances have customarily been recorded on video in long shot for company records (dynamics and detail are much diminished) and some have been televised. Most other dances of the 1970s have been lost, neither videotaped, nor filmed nor notated; some were never even reviewed or written about in any form. With the much wider access to video in the 1980s, records of small company work were made more regularly. The four choreographers focused on in Part 2 were all generous in lending me personal video records of their dances.

I gained most of my sense of history and rescued other lost, important dances for description from personal interviews with choreographers and participants in the organizations discussed. A large number of very busy people were extremely generous with time and information, and their assessment, either recalled from the time when work was first shown or made in retrospect, has helped to determine what work should be singled out for discussion. Not surprisingly, I have had to deal with conflicting memories about what happened in a dance, when or where a work was premiered, and so on. Sometimes individuals would change their minds when I questioned them thoroughly, or for a second time. I also welcomed a range of views and opinions from those I interviewed. The result of assembling and interlacing many different viewpoints must, in the end, be my own responsibility, my own 'story', although, in discussing work and work situations with which I have had little or no direct contact, I have concentrated on bringing out the full range of opinion that exists. There are, of course, as many 'stories' as people involved in the subject matter of the book.

Other sources for the book were the archive material housed by companies, institutions and artists – there has been much digging into attics and cellars – publicity, programmes, choreographers' working notes, photographs and contemporary critical writings. I have brought in my own observations as a sporadic viewer of dance in Britain in the late 1970s, and a regular dance viewer and critic in the 1980s.

The intention is that each chapter could be read as a separate essay, a form that is well suited to the purposes of study at school level or in higher education as well as to a more general readership. However, it is also possible to trace issues across chapters. The reader will find recurring references to modernism and post-modernism, and to relationships and differences between movement styles. References to funding and to how it affects an artist's work also pass through the book. It is crucial to point out how choreographers and dancers outside the large companies have had to battle to survive, increasingly so in the 1980s, however widely their work might have been praised; many have stopped working or gone abroad since the 1970s. Some of these issues are presented in the manner of problems raised rather than fully debated.

Artists can also be traced across chapters: Richard Alston and Jacky Lansley, for instance, feature strongly in several chapters. The chapter devoted to Alston in Part 2 concentrates on his post-Strider work, while also mentioning his early pieces for LCDT. Dartington College and the American Mary Fulkerson's work there are almost a leitmotif through the book (Chapters 2–5, 7–8). They could easily have merited a chapter of their own, but my chosen method was to indicate the breadth of their influence and support as, at various times during the 1970s, the British dance scene 'discovered' Fulkerson's work.

Perhaps, too, the essays might have a broader application, suggesting ways of looking at other dance institutions and other work. Finally, I hope that, without it being at all forced, something of the smell of the period discussed comes across ... or, more accurately, of what this writer, in 1990, now perceives as our recent dance history.

PART 1

CHAPTER 1

The Contemporary Dance Trust
Centre of the ferment

The background to a counter-movement

Within only a short time of the philanthropist Robin Howard's setting up the Contemporary Ballet Trust and founding of the London School of Contemporary Dance (LSCD), a centre for artistic experiment had been established. Far more than a school for training dancers and dance teachers in Graham-based work, the LSCD spawned its own creative counter-movement and became the centre for choreographic experiment in Britain. This chapter is a discussion of radical developments at the School during its early period of creative enterprise, from the official opening of the School in 1966 to the mid-1970s. It is also a discussion of the context of this work at the School, other experimental activity of Contemporary Ballet Trust (in 1970, renamed Contemporary Dance Trust) and of choreographers closely associated with the Trust. This was a period of rapid growth and change at the School: 1966, its establishment in one studio in Berners Place; 1967, the beginning of the full-time course (11 students); 1969, the move to The Place premises, which included The Place Theatre; then the large increase in student numbers, by 1970–71, 63 full-time students, 32 first-years (the Inner London Education Authority now recognized the School, and most local education authorities were prepared to offer discretionary grants); until the mid-1970s, when the number of full-time students stabilized at about 120.

Several reasons may be given why the School became so important as a centre for experiment, but undoubtedly the most crucial was the inclusion of dance composition as a regular part of the full-time course from its inception – classes from the first week of the first term[1] – and plentiful workshop opportunities for students to show pieces. Composition classes and workshops were not quite new to Britain. Balletmakers Limited, an organization begun in 1963 by Teresa Early, had run weekly composition classes and workshops for student and professional choreographers (the LSCD joined forces with Balletmakers for two early workshops in 1967). At Ballet Rambert in 1967, Norman Morrice instituted the *Collaborations* programme to give young choreographers an opportunity to present work, in conjunction with design students from the Central School of Art and

Design. However, in a school for dance training, structures that enabled creative work to take place were a radical departure. For the first time too, there was a sustained course for would-be choreographers. The School workshop series developed from occasional performances to a steady stream of presentations at The Place in the 1970s.

It is important to realize that, as well as having a passion for Graham's work, Howard took a great interest in experimental dance. He had brought Twyla Tharp over in 1967, in the days before she was a 'proscenium' choreographer. In the late 1980s, reflecting upon the development of the School, he reiterated his belief in cultivating opposition, that one of the purposes of such an institution was to stir up counter-movements, in order that a 'dialogue' between differing schools of thought could be kept going.[2] Howard invited Patricia Hutchinson to be first Principal of the School in 1967, an important decision: students remember her as a woman who responded openly and with flexibility to their needs and creative ambitions.[3]

Students at the LSCD during this period recall the energy of those early years, with a new institution in its formative stages, the feeling in the 1970s like a hang-over from the excitement of the 1960s,[4] and the persisting enthusiasm to overturn convention, to make an artistic virtue of plunging into the unknown and attempting the extraordinary. This was the period that stressed personal liberation and the period of an oppositional underground or counter-culture. There was a heightened political consciousness amongst many of the student generation after the momentous events of 1968 and, around 1970, the women's movement got under way. The more radical students at The Place were not only dancing, they were considering the politics of the structures that surrounded their dancing and viewing the institution within which they worked with a critical eye. The women were sensing a new power and freedom to make and present work.[5]

This was also the period of art school power. Art schools encouraged experiment with style and, well beyond the confines of a fine art tradition, stimulated developments in pop music, for instance, or forms that broke down boundaries between the arts: events, happenings, light shows and mixed-media events. A new generation of fine artists was extending the definition of sculpture to include event structures or environments, or moving out of the isolation of their studios to confront their audiences in performance: like Stuart Brisley, Bruce McLean, and Gilbert and George.[6] Some were interested in collaborating with the creative dancers at the LSCD. After all, dance responded to the call for physical immediacy and liberation that was so much in the air at the time. The alternative 'fringe' theatre movement, which had rapidly gained momentum in Britain after 1968, likewise offered scope for interaction. As well as political and feminist theatre groups, the movement included groups that were working in the genre that was gradually becoming known as performance art: The People Show, Welfare State and John Bull Puncture Repair Kit. Turning their backs on the tradition of literary theatre, suspicious of verbal communication and the culture that it structured and described, many fringe groups discovered a new potency in physical and visual approaches.

The LSCD attracted a very mixed group of students in those days, some with classical training, many without any dance background (after all, hardly anyone had had a modern dance training by then) – 'sculptors, accountants, mechanical engineers and gymnasts'.[7] Some were mature, experienced in another art form, and as interested in making work as in learning to dance. Richard Alston and Siobhan Davies were amongst the first of the full-time students, enrolled on the 1967–70 course. Both were straight from art school, like many LSCD students at the time, and they were perhaps the most interesting products of the Berners Place days. Alston immediately established himself as an independent choreographer, ignoring Graham models. But there were others instrumental in forming connections between dance and the new sculptural environments: Alan Beattie and Primavera Boman (daughter of the Austrian modern dance pioneer Hilde Holger).

Later, at The Place, a steady wave of rebels arrived, many interested in alternative theatre and performance art, and women among them who became involved with the women's movement. Perhaps the most powerful and creatively energetic were those who formed the dance group Strider for its first season. Sally Potter, who is now a distinguished film-maker, was already experienced in film and performance art when she came to LSCD (she was a student there 1971–74), and had been a member of Group Events, a co-operative directed by Tom Osborn. Jacky Lansley (1971–72, 1973–74) had danced with The Royal Ballet since 1967. Diana Davies (1970–73) had trained in fine art and lectured at Edgehill College of Education in Liverpool. Dennis Greenwood (1970–73), a Canadian who had come to England in the late 1960s, had trained in ballet and a range of modern dance techniques and was ready to move into areas of experiment.

Contexts of curriculum, performances and visiting artists

Throughout this period, Graham-based work formed the core of the dance technique teaching at the LSCD, and the basic composition training method was the one devised by Louis Horst, Graham's long-time musical director. Howard brought over two American teachers to strengthen these inputs, Jane Dudley in 1970 as Director of Graham Studies, and Nina Fonaroff in 1972 to establish a new Department of Choreography. However, student experience was much broader than this might suggest.

Michael Finnissy, the composer, who had arrived as an accompanist in 1966, was soon teaching a course in the use of music for dance, and ultimately promoting the more independent kind of relationship between music and dance that John Cage and Merce Cunningham had pioneered. Later, when he made it clear to his students that the Graham/Horst relationships were not of interest to him, they listened. He was of the same generation, still a student himself at the Royal College of Music when he taught in the LSCD's early days.[8] From the start, Finnissy also identified himself with all that was innovatory at the School. Many of the alternative choreographers collaborated with him before he left in 1974. Then, for the academic year 1971–72, Alston taught a composition course that drew on a post-Cunningham aesthetic, radically different from the Horst-based courses.[9]

Fergus Early, ex-Royal Ballet, ex-Ballet for All, and a member of Ballet-makers in the 1960s, came to the School to teach ballet in 1971. Soon, he was teaching not only ballet, but also folk dance and composition. The works for students that he directed with Michael Finnissy were notable for the manner in which performers crossed disciplines, singing, speaking and playing instruments as well as dancing: *Circle, Chorus, and Formal Act* (1973), based on the English folk play, and *Incidents from the Life of Jesus of Nazareth* (1974). Early worked outside the Graham mode, and had a way of engaging the least experienced students comfortably within a performance.[10]

Also in 1971, John Roche arrived as visiting drama tutor. The students had asked for drama experience, and he introduced a breadth of techniques from the new fringe theatre movement: improvisation, wordplay, trust games, circus skills, and the notion of street theatre production.[11] In 1972, for instance, he took charge of open air student performances at Euston Station and various Camden and Islington squares. The dance administrator Dick Matchett, who worked at The Place during this period, remembers Roche as a seminal liberating force at the time, like Early, especially important for the less technically inclined students: 'With John, everyone could have a go.'[12]

Teachers and choreographers visiting from overseas introduced a further range of ideas. There were teachers from the Graham school and company, but there were also some who had come from Cunningham's area of thinking: Cunningham himself, Viola Farber and Margaret Jenkins all taught briefly at Berners Place, and later Rosalind Newman taught at The Place. Alwin Nikolais and Murray Louis offered lecture-demonstrations at The Place. Nikolais-trained Carolyn Carlson and Robert Solomon taught techniques and composition. Twyla Tharp held open rehearsals at The Place during her season at the Round House (1974). In 1972, Meredith Monk incorporated 30 students in a performance of *Juice*.

In the 1960s, the course structures at the School were still relatively unformed and flexible. As Alston has noted, 'you had to find your own centre

16

in those days',[13] and there were those, like Alston himself, who thrived on the opportunity to do so. At The Place in the early 1970s, while the course itself was becoming more stable, there were still many occasions when students could set up their own independent working groups and rehearsal situations, and now excellent facilities for presenting work, a 260-seat theatre setting with lighting sometimes available and a large cast of performers at hand if a student wished to employ them. A typical programme might contain ten or so short pieces by different students. Most important, all kinds of work could be shown. The rebels who collected at The Place in those days grasped their opportunities readily. For some too, there were occasions to make work for the small touring groups run from the Contemporary Dance Trust: Alston took out a group (1970–71), touring a lecture-demonstration of Graham technique and a programme of short works by himself that had nothing to do with Graham.[14] Later, the X group and the School's Lecture Demonstration Group took some student work into the repertory.

Such was the energy and spirit at the time that many students were also active in forging their own links with fine artists, musicians and theatre groups, setting up their own performances, touring, pursuing their initiatives outside the School programme. Pat Hutchinson encouraged these external activities.[15] As an example, Davies, Potter and Greenwood performed with Strider during the period that they were at the School (1972–73, primarily during holidays) and also found time to establish with Lansley their own performance group Rescue Principle (in 1972). The same year, briefly, Davies performed with the John Bull Puncture Repair Kit at De Lantaren in Rotterdam, a group that she was later to work with more extensively. Sally Potter continued making films.

As for the professional activity at The Place Theatre, it could not have been a more lively adjunct to the student life. It was Howard's policy to promote experimental activity in all the arts there, and the theatre rapidly became one of London's liveliest arts centres, an international centre and locally, Camden's arts centre, one amongst a group of such organizations that sprang up in the late 1960s. Publicity containing a list of what had been put on in the theatre between 1969 and 1971 demonstrates well the range of work shown quite apart from dance (see Appendix 1): the list bears the slogan 'Barriers between the arts are disappearing. The Place is where they meet.' Art exhibitions were also housed in the building. Most visiting artists who presented dance at The Place in the early 1970s represented alternatives to Graham-based thinking: from New York, Dan Wagoner and Dancers, Meredith Monk, James Cunningham and the Acme Dance Company, Z'eva Cohen, Elaine Summers' Experimental Intermedia Foundation and, from Holland, Pauline de Groot.

Howard offered rehearsal space to outside performance groups and musicians. Based at The Place were, for instance, the Pierrot Players (later The

17

Fires of London) directed by Peter Maxwell Davies and Harrison Birtwistle, and Geoff Moore's mixed-media group Moving Being, until it moved to its present headquarters in Cardiff in 1972. The film-maker Ken Russell and visual artist/film-maker Derek Jarman were regular visitors;[16] Barry Flanagan, the sculptor, attended Carolyn Carlson's classes.[17]

Creative developments: examples of the new radicalism

Now, turning to a discussion of the creative developments associated with the Trust and School during this period, the focus is on work that moved most boldly away from the Graham impulse. It should not be forgotten that a good deal of work did not attempt to do this, and some work modified the Graham movement style without being conceptually exploratory. Topics have been selected to illustrate a range of experiment, and some lead towards the later developments of the 1970s that are discussed in this book.

If there is one thing that linked these various projects, it is that they engaged audiences in a 'cooler', more objective manner than expressionist work.[18] Many choreographers also reflected what Susan Sontag, the eminent American critic, called 'a more open way of looking at the world',[19] embracing, for instance, pop, everyday, as well as 'high' culture. There was in dance, as elsewhere at the time, a new democratic model for art, the old hierarchies of taste being broken down to reveal a 'long front of culture'.[20]

Sculpture and dance: some new connections

It is significant that the establishment of the School coincided with the period in British sculpture of expansion into performance and mixed-media. Students came to the School who had an artistic foot, so to speak, in both camps, sculpture and dance. Primavera Boman had trained in sculpture at St Martin's School of Art, the most influential school for sculpture during the 1960s, and also as a dancer at the Graham School and LSCD.[21] Alan Beattie, a scientist, had studied art, design and dance, and later enrolled at the LSCD. He had also taught courses and workshops integrating different media at a variety of art schools – Hornsey, Hammersmith, Central, St Martin's. These students who crossed the disciplines of sculpture and dance proclaimed their intention to bring dance into contact with the current temper in the other arts. The note for the *5 Situations* programme at the Mermaid Theatre, devised and directed by Boman in 1968,[22] pointed out that they were

> trying to use dance aesthetics which are relevant to other contemporary arts, especially those of sculpture and music. They all want to get away from the proscenium arch with all its Victorian connotations ...

18

Boman created her own sculptural environment and Beattie used a neon-light structure devised by Stuart Brisley, Beattie's colleague at Hornsey, and Bill Culbert. They were joined in a third sculpture piece by Peter Dockley, who had been a student in the Hornsey mixed-media workshops.[23]

These pieces presented the multiplicity of focus and independence of sound and movement that are very reminiscent in concept of John Cage, especially as they were intended for an audience free to move within or around the event. Thus, the work appealed 'to an audience's structuring facility'.[24] Sometimes the dancers were encouraged to collaborate, even to improvise in performance, and the environment had an effect on the movement choices.[25]

It is crucial here to consider the influence of Cage and Cunningham on visual artists in Britain at this time, arising from the Cunningham company visits of 1964 and 1966, before they had any major impact on the dance world. Supporting their ideas were the art exhibitions of Jasper Johns, Robert Rauschenberg and the American minimalists, and also the retrospective exhibition of the Dada artist Duchamp in 1966. British artists likewise became interested in finding alternatives to subjective creative methods.[26]

Clearly, Beattie, Boman and Dockley considered themselves out of sympathy with an expressionist aesthetic. They used the professional look and training of their dancers, stretched legs and feet,[27] but rather than allowing the dancers to give the appearance of expressing anything about themselves, they emphasized structure, conceptual concerns and functional behaviour:

The 5 *Situations* programme note stressed the dancers' 'kinaesthetics and visual impact: how they function in a given environment – a polyrhythm, for instance, going against the dancer's rhythm – how they are activated by light or objects. Every movement has a function other than the emotional expression of the dancer, and visual and sound structure therefore become very important.'

Primavera Boman: '[The dancers] must become aware of the fact that they are defining space, defining an idea rather than defining themselves. It is not a direct communication between the dancer and the audience but the communication of an idea by the dancer to the audience.'[28]

Peter Dockley (discussing how he made 4 *Sounds 4 Structures*): '[The dancers needed to be clear] that they were demonstrating space and that they were not expressing anything on an emotional level, that they were being purely functional.'[29]

As well as their multiple focus, the *5 Situations* environment pieces resulted in a patchwork of fragmented action, non-developmental and non-climactic structures. They were also cool examinations of form, reflexive in manner, inviting the viewer to adopt a self-consciously analytical stance and making an issue of revealing their own structures. Beattie's collaboration with Brisley and Culbert, *Four Dancers, Four Colours and Three Dimensions* used a programmed neon light sequence and set of dance responses to the lights, each dancer responding to a particular colour and with the dynamic quality of movement that the colour suggested to Beattie.[30] Boman's *Momentum in Quadrille* had the dancers manipulating rectangular blocks 'like a baby giant's construction kit':[31] these were a series of blocks hinged together and akin to the fundamental repetitive structures that American minimalist sculptors favoured.[32] Dockley's *4 Sounds 4 Structures* used four dancers, each in a different structure and investigating the particular characteristics of the structure – moving along its lines, complementing the planes suggested – in a sound environment that used the spatial dimensions of the performance area.[33]

Significantly, the *5 Situations* programme was first put on at a sculpture forum at St Martin's School (when Peter Dockley showed *Pyramid*, a part of *4 Sounds 4 Structures*). On both that occasion and at the Mermaid Theatre, the dancers used were from the LSCD, and the programme stated the Contemporary Ballet Trust's interest in helping such projects.

When Howard opened The Place in 1969, he declared his firm interest in this kind of work by inviting several artists to take part in two programmes of his own devising, *Explorations*,[34] his statement as to the kind of experimental ambience that he wanted there. The programmes took the audience through the various studios as well as into the theatre.[35] Some events were in the spirit of happenings. Beattie offered *Green Maze*, 'an environment for dancers and pedestrians', which involved three dancers moving 'in green mood' amongst a forest of green plastic sheets.[36] Dockley staged *Event with Air Structure and Costumes* with dancers emerging from a plastic air bubble and tubes connecting the participants and the bubble. Peter Logan, who had staged a mechanical ballet at the New Art Centre in Chelsea earlier that year now extended this idea into *Corridor and a Room for Robin Howard*. Spectators walked down a long corridor brushing past various moving objects, including a huge coiled spring from which emerged coloured streamers, and a naked leg protruding through an apparently solid wall. Then they entered a room where a mechanical ballet took place. Derek Jarman, then a visual artist interested in designing for dance (e.g. for Ashton's *Jazz Calendar*, 1968), provided a 'guest costume' for the piece, 'constructivist, Bauhaus-influenced, with a mask,' Logan recalls.[37] Alston provided the leg. Some South American artists were also invited to show work in these programmes: Leopoldo Maler incorporated sixteen dancers

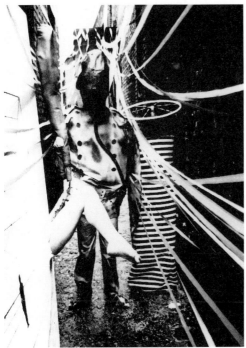

1. ABOVE: *Momentum in Quadrille* (1968), choreography and sculpture by Primavera Boman, danced by Clare Duncan, Xenia Hribar, Anitra Shore and Franca Telesio. (Photograph: John Dougill)

2. LEFT: Outdoor rehearsal for the 'Corridor' section of Peter Logan's event *Corridor and a Room for Robin Howard* (1969). In the foreground, Richard Alston's leg extending from Oskar Schlemmer's treatise on space (on canvas); in the background, Derek Jarman in ribbon costume. (Photograph: Roy Round)

3. *Signs* (Moving Being, 1971), by Geoff Moore. The performers are John Cassady, Kiki Obermer, George O'Brien and Pamela Moore. (Photograph: Geoff Howard)

4. *Busy Line* (1973), choreographed by Diana Davies for a student workshop at The Place. Dancers, from left to right: Belinda Neave, Diana Davies, Dennis Greenwood, Peter Bent, Mikloth Bond.

and two fork-lift trucks in his *'X' It*, and a group called Taller de Montevideo moving in a white environment, performed *Chronus III*.

It is doubtful that experiments such as these were in any way directly responsible for taking choreography *per se* into new territory. Critics allege that the movement content was unsophisticated. But it seems that choreographic complexity was never a prime intention for such work. Instead, these events suggested alternative conceptual directions for dance and opened up a new context in which dance could take place.

Geoff Moore and Moving Being

Geoff Moore, director of Moving Being, was another to come from an art school background and also showed work in the *Explorations* programmes, but his idea of crossing disciplines led to far more of a media mixture than in most of the sculpture events.[38] Moore never had any formal training as a dancer or choreographer, but was interested in the physical intensity of dance and the fact that dance, he says, 'is open enough to bear allusions'.[39]

In its first year, 1968–69, Moving Being showed several pure dance pieces, after which Robin Howard gave Moore a home at The Place, where he fell straightaway into a dance culture, to be reviewed primarily by dance critics. However, the pure dance pieces soon disappeared. Moore's main style was collage, using film, slides, speech, recorded text, music and sound effects, as well as dance, and his work bristled with multiple reference, often to contemporary issues. Moore spoke of a truly 'multi-dimensional language . . . very necessary,' he maintained, 'to our way of life now . . . people are needing to develop a sort of cubist compound way of living.'[40] Accordingly, when he founded Moving Being, he took in performers and collaborators from diverse sources: Berners Place, The Royal Ballet School, the Laban Art of Movement Centre, Dartington College, as well as the drama and art schools. Moving Being made an immediate impression, so much so that in May 1969, the year after its inception, John Percival could proclaim that 'almost single-handed, Geoff Moore has provided British ballet with its avant-garde'.[41] The group was soon firmly established as a touring ensemble with regular London seasons, and Moore's output remained prolific. Then, in 1970, the American theatre director and writer Charles Marowitz reported on Moving Being in the New York *The Village Voice* as 'the most committed attempt in England to refertilize the archaic notions of dance'.[42]

Moore was another artist to exploit Cage's principle of a 'multiplicity of centers' or 'things going on simultaneously',[43] but he applied it to work with meaning. Performing pieces in this style, Moving Being was similar to many fringe theatre and performance art groups at the time. Moore says that his early work celebrated the principle of radical juxtaposition for its own sake, according to the uncontrolled spirit of some sixties happenings.[44] He wanted to discover the effects of collage by simply 'letting things happen'. He cites the full-length *Accumulator* (1969) as one of the last examples of such open collage, involving as it did a hotch-potch of texts, films and slides projected on to three screens, music, dance, references from everyday life, high and pop culture. There were some bizarre visual puns on aspects of contemporary living, such as a television playing within a huge mouth, or a microphone seen inside a vast ear. However, Moore later used the discoveries from experiments such as this to arrive at far more controlled structures. There was now no arbitrary proliferation of information: images and ideas were carefully selected to have some kind of meaningful resonance or, as Marowitz encouraged, to 'collide ... in interesting smash-ups with one another'.[45] At the same time, by presenting material in an unfamiliar context, he sought to put a new slant upon it.

The early *Trio* (1969) is an example of more controlled juxtaposition. With the connecting idea of dreams, two men and a woman in a white hospital gown are seen in a V-shape of light spots, in stillness, minimal or slow motion, changing light spots and shifting into new choreographed arrangements during blackouts. Accompanied by jangling interruptions from Bach,[46] these blackouts are punctuation devices or jolting mechanisms as if to renew the attention, like the formal alienation devices that Moore observed in the work of Bertolt Brecht and of Jean-Luc Godard, a central influence. There are three texts: a passage from the opening sequence of Marcel Proust's *Remembrance of Things Past* (1913–27), when the author recounts his dreams as a child when his great uncle terrified him pulling his curls, or his erotic dreams of women; an account of the dream state by the cult psychologist R.D. Laing, from his *The Politics of Experience* (1967); and a doctor's physiological account of sleeping patterns, rapid eye-movements, nocturnal erections and increased heart-rate. At the end of the piece, Bob Dylan's *Talking World War III Blues* is introduced, in the manner of a signing device.

Looking at meanings, the woman could be seen as fighting her childhood past, as the author's mistress, or as a victim, merely a figment of man's imagination. She acquires meaning from the texts. At one point she is suspended upside down between the two men, an image of being compromised.[47] It seems that she gradually establishes her own independent identity as the dance movement develops, and, perhaps as a force of liberation, the movement becomes, according to the critic John Percival, less an illustration, more a visual counterpoint to the text.[48]

Placed in such a context, the texts took on a new significance, and the movement was open to being coloured, to acquiring meaning. But another issue is the unspecific nature of the statement, verified today by Moore and his collaborators,[49] the many half-formed meanings, the ambiguities. Although the elements of the work have been chosen carefully to encourage rich resonance, this is the kind of work in which spectators are invited to play with many possible readings and to enjoy using their own experience. Even then, nothing seems secure, fully firmed up. The uncertainties proposed between signifier and what is signified seem to have parallels with the uncertainties proposed by much new art of the 1980s.

Likewise *Signs* (1971) provokes questions about dreams and consciousness, madness and sanity, without attempting to give any answers. Like a cultural cabaret or visual LP, it brings together the characters of Alice, Hamlet, Ophelia and Artaud, four historical or fictional figures connected by crises of identity or madness. We hear texts associated with these characters and with many others, such as Plato, Shakespeare, Germaine Greer, R.D. Laing. We hear the music of Joni Mitchell and The Incredible String Band as well as of Elisabeth Lutyens.[50] The familiar is broken open in a new context; references act upon each other in mutual illumination. A quartet of dancers presents the 'other', inner and physical aspects of these archetypes.

It seems that, in his exploration of lively meaning resonance and ambiguity, Moore was a pioneer of a style that became commonplace years later (see p. 206).[51] His mixed-media techniques too were pioneering in production involving dance: they presage developments in dance theatre in the 1980s. However, critics noted the excitement and vitality of his productions as a whole rather than of his choreography. Moore's own inclinations, it happens, were to shift gradually more and more towards text-based drama and away from dance during the 1970s.

Henrietta Lyons

One of the earliest choreographers to find an alternative to the Graham/Cohan model was Henrietta Lyons. Lyons and her sister Jacqueline, also a choreographer, were two of the students sponsored by Howard to study in New York (1965–66) and they had experience and interests well beyond that which was happening at the Graham studio. It was Cunningham's abstraction and humour and the liveliness of his experiment that made most sense to Lyons ever since she had first glimpsed his company in London in 1964.[52] As much as the Graham work was emotional and theatrical in tone, she hankered for pure movement and abstraction.

In the late 1960s, while taking classes and teaching at the LSCD, Lyons collected a steady group of dancers around her, including the young student Sue Davies, and made a series of short dances. Some were 'expressive' pieces to pop music, but those that stood out at the time[53] were abstract, spare in construction, with more than a passing reference to Cunningham's vocabulary, and dressed simply in leotards and tights: *Song 7* (1969, music by Finnissy), for instance, in the making of which Cunningham-style chance procedures were used.

25

Richard Alston: choreographer and teacher

Alston, while he was well aware of the developments in mixed media at this time, recalls that his first inspiration to find an alternative to Graham came from the work of Lyons,[54] significantly a choreographic rather than mixed-media source. When Lyons eventually stopped making work regularly for her group, Alston continued, using several of her dancers. For Alston, another turning point was Viola Farber's arrival at Berners Place to teach a three-week course, in April 1969. At that time, recently a member of the Cunningham company (she left in 1965), Farber taught a class much along the lines of Cunningham, and Alston, who had had problems making his body meet the demands of Graham technique, realized that there was another way to move, much more suited to a 'long, skinny, puny physique'. After that course, he says, he never took another Graham class.

As a would-be choreographer, Alston also read avidly about Cunningham's work. His key sources were the *Dance Perspectives* issue 'Time to Walk in Space' (1968),[55] which contains many photographs as well as articles by Edwin Denby, Arlene Croce and Carolyn Brown, and John Cage's essay 'Grace and Clarity' (1944),[56] which espouses the virtues of rhythmic clarity and vitality in dance. Alston had seen the Cunningham company in London in 1966, as an art student, but not with any understanding of the work. By the time he saw him in the south of France in 1970, he was convinced that Cunningham held the key to the way forward.

At this point, with the exception of Cunningham, Alston's conceptual challenges came only from the other arts, and especially, stemming from his previous training, the visual arts. Like Lyons, he reacted against the emotion and high drama of the Graham/Cohan aesthetic, turning to abstract sculpture and painting and particularly to work that displayed the utmost formal simplicity.[57] If he sought imagery, it was not of the expressionist kind, but from the everyday sensibility of pop art, or of the precursors of pop, Robert Rauschenberg and Jasper Johns.

His choreographic inclinations were immediately obvious, although he admits that for several years the field lay open, his interests being broader than his direction was clear. *Transit*, his first piece, presented at the LAMDA Theatre in 1968, was no dramatic statement: it concentrated simply on the four women dancers crossing the stage space, its title 'found' from a Ford Transit van which happened to precede him one morning in a traffic jam. Cool simplicity was an objective behind several early works, like *Departing in Yellow* (1970, to a score by Finnissy), a solo inspired by Josef Albers' eponymous piece in his *Homage to the Square* series, and revealing a blown-up photograph of the painting as back-drop, or *Nowhere Slowly* (1970), modelled on the image of line-drawings.

In Cunningham's manner, any drama in Alston's work was understated or deliberately left wide open to interpretation, the focus being on motion and pattern, clarity in rhythm and space. Fundamentally, he shared Cunningham's concern for movement to stand without signifying anything beyond itself:

> something being exactly what it is in its time and place, and not in its having actual or symbolic reference to other things. A thing is just that thing. We don't ... have to worry ourselves about providing relationships and continuities and orders and structures – they cannot be avoided. They are the nature of things.[58]

Alston's programme notes stressed physical activity rather than meaning: '*Fall* (1970) moves through 4 phases, in which the dancers gradually succumb to the pull of gravity ... '; '*Still Moving Still* (1969) is concerned with the dancer's shifts of balance and equilibrium round a still centre point ...'. The title and text accompaniment of *Something to Do* (1969) did likewise. This was a fugal duet with text by Gertrude Stein: 'It is awfully hard for anyone to do anything ... some one has done something ...'[59] Alston openly admitted his debt to Cunningham and Cage. He used Cage's music for two early works, *Fall* and *Winter Music* (1970), maintaining the independent relationship between dance and musical structures that Cage and Cunningham had pioneered. The scheme of *Nowhere Slowly* (1970) allowed a measure of indeterminacy, another Cunningham/Cage device: its sections could be performed in any combination or order. *Nowhere Slowly* is also an example of a piece that appeared in several different versions and with several different musical scores, displaying the same matter-of-fact attitude towards dance material that Cunningham might have shown: material, like an object, could be re-cycled and placed in new contexts. Thus too, the solo *Departing in Yellow* became a double solo *Broadwhite* (1970) for one performance (now using the title of Finnissy's music) and then, as a solo again, it became a section of *Nowhere Slowly*.

Alston's creative talent was soon noticed and, given his maturity and articulateness, he was not only encouraged to choreograph for workshops (and a series of pieces for LCDT) but given early responsibility to teach others the ideas that he found interesting himself. Hence, in the early 1970s, he toured his own lecture-demonstration group and taught his own course in composition. By this time, again from second-hand experience and personal research, Alston had become acquainted with post-Cunningham, American post-modern dance ideas of the 1960s, ideas that emanated from the Judson Dance Theater in New York and from the new style dance composition classes that composer Robert Dunn taught at the Cunningham studio. Alston had read a 1965 issue of the *Tulane Drama Review*[60] which contained articles by Yvonne Rainer and the sculptor Robert Morris (on performance) and an interview with Anna Halprin, as well as Don

McDonagh's book *The Rise and Fall and Rise of Modern Dance* (1970).[61]
He devised a course in which the notion of dance could be expanded to include pedestrian movement and task-like activity, an extreme reaction
against the highly stylized emotional gestures of the past. Inspirational
approaches and value judgements took second place to questions and further exploration. Many students were impressed by Alston's composition
teaching, including a strong, regular group of collaborators who were
working 'outside the system', experimenting with alternative choreographic
ideas.

Meanwhile, Alston began to embrace in his choreography the
pedestrianism that he taught and the reflexiveness of some Judson work. He
made one extreme essay of this kind, *Shiftwork* (1971), a dance that has
stayed in the minds of many who saw it. Two women, one at a time, walk
round a wardrobe, the first nine times, the second once, the first eight times,
the second twice, and so on, while Alston paces out a series of squares of
ever-decreasing size in a corner downstage. The treatment of time was flat,
without any sense of climax and release. Pedestrianism and exaggerated
formal simplicity gave prominence to the actual workings of the piece.
The music was an interlude from Rossini's opera *Le Comte Ory* and chosen
precisely so that its warm romanticism would contrast with the mun-
dane stage activity. Alston maintains his influence was the dissociation of
music and subject matter in certain Italian films, like Pasolini's *The Gospel
According to Saint Matthew* (1964), but the device also relates to Rainer's
use in the 1960s of fulsome romantic or popular music.[62] Both
choreographers made an issue of the distance between plain, matter-of-fact
statement and conventionalized high sentiment.

Another work of 1971, *After Follows Before*, was plainly programmed
as 'prefabricated dance', with the performer (Christopher Banner) now
making choices about the order of sections within the performance itself,
in the manner of some Cunningham and Judson work. Like *Shiftwork*, this
piece too was juxtaposed with a romantic score, no less than the Prelude
from Act I of Wagner's *Lohengrin*.

Nevertheless, despite his debt to American models, Alston had already
begun to develop certain movement interests of his own, a style, for instance, that incorporated play with gravity.

Three women dance-makers:
Diana Davies, Jacky Lansley, Sally Potter

Leaders in setting up an alternative workshop within the School were
Davies, Lansley and Potter; their work is discussed here as examples of the
new areas of exploration.

While they were at the School, these three women choreographers enjoyed
the freedom of expanding their medium, bringing to it their previous

28

experience and what they learnt from each other.[63] Their ideas did not stem from what they saw around them in dance and, most important, while they had an idea of what was happening in American post-modern dance (Potter, for instance, had read Jill Johnston's collected criticisms of post-modern dance *Marmalade Me* (1971)[64] and, through the film world, had heard about Rainer's work), they did not look to the USA for inspiration. In this respect, these women differed markedly from Alston. They also tended to work more theatrically than he did, with images and some sort of semantic content.

However, a few works concentrated on dismantling or subverting the conventions of the dance medium itself, reflexive works, teasing the spectator to examine the structures of a piece in a self-conscious manner. Potter learnt this style from her background in the British structural/materialist film movement which, with a polemical Marxist intention behind it, set about deconstructing or revealing the nature of film.[65] Emphasizing rather than disguising editing procedures, structural/materialist film encouraged a critical and apperceptive stance from the spectator. There would seem to be a direct parallel between this kind of film work and Sally Banes' category of analytic post-modern dance (see pp. 4–5). It is important to recognize the influence of structural film through Potter at The Place, where she continued to make films, sometimes incorporating a dance element (see p. 106 for the discussion of *Combines*, Potter's collaboration with Alston for LCDT). In an early film in this genre, *Hors d'Oeuvres* (1972), she analysed the relationship between dancing figures and an angular space, while alternating colour, black and white, negative and close-up versions of the same film footage. Such alternating back and forth undermined any attempt to follow through the film as linear experience.[66]

In a live and more theatrical situation, Davies set up procedures that encouraged spectators to consider actual time and space rather than theatre time and space, to measure the time of an activity in relation to something else, to its space or to another activity. Thus *Brief Lives* (1972) shows dancers gradually progressing in private channels across the space, finally reaching the far side (except for one), while two people sit drinking tea very slowly, their cups reaching their lips only as the piece concludes. Finnissy provided the score for this piece, presenting the five musicians on stage, each playing his own refrain, joining in accumulatively at 30-second intervals and cueing the dancers.

The works by these women that used imagery for semantic content often proposed a gentle subversion of traditional representations in dance: relationships between the sexes, between members of the same sex, and between soloist and chorus. In this respect, the work pointed the way to the New Dance of the late 1970s (see Chapter 3). The women drew upon a range of dance styles. Potter's *Leave* (1973) was a gentle, lyrical duet for two men to Vaughan Williams' *Fantasia on Greensleeves*, a bold statement

29

at the time, as Clement Crisp observed, 'their relationship disquietingly ambiguous as they watch each other and manoeuvre with deliberate lifts and
falls'.[67] Lansley was exploring her wide dance and theatrical heritage as a
choreographer for the first time – singing, acting, tap, ballroom, flamenco
etc., her English Stage school training, and then her experience at The
Royal Ballet School and Company. But she took a sideways glance at what
she knew. Her gentle subversions of sexual stereotypes were a foretaste of
later investigations. She used ballroom routines in *Formations* (1973), but
an oddly assorted cast of two women in huge dancing dresses and one
diminutive escort between them. In 1972, to Helen Pope's *Fifty Million
Robins Can't Be Wrong* (lyrics by Billy Tracey), Lansley co-choreographed
and performed a tap dance with Early, a thirties-style number, but with
both of them dressed as men, in identical evening suits. *Getting Stronger*
(1974), a trio for Potter, Terry Berman and herself, and one of the last
pieces that she made as a student was, she maintains, her first outright
feminist statement.

Partly as an exploration of the relationship between chorus and soloist,
Potter made *Who is Sylvia? Three Clues* (1974). It was prompted by visits
to the Royal Opera House, Covent Garden. In it Finnissy plays Schubert's
setting of *Who is Sylvia?* three times, while being pushed, complete with
piano, to a new point on the stage for each rendering. There are three
soloists, Terry Berman in pyjamas, seen beating a pillow relentlessly,
Lansley, who sings the Schubert song in a surprising low voice, then Potter
herself (or Belinda Neave in the same role). A chorus in evening dress enter
('this was the first black dress and pearls piece', one of the dancers, Betsy
Gregory recalls[68]). Each member carries a sandwich box and, with
minimal and identical motion, removes a sandwich, brings it up towards
her mouth and then places it on the shoulder of her dress as a corsage;
later, the chorus members lay out their sandwiches in a neat circle around
Potter. Finally, Potter opens up each sandwich in turn until, in the last, she
finds a rusty key. This was a lively theatre of bold juxtapositions, but also,
according to Potter, a statement about the strength of a chorus or community, a reversal of the chorus role in traditional dance organization. In
lightly absurd fashion, the chorus here provides the soloist with the key or
clue to the question that has dominated the piece.

Davies broke new ground at the School by making *Band 7* (1973), which
mixed two non-dancers with two highly trained dancers. She found that,
rather than diminishing the non-dancers, the piece made them look as interesting as the others. It also opened up what she described at the time as
the 'fundamental socialist philosophy of interdependence and indispen-
sability of each person to another'.[69]

Not all the work by these women was so questioning in its bias. Another
piece by Davies that has remained especially vivid in the memory of those

who saw it, *Five Week Piece* (1972), was an accumulative happening performed in the entrance to The Place and up the four flights of stairs, at the
same time each week for five weeks. It involved activities as diverse and absurd in juxtaposition as a wedding party passing through, a woman strap-
ped to a board and dragged up one of the stairways, performers in bathing
costumes 'rescued' by a lifesaver, all close at hand and where one least expected to see them.

While none of this work was polemical in any overt sense, unlike later
work by each of these three women, its demystifying, deconstructive
characteristics in relation to establishment dance made a kind of political
statement. It encouraged a questioning audience response, and it used as
sources the homely and the familiar, what was 'real' to these choreographers, in movement, props, costumes and sound.

Potter recalls the tight timing of the student works in those days, an intellectual muscle presented economically and with humour. She contrasts
the work with the more time-indulgent dance experiences of the New Dance
of the late 1970s and 1980s.

The women, together with Dennis Greenwood, explored all the aspects
mentioned above, and the possibility of presenting work in a variety of locations, in their independent group Rescue Principle. They took School
workshop pieces into the repertoire, but a new development was the use of
scripts as a framework, scripts by Mick Banks of John Bull Puncture Repair
Kit. The two pieces of this kind, *Auk* and *Fallen Angels* (1972–73), darted
vigorously and humorously from one idea to the next, using narrative
thread at its most tenuous, repartee, improvisations, props, lighting effects
as well as dance, a multitude of resources to match Banks' Monty-
Pythonesque anarchy. The excerpts below from the *Fallen Angels* script
illustrate this:

> Diana: An aeroplane came over the house . . . The object it had dropped fell very
> fast and, as it got closer, I could see it wasn't a part of the aeroplane at all – it
> was a ball. *(Diana produces a small Black Rubber Ball and holds it up)* . . . And
> then suddenly it changed. It wasn't a ball any longer. It was a man . . . A man fall-
> ing out of the sky and rolling over and over as he fell. Over and over and over.
> *(She throws ball and it bounces off Stage, up into Roof and out into Audience)* . . .
>
> Dennis as the fallen angel dressed in:
> White Bathing Cap – which hides all his hair. He wears a pair of Flying Goggles,
> White Underpants and is otherwise naked. He has a pair of White Angels
> Wings strapped to his back. His body is patterned with 'FRAGILE' Sticky-backed
> Labels . . .

Potter and Lansley continued with Rescue Principle when they left the
School and later formed their own duo Limited Dance Company (see

Chapter 3). Davies, who won a Gulbenkian Dance Award in 1973, continued to move towards theatre: she used her dance knowledge as a performer within established fringe theatre companies, and in 1974 joined Welfare State.

The end of a creative era

By 1974, the ethos of the School had changed. It seems that the innovation of the first eight years did not last. The creative radicals at the School in the early 1970s recall that they had to fight increasingly hard in order to make an independent statement. The pull towards discipline and curriculum coherence, while undoubtedly necessary as the student numbers grew, turned out to militate against student experiment. Students were still exposed to a vast range of experimental ideas, but many felt unable to use them in their own explorations. As Robert Cohan noted at a meeting of the Contemporary Dance Trust (3 June 1971) – and his points were generally agreed upon – the biggest problem the School faced was to 'allow the students the maximum amount of freedom within the structure of the School and to [determine] what extent their work should be disciplined within the School's structure.' Diana Davies maintains that students had to be exceptionally strong and mature to survive as a counterforce in those days.

Another problem was that the School curriculum seemed geared strongly towards a career in the LCDT. Dick Matchett maintains that, as the company – the focal point of the Contemporary Dance Trust enterprise – became bigger and more demanding on time and resources, other projects that had developed personalities of their own suffered, or had to change to meet company requirements. Whether, of course, several very diverse organizations could have lived happily under the same umbrella is doubtful. The School was 'brought back into line. There was a chance for it to have been a living alternative theatre school at one point [embracing dance amongst other things], and it was decided not to take that alternative because it [the school] would have been setting itself up in opposition to the aesthetic that was demanded by the company.'[70] However, many students never had the ambition to join LCDT, seeking a dance education for other reasons. A Contemporary Dance Trust newsletter of 1 January 1974 reported that well over half the full-time students then at the School had stated their preference to find work outside the company: 38 to dance with the Company or one similar; 21 to dance in a small company; 18 to teach; and 21 especially interested in mixed media, drama or youth work.[71]

The emphasis on technical expertise increased, and with it came a selection process such that some of the most imaginative students of the 1960s and early 1970s, had they applied to the School later, would probably never have been accepted. While undoubtedly technical standards at the School

32

rose during the 1970s, the School's drive as a radical creative force lessened. Speaking in retrospect, Howard himself was the first to agree with this view.[72] Pat Hutchinson resigned as principal in 1974.

In terms of the future of dance in this country, what the Contemporary Dance Trust and the School had already achieved by the mid-1970s is extraordinary. Within a few years, they had demonstrated several alternatives to Graham-based expressionism and proposed the framework for the dance experiment of the late 1970s.

The term 'post-modern' was certainly not in currency at that time, but much of the work discussed here seems to demonstrate what we might now see as post-modern tendencies. I use the term post-modern in the broad sense in which Sally Banes uses it (see pp. 4–5), to encompass both work that foregrounds the nature and structures of the dance medium itself, 'modernist' post-modern work, and the kind of work that eventually in the 1980s became predominant, directing itself outwards towards meaning, while using structures of radical juxtaposition. Some of this work was directly influenced by American dance models. Some sprang from European or British sources, from arts other than dance, from the new counter-culture, or indeed from the shared international pool of ideas about new art. There was also exploratory work of the new modernist orientation, some with a brave conceptual thrust, testing out Cunningham's structural principles, a far cry from the Graham model. These developments are surprisingly early, at a time when a more traditional form of contemporary dance was only just starting. They were prompted by Howard's enthusiasm for an experimental dance movement and the presence of students who arrived at the School well-versed in new developments in the other arts.

It is important too to recognize how some of the work produced at the School and The Place expanded the boundaries of dance as it was generally characterized at that time. They extended it beyond a high art of steps and larger-than-life personalities, and brought to it a mixture of media as well as a hearty dose of ingredients from popular and everyday culture. A sign both of their achievement and of their times, a number of students functioned under the headings of performance art or fringe theatre when they left the School.

On the other hand, it was the ex-LSCD students who were largely responsible for the independent dance scene of the 1970s outside Ballet Rambert and LCDT. The following list of names testifies to this (it is a selective list, and those already mentioned have been excluded from it): Christopher Banner, Maedée Duprès, Kate Flatt, Craig Givens, Betsy Gregory, Julyen Hamilton (known as Peter Page at the School), Christine Juffs, Timothy Lamford, Shelley Lee, Tamara McLorg, Belinda Neave, Miranda Tufnell. Several small, experimental groups had been started by the mid-1970s:

Lansley's and Potter's Limited Dance Company, formed in 1974; Dance Organisation, in 1974 – with core members Early, Duprès and Emilyn Claid, it led to the founding of the X6 Collective, spearhead of New Dance, in 1976; Cycles, in 1974, a co-operative based in the West Midlands, formed by Rosanne Donahue, Cecilia Macfarlane and Sally Mason; the earliest of all these, established in 1972, was Alston's Strider.

CHAPTER 2

Strider
Pioneers on the move

From excited curiosity and intellectual stimulation to wrathful dismissal or blank incomprehension, Strider, the first experimental and 'independent' dance group to emerge from the LSCD, provoked extreme reactions during the years that it existed (1972–75). Yet it received strong critical support over its three-year lifespan, and its significance was soon generally recognized. Today, not only is the work that was produced seen as important to the development of British dance, but the very ambition and ethos of the Strider organization are considered exemplary by many who remember it. Strider's vitality was immense, both in terms of productivity and organizational procedures. It presented some sixty works, some brief, some extended, within only three years (see Appendix 2). Throughout its existence, the group maintained an impressive flexibility and progressive impetus in personnel and artistic interests.

The beginnings of Strider
In principle, Strider was a co-operative, like many fringe theatre and performance art groups at the time (see Chapter 3, on X6), but it was Richard Alston's brainchild, and he remained chief spokesman for the group throughout its existence. By 1972, Alston had already begun to contribute pieces regularly to the London Contemporary Dance Theatre repertory, but he wanted an independent outlet as well, not always, he says, to be compromised by the restrictions imposed by an 'establishment' company.[1] He wanted time to find his own feet before making the by then traditional study pilgrimage to New York (he eventually went to New York when Strider disbanded in 1975). Offered a Gulbenkian Dance Award of £1000, Alston had enough money to set up Strider for an initial 9-month period. Its beginnings were auspicious: Strider gave its first performance at The Place amidst the clamour of the ICES festival (International Carnival of Experimental Sound),[2] 14 August 1972. Soon after, it could be seen at the Edinburgh Festival when ICES transferred there. In September, the group appeared at the British Thing exhibition in Oslo, in October and December at the ICA (Institute of Contemporary Arts),[3] London's most important experimental arts venue, and in November in Rotterdam and The Hague.

35

Presenting a bold, progressive image, the title *Strider* had already been used before for a 1971 solo for Christopher Banner. But it had resonance beyond the dance: Alston had taken it from Gerard Manley Hopkins' 'The Windhover' (1877) which refers to the falcon

> ... in his riding
> Of the rolling level underneath him steady air, and striding
> High there, how he rung upon the rein of a wimpling wing
> In his ecstasy!

He had noted the connection in image with a drawing from William Blake's *Book of Urizen* (1794), in which an angel is seen 'striding' across the sky.[4]

When the company gave its first performance, Alston made his intentions for it clear, with a manifesto declaring the group aesthetic as one that countered that of established modern dance. It also demonstrated the group's allegiance to post-Cunningham thinking:

> In the fifties Merce Cunningham and John Cage proved that dance could be valid as movement in time and space, without dramatic associations. From this objective approach arose a generation of post-Cunningham dancers; if Cunningham brought movement *per se* to light, they re-examined it by setting it in new contexts. It is this kind of work, of which we aim to be a part.

Outline of developments within Strider: personnel, influences, the style of programmes

Besides Alston, the core of Strider in its early days consisted of leading radicals from the LSCD, Christopher Banner, Jacky Lansley and Wendy Levett (a dancer who had a particular interest in T'ai Chi), and volunteer students Dennis Greenwood, Diana Davies and Sally Potter. The work ranged from essays in extreme dance abstraction to highly theatrical pieces in which costumes and props played an important part. Performances included humorous and entertaining pieces as well as works of a more serious nature. As in LSCD workshops, programmes proclaimed variety in a series of eight or so pieces, most short, ten minutes or so in length, although a few pieces ran to about twenty minutes. Immediately, an informal tone was established which was quite at odds with the LCDT aesthetic, and which Strider continued to adopt until 1975. Dancers presented themselves as dancers or as life-size (rather than larger-than-life) people. For pieces that did not demand any specific theatrical costume, performers wore simple leotards and tights or casual clothes: boiler-suits, dungarees, tank tops and loose trousers or tracksuit bottoms, bare feet or plimsolls.

With frequent changes of membership, Strider was constantly in flux (see Appendix 3). Early dancers left, first Davies and Potter and, after a year, Lansley and Levett. An example of its flexibility, Strider began to admit dancers and choreographers from different dance backgrounds, outside the LSCD, the new members introducing very different kinds of work.

Nanette Hassall, an ex-Cunningham dancer, joined the group in 1973. She had been dancing with Ballet Rambert briefly, but was alienated by the expressionist nature of its repertoire.[5] She joined Strider at the time when its work was becoming less theatrical, more abstract and more Cunningham-oriented in its vocabulary. These were Alston's own inclinations, and Hassall introduced regular Cunningham technique classes to the company, its first regular experience of this way of moving. Open Cunningham classes were held at Strider's regular rehearsal base, the White Lion School, Islington. A unique opportunity for classes in this style, there was a regular attendance of 10–15 people.[6] In an application to the Arts Council, 14 January 1974, Strider's administrator, Paul Chandler, stressed the change: 'our de-emphasis on equipment and technical effects ... our focus on the essential "vocabulary" of dance'. Alston became the regular Cunningham technique teacher after Hassall left later in 1974.

The Rambert dancer Pietje Law joined Strider in 1973. Then, in 1974, Mirjam Berns joined from Dan Wagoner and Dancers. Berns had taught at the Cunningham Studio in New York, and she too offered Cunningham classes. So later did the Americans Ruth Barnes and Daniel Press, each of whom linked up with the group for some performances in 1975.

However, only shortly after Hassall's arrival, Strider began to undergo another aesthetic change, perhaps the most considerable of all, as the group came into contact, in autumn 1973, with the work of the American, Mary Fulkerson, dance tutor at Dartington College of Arts. Hassall was Strider's connection with Mary Fulkerson: she had known Fulkerson from their days together at the Cunningham Studio.[7] It was Strider, in fact, that had originally been invited to Dartington as a company that would visit regularly and form the core of the dance work. They could not accept the offer but, as an alternative, Hassall recommended Fulkerson as a full-time teacher and artist. In 1974, a year after her arrival in England, Fulkerson relinquished her teaching position at the University of Rochester in New York State and the directorship of her group there, the Tropical Fruit Company.

It was as if the company 'went from upright to horizontal', Fulkerson said of her experience with Strider. She introduced what has since become widely known as release work, and certain approaches to movement that had originated from the post-modern movement in the USA: moving the awareness inwards, extensive use of the floor; and also the democratic duet form known as contact improvisation, barely two years after its invention by Steve Paxton. The importance of Fulkerson to Strider during this period can hardly be overestimated. Whenever possible, after their first meeting with her, the group made study and performance visits to Dartington. They visited three times in 1974, giving up their summer vacation period to study with her and to be in residence with the Tropical Fruit Company for 1½ months. One additional autumn visit was pencilled into the Strider diary.[8] Alston wanted to expand beyond judging his dances 'externally', and likewise Hassall (who left Strider and stayed on to teach at Dartington after summer 1974), who was impressed that the method had 'at its centre' a regard 'for each individual's growth and development'.[9] Strider also commissioned two works from Fulkerson.

During its final year, Strider became an intimate group of three core performers: Alston, Greenwood and Eva Karczag. Besides Alston, Greenwood was the only Strider member to remain with the group for the three-year period, except for a few performances during the 1972–73 season when he was still a student at LSCD. Karczag came from a wide background of dance techniques and performing experience, from a traditional ballet company (London Festival Ballet) to small experimental dance situations and, since, 1971, had become very involved with T'ai Chi. The Strider work now developed from the movement principles and possibilities that Fulkerson had introduced. By this time individual programme items tended to be more extended than in 1972. It seems too that, over the years, the co-operative and improvisatory content of the work increased. A few early works were co-operatively choreographed, the dancers having contributed material. Some late works contained considerable passages of improvisation.

Sometimes, material from different pieces by different company members was mixed in performances called 'Events'. Events were a Cunningham invention, dating from 1964, and Strider publicity pointed this out. Sections from the current Strider repertory were mixed into a whole, stripped of their titles and of the significance that they had in their original context. The first such Event took place at Strider's second public performance, accompanied by a group of Swiss musicians called GERM (Groupe d'étude et de réalisation musicales). But later, from spring 1974, Strider's associated composers/musicians Jim Fulkerson and Stephen Montague being sympathetic to the concept, a series of such Events was presented. They used wide-ranging collage scores as accompaniment, music by other composers as well as themselves, and included improvisation as well as set material. The Event at the Akademie der Künste in Berlin (April 1974), for instance, was built around the ten rapid crossings from Alston's *Rainbow Bandit* (1974, the first version of this piece). Every five minutes, there was a visual signal, and the dancers marshalled themselves to perform one of the crossings. In between times they could improvise or perform other phrases from the repertory.

Policies

Despite the major changes in Strider's profile, certain policies were sustained throughout its existence. First was its kind of co-operative status, which included not only the dancers but others who were regularly associated at one time or another: Stephen Montague (composer/musician), Richard Johnson (sculptor/photographer), Charles Paton (lighting designer/technician), Paul Chandler (administrator). This co-operative social structure was most genuine during Strider's final year, when the company was at its smallest. Several members have referred to frictions within the group in its early years, and Alston admits that he was 'probably too much of a benevolent dictator. I function best when I am actually in charge.'[10]

Another policy was to emphasize company creativity and flexibility: to 'keep a situation where work could be made but not necessarily preserved ... each time somebody left we tried not to teach their work to somebody else but to go on making work and dealing with a new situation.'[11] Open rehearsals were scheduled as well as formal performances, and under the title 'Trailer', works in progress were presented. Another basic premise of Strider was to be open to new performance situations and not necessarily to be restricted to proscenium settings, although such opportunities were not offered as much as the dancers wished until the final year when they undertook a series of art gallery performances. Strider was the first dance group in Britain to carry out such a policy.

Teaching workshops and presenting lecture-demonstrations were other important aspects of Strider activity. The original application to the Gulbenkian Foundation stated Strider's aim to 'integrate the work of a dancer with everyday life ... to make more direct contact than a mere performance can allow (e.g. staying for week periods in universities carrying on their own work and involving it with the students).' Strider's residencies anticipated LCDT's first college residencies in 1976.

Strider dancers were also choreographers and, if 'outside' choreographers, like Fulkerson, made work, rather than merely delivering a piece, they would 'work alongside' the company for a while.[12] In other words, they would integrate the experience fully into company life. The group took in additional dancers occasionally, as circumstances required. There was Fergus Early, for instance, whose School workshop collaboration with Lansley *Fifty Million Robins Can't Be Wrong* (1972) was included in Strider's first programme, and who appeared as a Hell's Angel in Lansley's *Halfway to Paradise* (1972). Maedée Duprès joined the group for a performance of Potter's *Wings* in 1973; she was then a student at the LSCD and had danced in the piece when it was first presented in a School workshop. Miranda Tufnell linked up for performances at the Museum of Modern Art, Oxford, in 1975.

It is interesting that Strider never set the pattern for future dance companies, including Second Stride, which derived its name from the original group. (Second Stride was founded in 1982 by Siobhan Davies and Ian Spink, with Alston as a third choreographer.) Here again was a group dedicated to creating work rather than preserving repertory, but otherwise there are many differences. The frameworks in which the companies have performed are quite different. It is very important to see Strider in relation to its particular context. It has to be understood in relation to the pioneering state of experimental dance at the time, with a touring circuit for dance that did not even exist, and not least in terms of its peculiar relationship with the Arts Council.

Performance profile and touring

Apart from its regular London seasons at The Place, the ICA or the Oval House, Strider toured the circuit of venues carved out by fringe drama and mixed media groups in the 1960s. The group toured at minimum cost in its own van, with a floor and basic sound and lighting equipment. Strider was a pioneer of experimental dance, alone on the road for its first two years, with the sole exception of the mixed-media group Moving Being. It was the only experimental dance group to undertake a touring schedule that took it to colleges of education, small theatres, arts centres, and later art galleries (accompanying a touring exhibition of Jasper Johns drawings) all over the country.[13] Surprising situations presented themselves: the Friends Meeting House in Bath or HM Prison Wormwood Scrubs (both in 1973), or outdoors next to the Midland Group Gallery in Nottingham (1975). Many of these venues would now be considered unsuitable for dance performance with unsafe, hard floors, or the wrong shape; some of them have ceased to exist. Most impressive is the list of foreign performances for a new, small-scale company: in 1972, Norway and Holland; in 1974, Switzerland, Germany and France (on two occasions, performances in Angers and at the Paris Festival d'Automne). Few companies since have achieved a comparable schedule so rapidly.

A list of performances in 1974, the year in which the company performed most frequently, is instructive (see Appendix 4). Some 50 performances were given around England and Wales and abroad that year, many one-night stands as well as two-night to week-long series of performances. There was Arts Council pressure to maintain a heavy touring schedule and, with this in mind, 96 days of performances and workshops were projected in Strider's Arts Council application for 1974–75. But Strider neither wanted nor managed to achieve such a schedule. Company members found some of the regional touring hard, and audiences generally less understanding of the work than in London, although Alston remembers that college audiences were receptive, far more so than those in arts centres.[14]

5. *Corridor Walk* (1972), choreography by Christopher Banner, danced by Strider. (Photograph: Andrew Watson)

6. *Hundreds and Thousands* (1972), choreography by Diana Davies, Jacky Lansley and Sally Potter. Wendy Levett practising T'ai Chi in the background. Left to right in the foreground: Davies, Lansley, Potter. (Photograph: Andrew Watson)

41

7. LEFT ABOVE: *Wings* (1973), choreography by Sally Potter. Raymond Cook suspended. Dancers, from left to right: Nanette Hassall, Maedée Duprès, Jacky Lansley. (Photograph: Joy Chamberlin)

8. LEFT BELOW: *Common Ground* (1974), choreography by Nanette Hassall. Dancers: Dennis Greenwood, Eva Karczag. (Photograph: Eleni Leoussi)

9. ABOVE: *Soft Verges* (1974), choreography by Richard Alston. Dancers: Richard Alston, Eva Karczag. (Photograph: Eleni Leoussi)

43

When they performed abroad at this time, Strider dancers found themselves in a similar pioneering situation. Publicity suggests that they performed as isolated representatives of a European dance avant-garde. Thus they stood out at the Atelier Chorégraphique d'Angers. Elsewhere, they were seen as avant-garde next to the new American dance: in Paris, Robert Wilson, Andrew de Groat and Meredith Monk (she gave a vocal performance there); in Berlin, Pilobolus. Alston recalls Pina Bausch giving a late night solo performance in Berlin, but that she was then in the process of changing. She had not yet developed her post-modern style of dance theatre.

The funding of Strider

The initial Gulbenkian grant was of great significance, not only for Strider, but also for the Gulbenkian Foundation itself. Peter Brinson, then Director of the British and Commonwealth Branch of the Foundation, recalls that the grant signalled the beginning of the Gulbenkian's commitment to areas other than the establishment, to experimental work in the arts and, especially, to the community arts movement, which included community dance.[15]

After the initial Gulbenkian funding of Strider, supplemented by three small Arts Council grants (for equipment, administration and to help fulfil a series of performances, in total £1050), the Arts Council took over the annual funding of Strider, offering amounts far in excess of those offered to other small dance groups for some years: in 1973/74, £5000 for a 6-month period; in 1974/75, £10 000 for the whole year.[16] By 1974/75, Strider was receiving the sixth largest grant awarded for dance (excluding the two Royal Ballet companies) out of a total of thirteen awards. Strider was by then receiving a higher award than two well-established Arts Council clients, the educational dance groups Educational Dance Drama Theatre and Dance for Everyone. But Strider's appearance on the dance scene was timely. By the late 1970s, the growing number of small companies applying for money resulted in generally poorer funding; the cake was divided correspondingly into smaller and smaller slices, and the project system of funding supported a limited working period during any single year. However, it is Alston's view that the Strider experience helped to determine later Arts Council response to new experimental groups, and that Strider's demise after such generous funding was used as an excuse for funding groups very cautiously in the years that followed.[17]

Strider's relationship with Council was an odd one, the funding body's attitude ranging widely between enthusiasm and encouragement, worry, suspicion and guilt. However, first, it is necessary to digress briefly and discuss the background to Arts Council funding.

At this time, the body responsible for decisions on dance funding was a committee under the music panel, the Dance Theatre Sub-Committee. It had no allocation of its own, but the music panel gave money as each case was made for it. No forum for the specific consideration of experimental dance existed until 1978 when the New Dance and Mime Sub-Committee was established. For reasons of history, the Dance Theatre Sub-Committee tended to be weighted towards ballet, with several members of long standing. Dame Ninette de Valois of The Royal Ballet was in the chair until the critic Peter Williams took over in 1972.

From Arts Council documentation, it seems that the Dance Theatre Sub-Committee was a body that reacted to situations as they arose rather than looking ahead to an expanded art form, planning strategically and understanding that the cutting edge of an art should be given particular support in order to ensure the continuing development of that art.[18] The committee was traditionally cautious about taking on new groups and responsibilities, adopting the attitude that in order to do so, old groups had to be killed off first.[19] No strong concerted case was made by the committee to raise the amount of funding for dance as a whole or to plan for an expanded future. Alston recognized his debt to the Gulbenkian Foundation: 'If we had not been supported by the Gulbenkian Foundation we would not have been considered for Arts Council money.'[20]

London Contemporary Dance Theatre, for instance, had had its problems establishing a relationship with Council in the late 1960s.[21] It was only as a result of the three-year Opera and Ballet Enquiry (1966–69), when a strong case was made for a major contemporary dance company in Britain, that LCDT eventually received its first major grant (in 1970–71). In similar tone, committee members responded to Strider's initial application: the were 'very worried that Strider might become a new recipient of annual subsidy ... difficulties might arise over dancers wishing to leave London Contemporary Dance Theatre in order to join Strider, though still needed by the parent company', and wondered 'whether it would be better under the umbrella of the Contemporary Dance Trust'.[22]

It is sobering to remember that statements such as these were being made when in the USA there was already a flourishing experimental dance movement with a large number of small groups and individuals having proved the worth of their enterprise. It is also pertinent to compare the funding of dance with that of drama at this time for, within drama, there was a strong, vocal group acting on behalf of the fringe. It had fought for money since the late 1960s and won, and it had gained from making demands early. There was more money around to support new initiatives at that time, and building programmes then under way for a circuit of new theatres and arts centres responded directly to the needs of the new drama groups. Fringe drama took advantage of the general expansion in Arts Council funding during the decade 1963–73, before its levelling out, and then shrinkage after 1975.[23] The severe problems of dance funding from the mid-1970s might be seen to stem from the late arrival of an experimental dance move-ment (in comparison with drama) and the conservatism that seemed to greet its early demands.

The high level of Strider's funding was partly a result of the level of the initial Gulbenkian award. Jane Nicholas, then Dance Officer at the Arts Council, recalls that the Council was shamed into reacting to the Gulbenkian initiative in an appropriate manner and, after some discussion, it was recognized that the company needed to function independently of the Contemporary Dance Trust.[24] However, by January 1974, the committee was already voicing worries about the nature and standard of the work. 'In-sufficient progress' was the verdict on the January performances at the ICA. Committee members were more worried than many critics were. Never-theless, the Council increased the grant for 1974/75 to £10 000, with the proviso that Alston 'should be under no misapprehension that his group would be guaranteed continuing further subsidy'.[25] By the end of 1974, the committee was deeply concerned about Strider, more and more strongly influenced as it was by the principles that Fulkerson had introduced, and sometimes playing to tiny audiences.[26] The work was regarded as in-sufficiently communicative, and Strider members were called in to explain themselves.[27] Arts Council minutes do not suggest any ambitious commit-ment to supporting new, researching work – work that, in the first instance, might be ahead of general understanding or appeal only to small audiences. Certainly, committee members could have had no standards by which to evaluate post-modern or New Dance work at that time.

The reason why funding was increased for that 'difficult' final year is that the Arts Council favoured the idea of an experimental dance company as an alternative to Ballet Rambert and LCDT, and were impressed by Alston's previous record and articulateness as a choreographer and spokesman for experimental work. As Chandler observes, 'they were worried about being caught with their pants down'.[28] It is a paradox that, as much as the Arts Council was disturbed and admonitory about Strider's later work, it was at the same time encouraging the group to move towards revenue status, in other words, regular, year-round funding.

In the end, the Arts Council's plans for Strider did not come to fruition. Strider's co-operative organization militated against its achieving the necessary charitable status, there were strings attached to revenue status that did not suit the group (a greater accountability to the funding body, which also entailed a huge increase in administrative work) and in any case, by this time, the group planned to disband. One reason for this was creative exhaustion.[29] Peter Brinson believes that another factor was increasing competition from community arts in the venues that Strider visited.[30] There was at one time an intention for Strider to re-assemble after a year's break, but this never happened.[31]

The work: choreographers and collaborators

The lists of Strider dancers/choreographers and of repertoire provide a framework for examining Strider's work (see Appendices 2–3), its range at any given time and the broad changes in type of work between the years 1972 and 1975. It was Alston who produced by far the largest number of pieces, and second to him, Banner. Contributions by Potter, Davies, Lansley, Hassall and Fulkerson increased the stylistic range considerably. Associated composers and fine artists played an important role. Strider soon attracted artists sympathetic to its aesthetic aims and eager to be involved with a new platform for experiment in dance.

Anna Lockwood became associated with Strider during its first year, and provided Alston with three tape scores during the group's first year, for *Tiger Balm* (1972, music composed in 1970), *Windhover* (1972, a commission) and *Headlong* (1973, a commission funded by the Gulbenkian Dance Commissioning Fund). Gordon Mumma, one of Cunningham's composers, linked up with the group in its early months, providing sound for *Subject to Change* (1972) using an electronic trumpet which he played live on stage, and for Banner's *Pedestrian* (1972). Later, Jim Fulkerson, composer-husband of Mary Fulkerson, wrote and accompanied for the group; Stephen Montague became a sort of 'resident' composer/musician during its last year. Fulkerson and Montague provided both electronic and instrumental music.

Several sculptors keen to expand from the traditional nature and setting of the sculptural object attached themselves to Strider, but not to provide sets or costumes in any conventional sense. Barry Flanagan received a Gulbenkian award under the Dance Awards Scheme to enable him to work with Strider, 'to create one or more contemporary works in which human bodies and physical objects are combined and treated as a single created piece'.[32] He choreographed a piece himself, *Counterfoil* (1972), which explored the space within a 'court' area marked out by adhesive tape. It was he who organized the group's appearance at the British Thing exhibition in Oslo.[33] Flanagan joined in several pieces as a performer and, in *Hundreds and Thousands* (1972, jointly choreographed by Davies, Lansley and Potter), he had the task of shovelling grit from one spot to another, a material related to that used in his sculptural work at the time. The sculptor/photographer John Hilliard assisted Flanagan in this piece. During the last year of Strider, Richard Johnson joined the group, his primary function being to add an independent, adjacent element to the dance activity; but his taking of polaroid photographs was integral to the Alston/Greenwood *Split* (1974) – the dancers used the polaroids to generate movement. In the Musée Galliera in Paris, during Strider's week in the Festival d'Automne, he staged his own Event. He incorporated the Strider dancers and a musical collage with his own distribution of photographs, maps and geological materials drawn from various sites in England and Wales.

Richard Alston

Alston's choreography for Strider still looked to America, as it had done when he was a student and teacher at the LSCD. He continued to make a point of the matter-of-fact act of choreography and the lack of content inherent in his work beyond the dance material itself. An extreme example of the objective re-cycling of existing material combined with indeterminacy in performance was *Subject to Change*. Here, Banner, as dancer, took two solos – Alston's *Strider* (1971) and his own composition *Blue* (1972) – and mixed them in performance, first alternating chunks of material (taken in any order), later, alternating isolated movements until he had exhausted the entire content of each piece (an extremely taxing mental and physical process). The music for this amalgam was subject to change as well.

At this stage, Alston, like Cunningham, normally maintained the structural independence and autonomy of the dance and its accompaniment, hence the ease with which he changed his accompaniment for some of these early works. Yet, he did select music for its mood or atmosphere, and texts likewise for their connotations (he has always wanted more control than Cunningham in this respect). Thus, he chose recorded repartee between the popular American television comedians George Burns and Gracie Allen to accompany an 'automatic' duet called *Routine Couple* (1972), and an essay on traffic control and planning for *Traffic* (1972).[34]

Each of the works to a score by Lockwood had a distinctive kind of reference. However, *Tiger Balm* and *Windhover* step out of line somewhat from the other Alston work described, in that, although rarefied and understated, both transported the viewer into a definite unified theatrical world. Assuming the qualities of 'animal fear and a somnolent calm'[35] in Lockwood's already existing score of nocturnal noises, Alston evoked in *Tiger Balm* a mysterious, dream-like mood with sexual overtones, a ritual group in white robes, a solo by a naked man 'the vocalized orgasm ... a dance of tensions, of energy poised and then released in a body stripped so that the play of forces can register directly'.[36] *Tiger Balm* was a twenty-minute piece. It proved to be one of Strider's most acclaimed works, and was soon taken into the LCDT repertory. For *Windhover*, Lockwood drew from a collection of environmental sounds – birds, wind, running water – and again, Alston kept 'within' her sound world. Alston's interest in Hopkins' *Windhover* had led him to create this work, an eponymous duet which was opened by the *Strider* solo and took off from the bird image in the poem. The new work was a greatly abstracted account of the slow, ritual, approach of courting birds, based on information in Julian Huxley's *The Courtship Habits of the Great Crested Grebe* (1914). *Headlong* was a collaboration between composer and choreographer based on the idea of being at a great height and 'down-rushing flight'.[37] But this piece left behind fragmented meanings, its music a collage of roaring engines and verbal information, a rocket launch countdown, velocity statistics in parachute jumping, the tale of a woman shot from a cannon as a circus stunt.[38]

A few pieces that Alston made at this time were unusual for him in using popular music and responding directly to its rhythms and contextual connotations. Looking back now, Alston suggests that he might have been paying tribute to Twyla Tharp, whose *Bix Pieces* he had seen premiered in Paris in 1971 (under its first title *True Confessions*). To the music of Bix Beiderbecke, Tharp's dances drew on the vernacular of period social dances. Alston's own *Thunder* (1972) was a corresponding exercise in style, evoking an atmosphere of lethargy through a loose, floppy kind of movement, his dancers dressed as 'people' in forties dresses with additional period props and furniture; it was a series of dances to three recordings of the song *Stormy Weather* by Harold Arlen. After the first year of Strider, Alston ceased to make pieces of such specific theatrical reference. His later Strider work is so different in nature that it will be discussed separately later.

Christopher Banner

Like Alston, Banner was interested in abstraction and in developing dance material for its own sake. The structure of his *Corridor Falls* (1972), for instance, was a series of phrases of falling movements in corridors of light; in *Pedestrian* (1972, reworked in 1973) 'energetic movements broken by stillness' gradually pared down and simplified until the dancers became pedestrian.[39]

But Banner also had an eye for theatricality obtained by means other than pure movement. In his other corridor piece *Corridor Walk* (1972), a favourite with audiences, the dancers performed phrases that they had made up for themselves in a corridor across the space, picking up items from piles of clothing at either end and gradually assembling the oddest and funniest mixtures of costume. The soundtrack was correspondingly various, a collage of popular and classical music. In his solo *Blue*, Banner, in blue shorts, slowly and ceremoniously took blue paint from a pot and applied it to his face. Then, in the glare of a follow-spot, he performed a wild, savage dance with much slapping, so that the blue on his hands was plastered all over his body.

His solo *Strawberry* (1973) for Lansley commented on the ritual of the secretary painting and dressing herself 'to the nines' before going to work. An essay in pink, the piece showed Lansley's gradual process of transformation between fragments of dancing. Through various stages of make-up, undress and dress, she turned from a woman in underwear into a painted, clothed and artificial 'mannequin in pink'.

Diana Davies, Jacky Lansley, Sally Potter

Potter and Davies were still students when they were in Strider; Lansley joined Strider full-time for a year and returned to the LSCD as a student from 1973–74. All three contributed work to Strider of the sort that they were pursuing as students at the LSCD: theatrical work with meaning content, some of it 'deconstructive' in nature, gently subverting the usual codes of practice in dance, and examining images of women. The three women collaborated on *Hundreds and Thousands*. Early recalls the event at the ICA:

> The audience is banked on two sides of the action, confronting each other over the heads of the performers. To the incompetent strains of the Ross & Cromarty Orchestra (child of the Portsmouth Sinfonia) as they sawed their way through a remorseless waltz (keeping playing oom pah pah anywhere you want, or can, on your instrument) three women, clad in white tunics, swing white Indian clubs in unison callisthenics.[40]

The sugariness of classical ballet was emphasized and mocked, the waltz tunes and later the 'Dance of the Sugar Plum Fairy' from *The Nutcracker* were given an eccentric twist by the discordant rendering of this Maoist Orchestra (which was dedicated to the notion of amateur performance). And the behaviour of the women was distinctly unballetic. These were not fragile, innocent fairies, but energetic athletes who later turned from club-swinging to lifting each other and being lifted – no men were needed for support. The men, Flanagan and Hilliard, were relegated to shovelling grit from one spot to another, a dull labour that lasted throughout the piece.

Lansley made two pieces of her own for Strider, *Halfway to Paradise* (1972) and *The Truth About Me* (1973). In *Halfway to Paradise*, while introducing a ballerina figure as an element from her own past (she played the ballerina herself), she also presented an interpretation of that image. The ballerina was a metaphor for woman as sexual object and object of potential violence, a metaphor that she explored more rigorously in her work of the mid- and late 1970s. Billed as an Event, *Halfway to Paradise* juxtaposed three distinct stereotypes: the ballerina, a narcissistic figure going through the ritual of preparing herself for dance (she was seen centre stage at the ICA, raised on a small platform, in tights and leotard, sewing ribbons on to her ballet shoes and easing herself onto her pointes); a fearsome crowd of Hell's Angels (Flanagan, Mumma, Banner, Davies, Fergus Early and Colette Laffont) who burst through the audience waiting to be let in, carrying knives and chains – later they laid down their weapons before the ballerina and crawled away; and a group of porters in overalls (Potter, Levett and Alston) who spent their time transporting empty cardboard boxes. Lansley now admits the crude interaction between these radically different images of people: she maintains that the piece did not have the threads of narrative connection and clear ideological basis that she later developed.[41]

There were similar features in *The Truth About Me* – stereotypes again – but the reference this time was to the 1950s, in an introductory tape of Elvis Presley talking about himself (in 1956) and in the three Everly Brothers songs that were used for the three contrasting character sketches. There was Hassall, a lively, popstar-obsessed bobbysoxer to 'Wake Up, Little Susie'; Levett, in pyjamas, in a gentle, sleepy solo to 'Crying in the Rain'; then, for 'Cathy's Clown', Russell Dumas (or Christopher Banner), all extroversion and macho arrogance in his glittering, padded costume and high boots. The final duet for Dumas and Levett introduced a sinister suggestion of violence from male aggressor towards vulnerable woman.

Davies contributed two pieces on themes of loss or unfulfillment, *Dry Dock* (1973), a solo for Lansley in life-jacket, sadly executing fragments of a hornpipe to a compilation of sea sounds, bird cries and ship's noises, 'an atmosphere of desolating emptiness',[42] and a fantasy with the telling title *Three Romances of an Unobtainable Nature Featuring Air-Hostess Housewife and Call-Girl* (1974). Davies returned to Strider to make these pieces, the second one under the aegis of her Gulbenkian Dance Award but, by this time, she says, she felt at odds with the increasingly pure dance emphasis of Strider's work and needed in any case to reassess her own work as a choreographer.[43]

Potter's student workshop piece *Wings* (1973) was taken into the Strider repertory. In it was a man in pilot suit and goggles suspended above the stage in a harness. Three women danced below, as if racing in flight but sometimes, perhaps this time in Potter's structuralist manner (see p. 29), echoing and drawing attention to the series of positions that the pilot passed through overhead.

Later, in 1975, Potter, by then a member of Limited Dance Company, collaborated with Greenwood in an extended work about 45 minutes long called *Wheat*. This was put on under the auspices of Strider, using performers from both within and outside Strider, and fantastical in the gloomy Dickensian surroundings of Green Dragon Court, a space in front of the arches of Southwark Bridge, London. Greenwood and Potter made reference to *The Firebird* ballet.[44] Greenwood appeared as a kind of firebird, dressed in a strange red rubberized suit with net tutu and black bird's mask, and the opening few bars of Stravinsky's score were repeated through the piece. But these balletic references were mixed in free association with imagery from a dream that Greenwood had had, of wheatfields in his native Canada, of farmers, of drought affecting the farmland and of fire seen as a destructive force. Like most other dance projects in which Potter was involved, this was much more than a movement piece: with singing, fire-eating and burning cans of fire, it contained many elements of spectacle.

Nanette Hassall

Hassall produced a series of relatively abstract works, related to Alston's choreographic areas of interest, and contributing to Strider's change of focus, to the 'essential vocabulary of dance'. She used the Cunningham vocabulary. *Common Ground* (1974), a trio set to a Philip Corner trombone solo, had arisen 'from the working relationship that exists between these dancers and the choreographer as company teacher'.[45] *Needless Alley* (1973), a 'co-operative piece', explored the notion of plotted journeys in sections called 'Underground map', 'Street map' and 'Aerial maps and signals'. Under moving beams of light, the dancers trailed coloured powder from tins, marking out patterns of lines and curves. True to the Cunningham spirit, the title was 'found'.[46] Needless Alley is a street off Corporation Street in Birmingham, and the piece was premiered at the University of Aston, Birmingham. The music was by Cage. In two Strider performances at the Oval House in November 1974, a few months after she had officially left Strider for Dartington, Hassall presented two solos *Sanction* (danced by Deborah Chassler of the Tropical Fruit Company) and *Bearings* (danced by herself) that demonstrated her developing interest in release work.

Mary Fulkerson

Fulkerson contributed three works to the Strider repertoire. *Small Brown Shell* (1973) was a group work including balancing and falling games and spoken instructions that revealed the performance process.[47] As John Percival noted at the time, it was 'based entirely on the sort of movement you would think of as non-dance movement'.[48] *We Love You, Dennie* (1974), for Dennis Greenwood dressed as a glamorous young woman, was a lonely solo of small feminine gestures and everyday gestures, three tape-recorded letters providing contact with the outside world. Fulkerson also performed once with Strider in her *Making Light Work* (1974), which was about three women at different stages of life, aged 27 (herself), 37 and 70 respectively. This sort of concept could well have been new to British dance: it showed the women as real people carrying out tasks familiar to them. *Making Light Work* was a precursor to Fulkerson's later explorations of the female psyche.

Fulkerson introduced to Strider a distinctive approach to movement through imagery. In release work's anatomical aspect, images are used to structure the manner in which bones balance or articulate in movement: images of lines, bridges and bowl shapes in the body, of paths of action-flow, all designed to release the body into easy efficient alignment and action. Fulkerson's teaching integrated her studies with Joan Skinner at the University of Illinois (Skinner formulated a method of application to dance of what she understood of the Matthias Alexander technique), with anatomical information and related imagery learnt from Barbara Clark, a student of Mabel Elsworth Todd, author of *The Thinking Body* (1937).[49] Only very few dancers carry all this physical information naturally, but others can be taught it and undergo fundamental physical change. This is not at all about learning a specific dance style from shapes, patterns and qualities produced and copied, but about turning inwards to the body, making the internal image the movement source and allowing that image a range of external realizations. Fulkerson recalls that Karczag took to the work 'like a fish to water'.[50] Supported by her T'ai Chi experience, the work 'released' a new peace and fluidity and potential for improvisation that has been much admired since, after Strider, in her dancing with Miranda Tufnell, Trisha Brown and indeed, in her own work.

Fulkerson also applied her imagery principles to a choreographic context. She communicated this possibility to Strider. Now, new possibilities for using the floor and for improvisation within performance were explored. There was fast work but, now too, spare material, much stillness and, especially important, a new easy fluidity or flow and a democracy in partnering derived from the premises of contact improvisation. Thus the first half of Alston's duet with Eva Karczag *Soft Verges* (1974) was entirely contact and floor-based work. Alston also fused the new fluidity with his former style of Cunningham-based structured steps.

The late gallery work
Strider's connection with the Cunningham/Cage tradition remained strong. Probably because of Alston's known debt to Cunningham, Strider was invited to tour with a travelling exhibition of Jasper Johns drawings; Johns had made several designs for Cunningham, and was Artistic Advisor to the Merce Cunningham Dance Company for some years. But the connection between Strider and Johns went deeper than this. Johns epitomized the neutral, impersonal attitude towards making work with which Alston was sympathetic: Johns' use of familiar, banal elements from everyday life (flags, numbers, targets) constituted a deliberate negation of the artist's supposed unique, expressive gesture.

Strider danced alongside the Johns exhibition between November 1974 and April 1975, interlinking with it whenever possible, and developed three works related to the drawings and to Johns' sketchbook notes. In Alston's trio *Slow Field* (1974)[51], the dance material of which had its source in several drawings and in two statements by Johns, both audience and performers were ambulatory; any material could be shown by any performer at any time, while relating to specific drawings. The work contained minimal movement. Alston recalls simple arc-like arm gestures reflecting the broad gestures in a 1963 Johns drawing, *Untitled* (based on his own painting *Periscope*). *Zero through Nine* (1975), Alston's solo for Karczag,

contained material that related to the number series 0–9 and traced numbers as floor patterns on top of each other as imaginary layers. Similarly, in the related Johns drawings, numbers could be seen literally through one another.

The Alston/Greenwood collaboration *Souvenir* (1975) was a piece of performance art, containing as it did much activity involving props, but no movement that could be labelled dance movement. Both choreographers remember the piece as highly obscure and hard to reason. The drawings, *Watchman* and *Souvenir* (a series of related drawings) and associated notes that inspired the piece suggested the props, the imagery and the cryptic programme note:

> A correspondence between the spy and the watchman.

> The action takes place between Edisto Beach, South Carolina and the Imperial Hotel, Tokyo.[52]

What Alston and Greenwood appear to have attempted was a visualization in performance of Johns' work. Thus they introduced torches, postcards, piles of Ritz crackers and a paper plate that had a photograph of Alston printed on it (Johns had bought a plate with a self-portrait photo at the Tokyo Hilton and used it in his *Souvenir*). Alston (the spy) watched through a rear-view mirror as Greenwood (the watchman) went through separate activity in an adjoining room. In a sense, objects were used as 'abstractly' as Alston had used dance material in earlier works like *Subject to Change*. They were not juxtaposed for their value as signs. In this respect, this performance work was a far cry from that of Davies, Lansley and Potter.

Alston devised another performance art piece *Standard Steps* (1975) for the Museum of Modern Art in Oxford, using three galleries on three floors simultaneously. The work drew on words and images from Duchamp and Satie, both figures who had been a strong influence on Cunningham and the neo-Dada and Pop Art movements. Alston again interpreted visual art in performance, for there was the Bride, Eva Karczag (also a nude descending the staircase) and three Bachelors Alston, Greenwood and Daniel Press stationed on separate floors. These performance ideas stemmed from Duchamp's *Nude Descending a Staircase* (1912) and *The Bride Stripped Bare by her Bachelors, Even* (1915–23).

Sample programmes

Gallery performances such as these represented a vast change from early Strider programmes, as the following sample programmes demonstrate. Presenting a broad view of Strider, these programmes highlight the changing nature of its presentations and the rapid turnover of its repertory during its three-year existence.

The earliest Strider programmes consisted of a string of pieces, most of them short, a mixture of abstract and theatrical work.

August 1972, The Place

Title	Choreographer	Sound	Dancers
Parable	W. Levett	M. Finnissy	1m, 2f
*Routine Couple**	R. Alston	George Burns, Gracie Allen	1m, 1f
Solo	W. Levett	M. Finnissy	1f
Fifty Million Robins Can't Be Wrong	F. Early, J. Lansley	Helen Pope (lyrics Billy Tracey)	1m, 1f

INTERVAL

*Afar**	C. Banner	M. Finnissy	1m, 1f
*Thunder**	R. Alston	Harold Arlen[53]	4f
*Subject to Change**	R. Alston, C. Banner	subject to change	1m
*Tiger Balm**	R. Alston	A. Lockwood	2m, 4f

3 and 5 October 1972, ICA

Tiger Balm	R. Alston	A. Lockwood	2m, 4f
Thunder	R. Alston	Harold Arlen	4f
*Trailer**	(work in progress, later part of *Windhover* 1972)	R. Alston	1m, 1f
Parable	W. Levett	M. Finnissy	1m, 2f
Blue	C. Banner		1m

INTERVAL

Traffic	R. Alston	Peter & Alison Smithson	1m, 2f
*Counterfoil**	B. Flanagan	T. M. Offredy	1m, 1f
Hundreds and Thousands	D. Davies, J. Lansley, S. Potter	Barry Flanagan, Paul de Feu, Ross & Cromarty Orchestra	2m, 3f

*Indicates the premiere of a piece.

55

Striding Out

The 15–19 January 1974 season at the ICA introduced the largest number of new pieces since Strider's premiere, and the greatest stylistic range, with Fulkerson's work now represented for the first time. Christopher Banner and Wendy Levett also presented work during this ICA season.

15 January 1974, ICA

Title	Choreographer	Sound	Dancers
Rainbow Bandit*	R. Alston	Charles Amirkhanian	2m, 3f
Common Ground*	N. Hassall	Philip Corner	2m, 1f
Solo . . . for myself	M. Berns		1f

INTERVAL

Title	Choreographer	Sound	Dancers
Three Romances*	D. Davies	Rasputin Compton	3m, 3f
There is and always will be*	M. Berns		3m, 4f

18 January 1974, ICA

Title	Choreographer	Sound	Dancers
Small Brown Shell	M. Fulkerson	J. Fulkerson	3m, 2f
Making Light Work*	M. Fulkerson		3f

INTERVAL

Title	Choreographer	Sound	Dancers
Common Ground	N. Hassall	P. Corner	2m, 1f
Headlong	R. Alston	A. Lockwood	2m, 2f

*Indicates the premiere of a piece.

By the time of Strider's performance alongside the Johns' exhibition at the Serpentine Gallery (1975), pieces shown were fewer in number, tended to be longer and all now developed from the movement principles that Fulkerson had introduced. The Serpentine programme was one hour in length.

9–16 April 1975, Serpentine Gallery

Title	Choreographer	Sound	Dancers
Souvenir	R. Alston, D. Greenwood	E. Satie	2m
Slow Field	R. Alston	S. Montague	2m, 1f
Zero Through Nine	R. Alston	S. Montague	1f

Looking back across the Strider repertory, its wide range and shifting profile during its three-year timespan are immediately striking. They are the product of Strider's determination to create rather than to keep repertory and, it seems, a passion within the group to embrace new ideas.

Strider choreographers can be seen as having been instrumental in initiating explorations that were continued in the late 1970s and 1980s in New Dance and in the new modernist contemporary dance. Release work was one of the most important of these areas of exploration. Born from the LSCD, Strider also formed the bridge between New Dance and the countermovement at the School. Now, to audiences around the country, Strider dancers introduced new kinds of dance content, abstract or political; new movement vocabularies, Cunningham or release-based; new forms, including improvisation and 'flatter', non-hierarchical structures in time; new relationships to music, using sound for mood or reference rather than for a structural basis. Perhaps most striking, the dancers presented themselves with a new directness and informality, preferring, where possible, to use non-proscenium spaces.

As an organization, Strider was an anomaly amongst experimental dance groups in Britain, never a model for future groups. Very much of its period, a pioneering experimental dance company, it thrived on exceptionally generous funding, and was able to develop a highly ambitious touring programme.

At the time of Strider's demise, its members were heading in different directions. Davies, Potter and Lansley were pursuing performance and theatrical interests. Banner had joined Dan Wagoner and Dancers in New York. Hassall had left to study with Fulkerson at Dartington and then returned to her native Australia. Greenwood, who had seen Strider through all its stylistic changes, stayed with 'minimal' movement work in his career with Rosemary Butcher and Miranda Tufnell. Two Strider members set off to New York to study – Karczag and, at last, Alston himself.

CHAPTER 3

X6
New Dance becomes a movement

'New Dance, A Celebratory Weekend': two organizations, Chisenhale Dance Space and the National Organisation for Dance and Mime (NODM) joined forces on 12–13 July 1986 to present a packed programme of talks, discussion and performance. The aim of the event, which took place at Chisenhale Dance Space, was to examine the form called New Dance and its development over the previous fifteen years. The publicity leaflet for the weekend claimed that 'New Dance in Britain goes back ... to the early seventies and even, in a few isolated instances to the late sixties'.

'New Dance': the power of a label is strong. The term was coined with the publication of the first issue of *New Dance* magazine in New Year, 1977. This was one of the projects to be initiated by a group of dancers who called themselves the X6 Collective, after their working base X6 Dance Space in the Bermondsey Docklands in London: Emilyn Claid, Maedée Duprès, Fergus Early, Jacky Lansley and Mary Prestidge. With the advent of the magazine, the term 'New Dance' was immediately applied to the work of these artists, to that of many others covered in the pages of the magazine and later, as we have seen, retrospectively.

Certainly, at the 1986 weekend, there was no firm agreement – if ever there has been – as to what exactly this term New Dance means. Indeed, by that time, there were new generations of so-called New Dancers, some feeling that they had little in common with those of the 1970s and worrying that the label New Dance might no longer be appropriate to what they were doing. Since that weekend, *New Dance* magazine itself has ceased publication (the last issue, no. 44, was in September 1988) and, perhaps symptomatic of its demise, the term itself seems to have become history. While labels of any kind seem to have been less of an issue since the late 1980s, the terms 'independent' and 'contemporary' have been perhaps most regularly used. However, the fact that a celebratory weekend took place under the banner New Dance at Chisenhale Dance Space, the direct descendent of X6 Dance Space, which closed in 1980, testifies to the significance of that label and to the seminal importance of the X6 Collective. It had spearheaded a movement and a kind of thinking that prevailed well into the 1980s.

The Collective existed as such from the time that its members moved into their space in March 1976, until they left it in September 1980.

The growth of an independent dance movement and its supporting organizations

It is useful first to place the work of the X6 Collective in perspective. The late 1970s was a time of considerable growth in the number of dance groups functioning independently of the large contemporary companies, in both London and the regions. By the time Strider folded, in 1975, this growth was already under way. It is virtually impossible to assess the precise number of groups that sprang up in the 1970s, because the only reliable annual figures that exist are for groups that received public funding. But they are, for instance, the main contributors to the steep rise in the total number of Arts Council dance and mime clients through the 1970s. The following figures exclude the two Royal Ballet companies, which were funded separately by the Arts Council, but include throughout the decade the four large English companies, London Festival Ballet, Ballet Rambert, London Contemporary Dance Theatre and Northern Dance Theatre, as well as Ballet for All, The Royal Ballet's educational company.

Arts Council-funded dance and mime groups.

1970–71	1977–78 (the year of peak numbers)	1979–80
9	38	30

Drawing upon a wider range of sources than funding records (but including Regional Arts Associations as well as Arts Council clients), Susan Davies has listed the number and names of new contemporary dance groups according to the year in which they first appeared – and some were short-lived – between 1972 and 1981.[1] These figures, too, demonstrate the growth of activity:

New contemporary dance groups.

1972	1973	1974	1975	1976	1977	1978	1979	1980	1981
4	3	10	8	12	9	12	10	9	13

But there were other groups in addition to these; the border-line between professional and amateur is very unclear at this stage. Some of these 1970s groups were hardly experimental in orientation, although they did not necessarily use the Graham-based vocabulary of the large contemporary dance companies. But there were others, like Strider, which reacted more strongly against established models. Several of these had come into being by 1975: Limited Dance Company, Dance Organisation, and the West Midlands company Cycles Dance Company (all three companies founded in 1974 by dancers who had met at the London School of Contemporary Dance), and the Rosemary Butcher Dance Company (founded in 1975).

The late 1970s was the time when this growing band of British independents began to develop support structures for its growth and survival. In September 1976, the Association of Dance and Mime Artists (ADMA) was founded, a kind of trade union for dancers that acted as an information-sharing body and a pressure group for funding.[2] ADMA looked to the model of The Association of Community Theatres (TACT, formed in 1974) and the Independent Theatres Council (ITC, formed in 1975), which had already achieved so much for fringe theatre groups. TACT and ITC were part of a wide move towards self-organization amongst radical artists since the early 1970s, a response to the growing economic difficulties of the period.[3] It was seen as crucial to combat what seemed as cautious, unsympathetic attitudes towards experimental and independent dance work at the Arts Council in the mid-1970s. The hegemony of establishment dance remained strong. Minutes of the Arts Council Dance Theatre Sub-Committee record:

> Members were concerned at the number of people ... who now wanted 'to do their own thing' in smaller and smaller units. *(15 July 1974, on consideration of an application from Limited Dance Company.)*

> The Chairman [Peter Williams] pointed out that experimental projects tended to end up not breaking any new ground but getting stuck in a rut. *(21 November 1975)*

> Project grants had not always resulted in improved standards, and had sometimes been a waste of money ... [one committee member] was worried about fragmentation. *(12 January 1977)*

And Peter Williams wrote in his influential article on the situation of British dance 'The Way Ahead' (*Dance and Dancers*, November 1976):

> Let us, for the present at any rate, forget about 'experiments' and 'experimental projects' in connexion with dance ... everything has been done before.[4]

Partly because of ADMA pressure, a New Dance and Mime Sub-Committee of the Dance Advisory Committee was established at the Arts Council in 1978, with a membership knowledgeable and supportive of experimental dance work. (This was also possible because, in 1978, dance had achieved committee status. It was no longer subsidiary to the music panel, and the Dance Theatre Sub-Committee became the Dance Advisory Committee.[5])

The late 1970s was also the time when Dartington College of Arts in Devon began to make a major contribution to the independent dance scene. Students of Mary Fulkerson, who had arrived there in 1973, were now starting to graduate from Dartington's theatre department, having trained in her release principles (see Chapter 2) and in a variety of post-modern techniques introduced by visiting teachers from the USA.

Since 1975 too, several polytechnics and colleges of higher education had begun to offer dance study at degree level, without a teacher training bias, emphasizing practice as well as academic content. Most courses that included dance as a major study offered it within creative or performing arts degrees approved by the Council for National Academic Awards (CNAA). In 1974, the Laban Centre for Movement and Dance launched its three-year dance theatre course for dancers and choreographers and, in 1976, the country's first BA honours degree in dance. Nationwide, the dance student population was increasing. Contributing both participants and audience, it fed the independent dance movement.

In the late 1970s too, a variety of venues began to present the independent companies, in single programmes or even short dance seasons: in London, Action Space, the ACME Gallery, Battersea Arts Centre, Jacksons Lane Community Centre, Riverside Studios, the ICA (at the last there was more regular dance programming now than in the early 1970s); in Bristol, the Arnolfini Gallery. Several dance festivals were initiated during this period, the first, ADMA, was followed by Dance at Dartington and Dance Umbrella (see Chapter 4, Appendices 5–7). The independent movement played a central role in the two Many Ways of Moving Congresses in London in 1977 and 1978.[6]

Other important projects outside established dance in the late 1970s had connections with independent dance. The community dance movement began during this period, with great support from the Gulbenkian Foundation. In 1976, the Minorities' Arts Advisory Service was established (out of which came the black dance group MAAS Movers in 1977), also Shape, the arts agency for the disabled.

However, for all this activity, these were formative days for independent dance in Britain, and many dancers were just out of full-time training, confused as to how, or whether they ought, to go about making and presenting their own work, or in the early stages of experimentation, with no developed performance circuit or audience, and a limited critical base to give them encouragement. The foundation of the X6 Dance Space by a collective of experienced artists (their preferred term was 'artist' rather than 'choreographer') who wanted a working base that they could call their own turned out to be the foundation of an important self-support situation for this new growing community of independent dancers.

X6 Dance Space as a new centre for dance: its foundation and early activities

The X6 Collective had found its space at Butlers Wharf in the Bermondsey Docklands amidst a community of artists who had been working there since 1973. At the top of X block, an old tea warehouse, was, Early describes, 'a dream space . . . a wide expanse of smooth maple wood floor, high gabled wooden roof, massive, red, wooden beams spanning the space',[7] although the space was basic beyond the essentials for dance (toilet facilities never existed). At the time, the Collective imagined that X6 would set the precedent for many dance artist-controlled spaces, the British equivalent to the artists' lofts in New York.[8]

During the four years of its existence, X6 occupied a pivotal position. It became the London centre specializing in alternative practice in dance, the radical end of the independent dance scene.[9] It forged a strong link with Dartington, becoming the London performance 'home' for several of its graduates. Except briefly through Strider, this was the first time that Fulkerson and the London dance community were in contact. There was, too, a strong link with Cycles Dance Company in the Midlands, founded by Cecilia Macfarlane, and likewise a collective organization. Early and Claid both contributed choreography to Cycles during this period (Duprès did so in 1975), and the full-length work that Early directed for the company, *Another Way of Living* (1979), was first performed at X6. The X6 Collective also had key connections with the funding bodies and with ADMA. Early was a member of the Arts Council's Dance Theatre Sub-Committee, 1975–77 (although he battled in vain to shift attitudes[10]), and also, from 1975, of the Greater London Arts Association (GLAA) drama panel, assisting in the formation of the first GLAA dance sub-committee. The Collective was well-represented within ADMA: Claid, Duprès, Early and Prestidge were all members of the first ADMA Steering Committee.

Immediately, there was a great energy generated at X6, encouraged by the freedom that the Collective had to determine exactly what it wanted from its space. It established alternative classes and workshops and began to develop a unique programme of presentations, much of it work that was never shown anywhere else. Within a few months of the public opening of X6 in March, the Collective had organized a grand scale outdoor happening in the vicinity, *By River and Wharf* (20 June 1976), as well as a radical dance summer course and a conference on experimental dance in Britain (the first of this kind). The first issue of *New Dance* magazine was prepared for publication; it has since become a prime source of documentation on X6 and related activities.

These initial X6 projects were specifically geared to involving a large dance community beyond the Collective itself and to developing contact with the local community.[11] *By River and Wharf*, for instance, which stands vividly in the memories of those present at its performance, involved a collection of dancers described by Early as a 'Who's Who' in New Dance at that time.[12] Each was invited to perform work in a chosen location. Participants included Rosemary Butcher, Sally Cranfield, Kate Flatt, Craig Givens, Martha Grogan, Julyen Hamilton, Judith Katz, Timothy Lamford, Miranda Tufnell, as well as the Collective members themselves. Two different pedestrian tours were organized (50–100 people in each), passing across Tower Bridge, down alleys, across squares and bomb-sites, even dangerously up over old iron girders.

Thus, to a great extent as a result of X6 energy, an alternative dance community was first galvanized into action, suddenly aware of its own existence (ADMA was formed a few months later). There was too a sense that an authentic British movement was beginning, British dance for the first time not looking to foreign examples.[13] Some dancers and choreographers at the time, like Richard Alston, felt that they had to go to New York as the world capital for modern and post-modern dance, for further study and to find support for their interests. But there were some now who questioned the need to leave home and decided that, as British artists, they would build directly from their experience in Britain.

Clearly, the impact of X6 Dance Space extended far beyond any public value given to the work born or shown there, or to the Collective who ran it. Its impact has to be assessed in different and much broader terms than this: in terms of ideas generated and shared within a dance community, some ideas initiated by the Collective, many received from other New Dancers invited to contribute to the work there. Certainly, interested outsiders found no tight hierarchical organization or single focus when they arrived for classes or performances. Early has described X6 in the loosest of terms: 'not a dance group, not a school, not a rehearsal room, but a body of diverse ideas, finding a form of collective organisation'.[14]

The X6 Collective: artistic background

The X6 Collective members remained together throughout the four-year period of the space, with the exception of Duprès, who left in 1979. She was replaced during the last year of X6 by Sarah Green, who came from a non-dance, art school background. Of the founding members, Claid (until the end of 1976 known by her original name Louise Harrison), Duprès, Early and Lansley had all met at the LSCD. Duprès had her initial training as a dancer there. The others had come to the School from extensive experience in large, established ballet or contemporary companies. Claid had danced with the National Ballet of Canada, later studied at the Graham School in New York and, after a break from dancing, became a Graham technique demonstrator at the LSCD. Early and Lansley were pursuing different directions in their careers after dancing with the Royal Ballet

(Lansley joined Strider 1972–73, see p. 30 and p. 50). Mary Prestidge, who came to know this group after they had left the school, had been an Olympic gymnast (at Mexico in 1968) and afterwards a member of Ballet Rambert.

All five were ready in the mid-1970s for a major reassessment of their work and lives as artists, and it was at this point that they decided to establish their own working base as a Collective. The background to this decision lies in the workshop experiments of Early and Lansley at the LSCD (see Chapter 1), Limited Dance Company (the Lansley/Sally Potter duo, 1974–75), and Dance Organisation (1974–76), the umbrella for a variety of working groups, with Early, Claid and Duprès as its core. Several principles of Limited Dance Company and Dance Organisation were similar: collective creation, the production of work specifically for the various indoor and outdoor situations in which it was performed ('street, stage, gallery or lawn'[15]), the expansion from dance into the broader theatrical arena of performance art. Dance Organisation members stressed:

> Although dance is the common root of the present participants, it is only one element. . . . Theatre, music, the visual arts, are seen as indivisible ingredients of the group's working and performing processes, to be used in any combination and proportion that a situation may demand.[16]

Limited Dance Company toured and taught workshops throughout the country, concluding with a US tour in 1975. The title of the company was meant to imply minimal dance content. Lansley says that she and Potter often used a lecture/performance format which enabled them to make performance a platform for political as well as artistic expression. The work, which came from a feminist starting point, incorporated reflexivity as part of the performance event, analysis of the context in which the work was being shown, the implications of the specific venue or site, the spatial relationships between performers or between performers and audience, as rigorously as possible, in order 'to be in control of our imagery'.[17]

Dance Organisation began in November 1974, when Early and Craig Givens devised and performed a duet for the Chile Festival at the Royal College of Art. In 1975, the group found a base at the International Arts Centre near Elephant and Castle in London, where members taught classes and prepared work for the building and vicinity. The same year, there was a generous commission to perform at the Royan Festival of Contemporary Art with a group of musicians. Dance Organisation presented *Light Matter/Light Music*, a piece directed by Early, Lansley and the composer Michael Finnissy. Early recognizes the important lead that Lansley gave to the group from her Limited Dance Company background, in terms of the performance art orientation, the collaborative method and the forms used:

10. A scene from *By River and Wharf* (1976), an outdoor event organized by the X6 Collective. In the background, Mary Prestidge on stilts. (Photograph: Geoff White)

11. Workshop at X6 Dance Space. (Photograph: Geoff White)

12. LEFT: *Gymnopédies* (1976), choreographed and performed by Fergus Early. (Photograph: Geoff White)

13. BELOW: *Going Back* (1976), created and performed at X6 Dance Space by Emilyn Claid. (Photograph: Geoff White)

events devised and performed independently by each of the artists involved, within environments that performers had constructed for themselves, loose linking devices between events, and occasional group episodes. All of these features were influential on the work that happened at X6.

Philosophy and organization

For the X6 Collective, when it came into being in 1976, there was a crucial philosophical emphasis. An examination of what art can be as form or media was inextricably linked with a new, fundamental concern for the individual, the person participating in art. 'We wanted,' says the Collective, speaking as a group, 'to move forward the very moribund and static forms of contemporary dance and ballet in this country, but we felt that the only way to move form forward was to look at the personal, the social aspects of the work ... and form cannot be liberated unless other things are liberated.'[18]

The Collective did not merely address the familiar question of relationship between artist and audience, but also new questions about how choreographers and dancers train and make work, how dancers' bodies are used, and what representations dancers are expected to comply with in their work and surrounding activity. Members shared the need to reconsider these issues in the light of their own backgrounds in 'oppressive' institutions; they looked back on hierarchical organizational structures within which predominantly male choreographers presided over silent dancers struggling to meet painful technical demands and succumbing to reactionary images of gender identity. It comes as no surprise, therefore, that at the 1986 Chisenhale/NODM weekend, Early pronounced 'liberation' as the one and only essential concept of New Dance. He went on to cite the specific liberation of dance artists and of the body, referring to their intimate connection with other current movements for liberation. And he insisted that style is useless as a definition of New Dance:

New dance is not:
baggy trousers, rolling about, chinese shoes, contact improvisation, ballet to rock music, release work, image work, outside performances, post-modern dance, martial arts, self indulgence, stillness, American, non-narrative ...

New dance does not exclude:
formal choreography, tap, ballet class, baggy trousers, rolling about, chinese shoes, jazz shoes, no shoes, army boots, self-indulgence, contact improvisation, rock music, virtuosity, stillness, narrative ... [19]

New Dance then, according to Early's definition, is about an attitude rather than a kind of work. Yet, for members of the X6 Collective, that attitude certainly led to making work with a particular kind of subject matter. While seeking non-oppressive working methods, members were committed to exposing the personal, immediate issues that informed those methods as the subject matter of their work. There was no time for art for the sake of art. Thus, Claid, in her editorial in *New Dance* no. 3 declares that 'there is nothing new to be discovered in dance movement ... What is new is now and what is *happening* now'. In order for dance to be new, she continues, connections must be 'made consciously' with the social, financial and political context.[20] New Dance then, for the Collective, was oppositional both in terms of how it was made and what was made.[21] This was certainly not the first occasion for a polemical element to be introduced into dance, but there was now an important renewed thrust of this kind within British work.

It is useful to understand the philosophy of the X6 Collective in terms of a much broader movement within the arts and society of the 1970s to find radical alternatives to existing social, political and working structures. Against a background of increasing conservatism during the 1970s, a small and mainly youthful minority sought in various local and fragmented ways to work through alternatives to the traditional power structures around them. This was undoubtedly a result of the spirit of enquiry of the 1960s. But it was also a symptom of growing social disillusionment during the 1970s as hopes raised by the Labour Government under Harold Wilson and James Callaghan faded, and, too, a symptom of the growing interest in Marxism and feminism (the latter movement gained ground in Britain after about 1970). The outlook was markedly different from that of the period of the early LSCD; it was the outlook of a far less positive era. The democratic collective or self-help organization became the most common alternative structure, sometimes used as a basis for living (as in communes), sometimes as a basis for consciousness-raising (the women's and gay groups, for instance), sometimes as a basis for working.

The collective as a basis for working is most relevant to a discussion of the arts. When X6 was founded, it became part of a network in 1970s Britain of arts collectives or co-operatives (of musicians, film-makers, writers etc.).[22] However, this kind of collective often served a second purpose as a basis for consciousness-raising within the working group. In this politically aware alternative arts scene, there was a concentration on working through politics at a local level within the separate collective arts organizations. The concept of the personal as political, which originated from the feminist movement, was widely applied.[23] X6 members who were knowledgeable about what was happening in the other arts (especially performance art, theatre and structural film) were attuned to the kinds of thinking alive across these communities as they formulated their own collective philosophy and working plans.

It is noteworthy that many radical artists at the time were involved in co-counselling. This is a technique that enables participants, amongst other things, to analyse personal politics rigorously in a spirit of self-help and mutual usefulness. The relevance of this for dance is that participants could apply what they learnt from co-counselling sessions to their work as artists. There are obvious parallels between social structures and structures through which art is produced. Just as Collective members made work that was about social issues, so they brought their personal discoveries and politics into their teaching and rehearsal processes.[24]

Working notes testify to the importance given to personal relationships and feelings as an integral part of an artist's research: they include not only plans for actual pieces, but essays on various aspects of personal consciousness that arose during rehearsal and performance. In the 1990s, and indeed the 1980s, such introspective attention seems surprising. Yet, for X6 members, this research as a part of making work was a priority, a crucial means of reclaiming oneself from an oppressive past and achieving a sense of responsibility for oneself as an independent artist in the present. One dancer Anna Furse, active at X6 from 1977 and informed by Marxist-sociological analysis from her recent university experience, goes so far as to say that for all the energy and initiative that X6 generated for the dance community, at a personal level, this was a time of 'terrible poverty' where 'things happened slowly . . . people were sore, angry, especially the women . . . it was a crisis-cum-healing period'.[25]

Personal politics were not necessarily of such importance to the outer circle of people drawn to X6. Nor by any means did all who benefitted from the activities of the Space lay such emphasis on New Dance as a force of opposition, and therefore define New Dance in quite the same terms. X6 represented a particular philosophy for the Collective, which might be shared to greater or lesser degrees by those outside it. There were many other useful things to draw from the Space. Yet it is significant that a group with such political motivations as these initiated the self-help situation for a broader dance community than themselves.

Obviously, it was of paramount importance to Collective members that they were in control of their own working space at this time. They took turns with the administration of X6 as a rehearsal, performance and teaching space, and earned money towards paying for the Space from teaching activities and collections held after performances. Eventually, the Arts Council realized the importance of X6 to a dance community much broader than itself, and it was pressured to change its funding policy: for the first time, instead of supporting a creative project, it funded the running costs of a space where the art form might develop.[26] X6 was also one of the first organizations to receive grants for a whole year's work: £3000 for 1978/79, and £4500 for both 1979/80 and 1980/81. It is important, too, to be aware of another matter of context, that certain aspects of life were easier for artists in the 1970s than in subsequent years. Although there was a growing need for subsidy in the 1970s in order to survive, artists now feel that there was more time in those days, and remember that it was easier then to 'squat', to find cheap, short-life housing or, if necessary, to live for a period on the dole.[27]

The class/workshop programme

From the opening of the Space, regular classes were held there according to a pattern of terms, daily classes six days a week during terms, weekend workshops, Easter and summer courses. At first, it was the Collective who taught all classes at the space but, by 1978, true to the policy of receiving as well as offering ideas, a series of special workshops given by outside teachers was begun. There were classes in movement technique, as well as creative workshops that drew from everyday personal experience.

For the Collective members themselves, teaching was an important area of research and in this open situation they evolved a new kind of class, re-evaluating existing techniques to encourage a healthier, less stressful and more efficient use of the body. Collective members were influenced by destructuring alignment methods: Alexander technique (which had been introduced at the LSCD – the Collective invited its own teacher to X6) and later release work (see pp. 52–53). Members incorporated information from these methods into their teaching. However, a core principle which stemmed from destructuring methods and the belief in taking responsibility for oneself, was to help individual students to find their own body truths through questioning and deep internal awareness, as an alternative to copying the surface of movement in rapid striving for a goal. Thus it was that Collective members reconsidered the manner in which they themselves had been taught traditional techniques and tried to introduce a more thoughtful, non-competitive class situation. This was also a context for mutual feedback and learning between pupil and teacher, relating, if indirectly, to co-counselling practices.[28]

The various Collective members specialized to a certain extent in their teaching: Claid and Early – ballet (in the new way described, and as 'barefoot ballet'), and Claid also taught improvisation; Duprès – a contemporary technique (also in the new way described) and, with Julyen Hamilton, dance and rhythm workshops; Prestidge and later Sarah Green – gymnastics (as non-competitive exercise, and incorporating release principles); Lansley – women's creative workshops, which began in 1977 and in 1978 generated their own performance group, Helen Jives. Different teachers attracted different students, although there was some overlap. Students who were either locally-based (from the Laban Centre, for instance) or on vacation came to classes, as well as ex-students who had completed a contemporary dance training, enthusiastic beginners, artists from other disciplines who wanted to extend their work into physical expression, and women from a variety of backgrounds who were seeking a 'safe' all-women situation for creative, collaborative performance work. Contact with the local community turned out to be less successful than the Collective had originally hoped. X6 classes functioned primarily as a support for New Dance enthusiasts.

Undoubtedly, the most influential guest teachers were the Americans, who brought with them attitudes to the body and approaches to learning that were fully in accordance with X6 philosophy. The X6 Collective invited Fulkerson to teach in January 1978. Other teachers of release followed: Kris Wheeler, who taught the method as developed by Joan Skinner; John Rolland, who later taught at the Amsterdam Theatre School; and Linda Hartley, a British ex-student from Dartington. Later in 1978, Steve Paxton, a regular visiting tutor at Dartington since 1974, introduced contact improvisation to X6, the democratic duet form that he had originated, in which participants must 'accommodate the movement of their partner, and together ... discover a course of action for mutual movement'[29] (see p. 37). Two other Americans, Lisa Nelson and Nancy Stark Smith gave contact workshops in 1979. For many participants, contact improvisation came as a breakthrough experience, physically liberating as it stressed the free giving of weight, potentially fast and energetic as well as gentle, a method that made the work itself the teacher, an opportunity to work with someone else without the traditional gender role playing. There was a burst of enthusiasm for contact improvisation that peaked during the late 1970s and early 1980s. Sometimes this was manifest in performance, as in Transitional Identity, the group formed by Claire Hayes, Laurie Booth, Anna Furse and Kirstie Simson in 1981, more often in workshop jam sessions. Patricia Bardi, an American who moved to Britain during this period, taught creative work that stressed use of the voice and of the organs in dancing, how body organs can be used to support and initiate movement through the skeletal structure.[30]

The performance programme

The performance schedule at X6 increased over the years. Guest performers were introduced, initially for a trial month in autumn 1977. For a start, most guest teachers were invited to present work. Performances rose in number from seven in the first year of the Space, all in-house, to forty during the financial year 1979–80 (noted in the 1980 application to the Arts Council), a large number for a venue in Britain at that time. By 1979 there were performances by visitors from many countries in Europe and from North America, as well as by British-based artists and the Collective members themselves. Concentrating on work outside the 'straight contemporary'[31] traditions (the Graham or Cunningham-based traditions), X6 presented a unique programme. For many foreign performers, it was the only place in Britain where they could be seen. Contacts were made through *New Dance* magazine, the American radical dance magazine *Contact Quarterly*, or through Paxton and Fulkerson.[32] The following artists and groups came from abroad to perform at X6:

1977: Russell Dumas and David Hinckfuss (Australia), Patty Giovenco (USA)
1978: Mimeteater Termiek (Holland), Ulla Koivisto (Finland), Peter Dudar and Lily Eng (Canada)
1979: Diane Torr (USA), Steve Paxton and Lisa Nelson (USA), Dumas, Hinckfuss and Eva Karczag (Australia), Donna Henes (USA)
1980: Jeanette Leentvar (USA), John Rolland (USA), Anne Crosset and Cher Geurtze (Denmark), Dudar and Eng (Canada), Anna Winteler (Switzerland), a group of five dancers and mimes from Holland (in work by mime Sjoerd Schwibettus and dancer Gail Dockery).

It would appear that the whole of the British New Dance scene of the late 1970s was represented. This included the following dancers and/or choreographers, to select perhaps the most prominent figures in 1970s and 1980s New Dance. Most of the following were involved in more than one performance at X6: Laurie Booth, Rosemary Butcher, Kate Flatt, Anna Furse, Craig Givens, Dennis Greenwood, Betsy Gregory, Julyen Hamilton, Claire Hayes, Tim Lamford, Sue MacLennan, Kirstie Simson, Yolande Snaith.[33]

Artists from non-dance backgrounds also came to perform at X6. These included Rose English, the performance artist, musicians from the London Musicians Collective, and Doug Gill and Philip Jeck, out of an art training at Dartington and interested in crossing into performance. Likewise, from structural film, crossing into expanded film (i.e. film with a live performance element), came Annabel Nicolson, William Raban (he also wrote briefly for *New Dance*) and other members of the London Film-Makers Co-op. Thus, there was a very open attitude towards what might be shown at X6 and no concern at all as to whether what was shown fitted established definitions of dance. Indeed, the 'choreographers' themselves regularly showed work that contained minimal dance content.

The ambience at X6 was fraternal and intimate, audiences seated on the floor as well as on chairs and numbering anything from a handful to a hundred. A large number of the spectators were themselves choreographers/dancers supporting their peers, and there was a regular core community around the Collective itself (at various times in X6 history Flatt, Furse, Givens, Gregory, Hamilton, Hayes, Lamford).[34] Often there was discussion and feedback after performances. Yolande Snaith recalls 'the tremendous atmosphere ... my favourite ever dance space': her interest in dance as a career was launched by X6.[35]

The Collective view is that much of the work shown at X6 was of 'extremely high quality', the result of a formal policy on programming and careful choice, although there were also more open weekends of performances.[36] Others interviewed prefer to stress the laboratory nature of X6. They remember a good measure of half thought-out – even 'terrible' – work. The important point here is that audiences were sympathetic to the processes and questions that performers addressed and prepared to acknowledge that, by its very nature, questioning, researching work might not be successful as a product to an outside eye. People often showed work in progress. Artists were allowed to fail in this situation of peer support; the arena was non-judgemental. There was no amateur/professional distinction; some presented their first work at the Space. And X6 was a situation where the work presented could be more useful to artists than to audiences. In this respect, some might have seen X6, as Anna Furse suggests, as 'an artistic therapy centre'. Years later, Sue MacLennan recalled a certain pressure to be creative during this period: 'Being just a dancer was looked down on – everyone was supposed to be a choreographer, or have the potential to be a choreographer.'[37]

Programmes at X6 might consist of a series of short works or just one longer work. Some of the pieces shown were movement pieces. Others were more theatrical, drawing on a range of materials, films, props, text, everyday activities, and sometimes including commentary on the piece itself. Subject matter was often personal, concerned with the real person in real space and time; there was a willing audience then for highly personal work. Episodic theatrical forms were favoured, a collage in time or simultaneous juxtaposition of different elements: similar frameworks, in other words, to those that choreographers used earlier in the 1970s. Most of the work relinquished conventional technical vocabulary, except to subvert it in some way. Some of it used the soft movement quality and free, easy contact with the floor that sprang from release classes, developing in this case from physical imagery, and this was usually complemented by loose, comfortable clothing. Occasionally, choreographers used folk and social dance forms – Kate Flatt, for instance, who reconstructed East European folk dances for performance and used folk dance as an inspirational basis for her own choreography. Some work was improvised, or included passages of improvisation within a fixed framework. Choreographers normally appeared in their own work, identifying with it as personal statement, while often inviting collaboration in the creative process from fellow performers.

Sometimes there was an element of audience participation, establishing a 'democratic', communal rapport between performer and spectator.

Much of the work met at some point with X6 Collective philosophy, usually in its emphasis on body movement without stress and on collaborative, creative process, 'listening' to colleagues. However, while often focusing on the personal, subject matter ranged widely, a good deal of the work laying no particular stress on polemical content. A strand of quiet, 'spiritual' work celebrating the released body was pronounced. A high proportion of the work was made for a single showing, partly because there was no other venue for it, but perhaps, too, as opposition to the accreditable, repeatable products associated with establishment dance. Improvisation could be seen as directly oppositional in this sense. Here, in some cases, pleasure for the audience lay primarily in following the process of a performer's spontaneous response to a situation.

X6 aficionados all remember certain magical 'products' presented at X6. One of these was the performance event *Nocturne* (1980) by Philip Jeck, Douglas Gill and Jessica Loeb. It took place on three floors of Q-block next door to X6: a variety of dimly lit, dusty environments, furniture, props, sounds and music carrying from other floors, a pigeon released, a torch dance, a chamber trio, anonymous coated figures, the audience moving in stages from top storey to bottom.[38] As an example of a pure movement piece drawing from the new movement practice, many have singled out Steve Paxton and Lisa Nelson in *Pa . . . rt* (performed at X6 in 1979, created in 1978). X6 hosted the first performance of this piece in Britain before it reached Dance Umbrella and Riverside dance seasons (in 1980 and 1981 respectively). It was a duet about the implications of opposites, East and West, apparent in Robert Ashley's score, Nelson's costume suggestive of Indian classical dance down to a pencil-line moustache, while Paxton was like a stray Californian in dark spectacles. Her movement was courtly and oriental in its fast, clear weight shifts and tiny gestures, his statuesque and bold.[39]

The performance work of the X6 Collective

Naturally, the work of the Collective members themselves exposed most clearly the philosophy behind X6. With a few exceptions, the Collective members tended to direct their own work independently during the X6 period, or to work in pairs, rather than make work collaboratively as a group as they had done in Dance Organisation. By now, Collective members were pursuing different directions in their creative work.

A major concern in Fergus Early's work at this time was to make informal contact with his audience so that the performer as person and the mechanics of performance would be revealed: 'more than image and movement is conveyed, there are actual occurrences, bootlaces snapping, sweat, breathing'.[40] Yet, he says, he also stressed dance as part of the broad tradition of theatre, rather than merely an opportunity for purely choreographic innovation. Thus, he devised a solo show *Dances for Small Spaces* (1977) that made an issue of intimacy between performer and audience, or demystification, knowing as he did the delights of the close audience/performer relationship at X6, but exploring this with non-specialist audiences. The show was devised for a Greater London Arts Association tour, 11 shows in 12 days, for spaces where the audience would be 'within a few feet of me',[41] often on three sides and invited to talk and challenge Early during and after the performance. Early introduced each dance verbally and invited the audience to choose the order in which the dances were performed. Choreographies to folk and court dance music using social/folk dance as a resource and an authentic Morris jig proclaimed dance as a common heritage, everyman's dance rather than dance as removed high art. In contrast, *Gymnopédies* (1976, incorporated in the 1977 programme), both played at and subverted theatre performance, a sort of musing in the privacy of a bed-sit setting, with minimal moves and big climaxes, undressing from overcoat to underpants, a tap step or two, outrageous falls, and acrobatics on a chair. Early's performance manner and execution of steps was easy, unforced and, with his immaculate timing, revealed a gift for dry but sympathetic humour.[42] With modifications, Early continued performing his solo programme for several years.

Two Man, One Man (1977) and *Manley Struggles* (1978), double acts with Julian Hough, an actor by training, continued the demystification process. Using the tactics of music-hall or performing players to negotiate with audiences, they drew from 'any available skills'[43] – dancing, speaking, acting, playing flutes – and including passages of improvisation, while juxtaposing story and the reality of performance. The structure was episodic (collage). The use of text and acting was, Early says, second nature to him, stemming from his earlier experience working with actors in The Royal Ballet's educational group Ballet for All. These pieces also examined the issue of manliness and friendship between men. *Manley Struggles* expressed the need to find alternatives to the male stereotypes of, for instance, businessman or explorer, all developed under the pun-name Manley Struggles.[44] And in his press release on this piece, Early acknowledged the 'enormous amount of emotion and need bound up in a buddy situation . . . men are made to feel ashamed of this supposedly feminine side of their character.'

Other pieces by Early commented on the ballet heritage. *Naples*, made for the three-week X6 season at Action Space (1978) after an earlier version for Cycles, demonstrated Early's affection for the nineteenth-century ballet choreographer Bournonville – 'in my days as a ballet dancer . . . the classical choreographer whose work I most enjoyed dancing'.[45] He introduced the *pas de six* from Bournonville's *Napoli*, the solo and group dances of which he re-organized, added to and fragmented, within a fictional contemporary Naples. The nineteenth and twentieth centuries rubbed shoulders. Dressed in Neapolitan ice cream colours, each of the seven dancers had created his/her own character and environment, making a setting that filled the space – an artist in her studio (Prestidge), a boy on a motor scooter (Claid), a man in bed (Givens), a glamorous lady making up (Lansley), and so on – all joining to eat spaghetti, cooked on stage, and from time to time to perform the set dance sequences.[46] This was the forerunner of the 1984 *Naples* for Extemporary Dance Theatre.

Two other pieces commented on *Giselle*. In *Sunrise* (1979), Early appeared in a white wedding dress and veil through a hatch in the roof of X6, removed his dress and, in Y-fronts, performed steps and gestures from the ballet. He then returned through the hatch, but not before throwing down his dress once and for all and leaving it behind. *Sunrise*, Early explains, was like a *Giselle* Act III in which the heroine decides that she no longer wants to remain a Wili. The comment was gently humorous, typical of Early, affectionate towards the ballet, while containing a gesture of support for the emergence of the strong and liberated woman. The Y-fronts, a recurring image in his work, were a deliberate means of making traditional masculinity seem vulnerable and slightly absurd.

Early and Jacky Lansley co-directed *I, Giselle* (1980), which took the main body of the *Giselle* story and was more explicitly critical than *Sunrise*, in the tradition of deconstruction, revealing and questioning an underlying ideology. It also reflected the feminist stance of the X6 collective, which was of a confrontational kind, intent on active intervention in patriarchal culture. *I, Giselle* went through the original narrative, turning it upside down in order to challenge the views represented by its characters. 'We wanted to remove Giselle from her eternal victim role,' the programme note explained, 'give her a voice, allow her to triumph.' Giselle is not taken in by the romantic hero Albrecht, and it is Albrecht who goes mad and dies in this version of the tale. The women are strong, the men feeble. The last piece to be rehearsed at X6, *I, Giselle* emphasized theatrical values: it was a group piece, with full set design by Givens and additional slide projections, including some of the original and later productions of the nineteenth-century *Giselle*, signalling the double-coding in this piece.[47] The score by Stephen Montague was an electronic transformation of the Adam original, together with electronic excerpts by a variety of other composers. *I, Giselle* was something like a pantomime in its resource, drawing on music-hall as much as ballet, speaking and singing as well as miming, referring to folk, jazz and chorus-line as well as to parodied classical steps. A piece of this scale, touring nationally, brought fresh visibility to Early and Lansley.

Lansley made pieces of her own that referred to the ballet classics, indeed the first of the series of works of this kind, for the public opening of X6, was a version of *Swan Lake* Act II with the Collective in baggy, beige tropical suits.[48] Later, Lansley and Rose English made *Juliet and Juliet a Duet, Romeo and Romeo a Duel* (1979), two duets to Prokofiev's *Romeo and Juliet* score, questioning the conventional role models for the sexes.[49]

However, far more of Lansley's work during the X6 years demonstrated a concern with the nature of performance in a broader sense, very often drawing parallels between the performance that occurs as part of being a woman and stage performance. Lansley was one of several artists and writers at this time to explore the notion of woman as watched performer.[50] Lansley's pieces subverted or deconstructed her medium in order to expose the medium itself and to emphasize the mask of performance. As in Limited Dance Company lecture performances, spoken or taped texts analysed what was happening live as movement. *Dance Object* (1977) was, the audience heard, a deliberate attempt to abolish any personality or mask with which to entertain her audience. She explained her feelings about performance, her insecurity, for instance, about intimate confrontation with her audience. She attempted to be, rather than act, in real space and time, and dressed herself in a manner – baggy trousers, a man's suit – that gave herself the opportunity to liberate herself from the conditioned female persona.[51]

Bleeding Fairies (1977), a collaboration between Emilyn Claid, Lansley and Mary Prestidge for the Women's Festival at Action Space, Lansley has described in terms of 'destructuring' performance, the attempt to experience or behave rather than 'present' themselves as performing women or women performers.[52] Provoking a controversial cover of *New Dance* no. 5, a photograph of a ballerina coloured in to suggest menstruation, *Bleeding Fairies* also drew attention to the reality of being female, questioning among other female stereotypes the pure, androgynous image of the ballerina (indeed dancers often do not, in fact, menstruate). In her working notes to the piece, Claid wrote of the new representations of women that they sought: 'we have buried the images of swans, nymphs, sylphs and earth mothers – and replaced them with strong vibrant images of women in action.'

It would seem that this series of pieces was polemical, revealing the mechanisms by which ideology is disseminated and, in another way from *I, Giselle*, focusing on and undermining the basic illusory and entertaining aspects of traditional dance theatre. Lansley also continued to use collage forms as a way of opening up a space in which an audience would ask questions and become active in making meaning, but in a more complex manner than in her Strider pieces (see Chapter 2). The object was to create an environment of disconnected images in which an audience would experience a change of perception.[53]

Many of Lansley's pieces during this period trod the narrow boundary between dance and performance art, with a very pared down movement content, perhaps because at this time she was trying hard to obliterate the traditional presentational manner that tends to arise with technical movement vocabulary. But she was also pursuing her interests in a broad performance art/theatre context. She continued to collaborate with Rose English and Sally Potter as an extension of Limited Dance Company, on *Rabies* (1976) shown at the Roundhouse, London, and on *Mounting* (1977) presented at the Museum of Modern Art, Oxford, amidst an exhibition of Frank Stella paintings, and questioning the patriarchal values of the gallery world. There was a more theatrical, narrative emphasis in the work of Helen Jives, the performance group that came out of Lansley's Women's Workshop at X6 in 1978. Anna Furse, a member of Helen Jives, recalls their work, loosely led by Lansley but largely collaborative, as anarchic, rude and boisterous: 'and we didn't ever talk about our work as dance'. It was in the spirit of work by anti-naturalistic feminist theatre groups like Cunning Stunts, and Beryl and the Perils, with divergent images racing from a shared theme and the deliberate negation of expected female behaviour: real menstrual blood confronting the audience from a sheet in *Vision Extracts of Bagwash*, large amounts of food consumed in *The Fast Supper* and *Edge City* (all 1978).

Early and Lansley were by far the most experienced choreographers in the X6 Collective. The other members were all dancers in the early stages of creating work. They speak now with great modesty about these first experiments. Interestingly, all felt the need early on to make pieces about their pasts. The urge was to come to terms with or exorcise their pasts, and pieces introduced excerpts from home movies and talking about personal history, while dance material indicated directions that these artists were taking at present. Examples of such works are Claid's *Going Back* (1976), Green's *Family Background* (1977), Prestidge's *Film Event* (1976) and *Fifty Million Robins Can't Be Wrong* (1979) by Early and Lansley. In her *Choice and Presence* (1977), for instance, Duprès introduced a chest on wheels, topped with model cows, bells and photographic reminiscences of Switzerland and her childhood background.[54]

Many of Emilyn Claid's pieces during this period were solos, drawing from personal experience, sometimes with one or two people supporting in some capacity. Like the work by Early and Lansley, her pieces emphasized real time and space. Perhaps her most striking solo was *Making a Baby* (1979), partly structured, partly improvised. Claid, now seven months pregnant, wanted to share her experiences of pregnancy. Sarah Green describes one of the performances beginning 'by focusing on how she was at that moment, only separating it from her normal speech and movement by placing it in the performance context'.[55] Then, in movement, Claid confronted misconceptions about pregnant women being ungainly or fragile. Lying down, balancing a dish of water containing a plastic swan on her stomach, she waited for the baby's movement to set the swan bobbing. The performance ended with audience participation in playing out customs of childbirth of other cultures.

In creating work for herself, Claid deliberately avoided using her ballet and Graham technical backgrounds and, she says, her pieces, like those of Early and Lansley, were experiments in theatre rather than in movement vocabulary. A thread through some of her early works was the exploration of emotional states in terms of body language and gesture, what she called 'the emotional functioning of the body – the physical expressions of our emotions'.[56] Working from emotional experience was one of the subjects of Claid's workshops in improvisation (as well as examinations of 'space design', gesture and rhythm, never, she insists, working from the physical images of release work). The mature realization of this working process came in *Solo* (1983) for Annelies Stoeffel of Extemporary Dance Theatre.

More than other Collective members, Maedée Duprès developed a strong profile as a performer independent of X6 during this period, in a series of solo programmes that began in 1978 and continued into the 1980s, and with a variety of groups, most notably the Rosemary Butcher Dance Company (1976–78) and Richard Alston and Dancers (1978–80). Her sensitivity and charisma as a performer and her versatility as dancer and musician (she also sang and played the piano) were widely recognized. Duprès' solo programmes consisted of pieces by herself and guests, including Alston, Butcher and Flatt, and X6 members Lansley, Claid and, in 1981, Early. For the 1978 programme *Dance and Slide*, Geoff White, the X6 photographer, provided slides as a connecting device.

Duprès recalls that she did not feel the same need as other Collective members to question existing dance traditions and was generally more inclined to abstraction.[57] She was concerned with finding how improvisation could stimulate movement invention[58] and establishing a comfortable rapport with her audience. Duprès' frequent method for her solos was to work from an improvisational basis, often improvising within the performance itself. In *Dance and Slide*, for instance, her own contribution *Body Obligato* was an improvisation based on a duet for 'cello and double bass by Rossini. In several other early pieces, there was an element of audience participation. In *Choice and Presence* (1977), she asked audiences to comment, or to co-ordinate raising and lowering the window blinds as she improvised, or to make any kind of noise that they wanted whenever she raised a foot.[59] And in *Overall White* (1977) at the Serpentine Gallery the spectators were issued with stick figure drawings ('statues') and instructions to throw various bits of paraphernalia on the floor at her whenever she formed one of these statues. Then they were to make the statues themselves and finally, on a verbal cue, to line up outside the Gallery.[60] Duprès singles out *Foot-falls* (1979) as her first major piece and her most thoroughly structured choreography to date. Created at X6 for her 1979 solo show, it developed from images of physical limitation, for instance moving around a hand fixed to one spot on the floor. It was a collaboration with Stephen Montague who, she says, transformed the sounds of her foot patterns and voice to make a tape score.

Choreographing for other people, Duprès offered her performers considerable creative freedom. In *Similar Instructions* (1976), she gave the same set of verbal instructions as the starting point for two couples who worked both with her and alone, and then, she says, juxtaposed the two different results in performance. For the X6 season at Action Space in 1978, she made *A Dance Score*, involving her beginners' dance class. With Duprès as conductor giving signals, some sequences were set and others improvised to specific instructions (e.g. 'solos on a floor pattern . . . "follow your leader" with the conductor shouting out the names'[61]). Finally, giant fruit salads prepared during the piece were shared with the audience, who were then also invited to take part in the dancing.

Duprès was the first Collective member to leave X6, becoming gradually less involved as her performance commitments increased. The main reason for the break, she says, is that she needed to assert her independence as an artist in control of her own work.

Mary Prestidge, experiencing a new confidence to make work after being what she calls an 'object dancer' at Ballet Rambert, enjoyed a range of environments, both outdoor and indoor. She made two pieces with Carol DeVaughn (a poet and dancer), using radical juxtapositions of image, object and functional movement. Elements, Prestidge says, were 'sometimes used symbolically and ritualistically', for instance, when she burnt a photograph of herself in *Did you know that a praying mantis sometimes sits between the toes of an antelope?* (1978). Prestidge was also interested in improvisation as a performance form, and worked for several years with Rough Rhythms, a flexible group of musicians, poets, visual artists and dancers.[62]

Sarah Green and Prestidge both made pieces, alone and together, that referred to their backgrounds in gymnastics: *Family Background* (1977) (Green) and *Film Event* (1976) (Prestidge), also *Olympic Athlete* (1977) (Prestidge), *Around Rolling* (1978: a collaboration), and *Kami-Kaze Gymnast* (1979) (Green). Work of this kind was often lighthearted. *Around Rolling*, performed at the 1978 ADMA Festival, included discussion about their past as girls developing gymnastic skills and their concern now about the pre-pubescent image of the female gymnast and the negative aspects of competition.[63] The new gymnastics that they performed was informed by feminism, and Prestidge recalls that her movement style now incorporated concepts from Alexander, release and T'ai Chi traditions, making for a less stressful, healthier approach.

X6 as a forum for ideas: New Dance magazine

A key part of X6 activity, extending beyond the Collective itself, was discussion, about teaching, movement techniques, pieces and the politics of being independent. Craig Givens remembers X6 as 'the place where people became aware ... a tangible place where you could go and think about dance in a new way ... find out what you were up against.'[64] It was entirely logical, then, that the magazine *New Dance* was set up as a forum for ideas.

As Lansley said in her editorial to *New Dance* no. 1, the magazine started because 'New dance needs a new language, it is time that we began to define ourselves and our work'.[65] Collective members felt that their work was either ignored or misrepresented by the mainstream press and that the only way in which it could be explained in appropriate terms would be for dancers to start writing themselves; hence, the *New Dance* slogan 'the only magazine by, for and about today's dancers'.[66] Dancers writing was another sign of dance artists asserting a sense of responsibility for themselves. In the same editorial to *New Dance* no. 1, Lansley also stressed that dance demanded to be related to an intellectual context well beyond that tapped by the professional critics at that time. The magazine was intended to be a vehicle for serious dance research and theory as well as for reviewing new work.

New Dance always relied on an unpaid commitment from the Collective running it, although it was supported by Gulbenkian Foundation grants in 1979 and 1982, and by an Arts Council grant in 1983. When the magazine began, it was the X6 members who did the editorial and production work and contributed the majority of articles. However, soon, this magazine Collective began to change and expand. Regular members and writers during the X6 period included Stefan Szczelkun, Claire Hayes, Anna Furse, and Doug Gill, and there were other members during the 1980s. Again, there are contextual reasons for the production of a magazine of this kind. *New Dance* was part of a whole community of alternative political and cultural publications, many of them short-lived, that sprang into existence in the mid-to-late 1970s, of similar meagre means of finance and collective means of production.[67] Perhaps closest to *New Dance* were the two magazines *Musics* (1975–79, put out by a group from the London Musicians Collective) and *Readings* (on expanded film work – it lasted for three issues, in 1977).

The flavour of *New Dance* was immediately distinct from that of other British dance magazines at the time, because of its New Dance focus and emphasis on the artists themselves writing about their creative and teaching

81

philosophies.[68] It was also unusual in its breadth of perspective, covering such areas as dance anthropology and history, gender issues in relation to dance (there were special men's and women's issues, nos. 14 and 15), social and folk dance, dance therapy, T'ai Chi, skateboarding, and the funding of dance. The philosophy underpinning the magazine was the same as the X6 Collective philosophy of relating dance to a context beyond itself.

During its history, *New Dance* was frequently criticized for insubstantial pieces, lack of clarity, an incestuousness that made writers less critical than they should have been and, in the long term, debates begun, reiterated, but left undeveloped. (Incestuousness was inevitable when the only way that many performers could get coverage was from their peers.) Some of these criticisms came from the writers themselves or sympathetic readers and were voiced within the pages of the magazine itself.[69]

However, *New Dance* did fulfil an important role in several respects. There were reviews and discussions of kinds of work that were largely ignored elsewhere and, if they lacked a certain distance from their work, artists undoubtedly provided useful insights into the nature of New Dance. Most significantly, *New Dance* initiated new critical frameworks that were appropriate to radical work and, so it turned out, that might be used in a reassessment of other kinds of dance. Writers examined whether, and by what means, work addressed itself to its cultural context, and evaluated working processes and questions asked as well as 'products'. With this emphasis, *New Dance* broached topics that were again ignored by other dance magazines, in the 1970s at least. The series of articles on women and dance is especially noteworthy: Lansley's 'Women Dancing', a discussion of new structures and performance modes through which women might reclaim their identity;[70] Anna Furse's examination of the image quandary in which the female dancer traditionally finds herself (trapped by the male gaze);[71] and Rose English's 'Freudian/Lacanian' analysis of the ballerina figure, drawing from feminist studies in the other arts.[72] In fact, *New Dance* introduced to dance the Marxist/feminist thinking that has been the basis of feminist and cultural studies in the 1970s and 1980s. In her editorial to the first issue, Lansley recognized that analysis of this kind was already taking place in film and performance art. It was important that dance, too, should take on board these arguments. *New Dance* played a significant role in opening up this process.

The X6 sphere of influence

Ultimately, it was within the New Dance community that X6 had the most profound effect. This far outweighed its effect as a publicly visible organization generating and presenting work. It was a movement for dancers rather than a movement with immediate consequences for dance audiences. X6 served mainly an audience of peers and friends. There are several reasons for this. For a start, there was no developed audience for experimental dance at that time and, as a centre, X6 was awkwardly situated geographically. Publicity through critical support was virtually non-existent. Furthermore, the influential Dance Umbrella Festivals of 1978 and 1980 put emphasis on work of quite another kind (see pp. 99–100). This is not the place for arguing the reasons for this lack of support for British New Dance in detail, only to list the impressions that were frequently reiterated by critics and assessors from funding bodies: poor quality, especially in terms of presentation; polemics at the expense of artistic interest; a lack of dance content; lack of originality – the work was too derivative of American work.

New Dance as a British movement

The notion that British New Dance work merely reiterated American in-novations deserves careful examination. The parallels with the Judson Dance Theater of the 1960s and the debt to release work are the examples most often cited.[73] Undoubtedly, there was a similarity of purpose with Judson: both X6 and Judson were co-operative, artist-run organizations dedicated to alternative ideas. And there were clear likenesses across the work, for instance, the wide range of materials incorporated into perfor-mance, the broadening of the definition of dance, the use of non-technical movement, the collage structures.

Some of the theatrical, collage-structured New Dance would seem to be distinctly post-modern, according to the later meaning of that term (see p. 5). Another body of work is harder to categorize within the main thread of dance post-modernism, seeming to embrace rather than distance the au-dience for analytical enquiry, encouraging the spectator's empathetic response to the performer as a like person, even, especially in work that in-cluded audience participation, involving an element of ritual. Perhaps such work bears some comparison with what Roger Copeland calls 'therapeutic' post-modern dance, the work in the US of Simone Forti, Anna Halprin and Deborah Hay,[74] although I would hesitate to use his term in the British context or to claim that British and American work looked very similar. In retrospect, there is sound evidence that much New Dance interlocks with the broad, international post-modern movement although, at the time, in their enthusiasm to create a British movement, it seems to have been hard for some New Dancers to recognize this.

But it is worth noting how the connections with American work, in-cluding post-Judson American work, came about. They resulted from osmosis rather than direct influence, information, for instance, gleaned via the British structural film movement. The Sally Potter connection was im-portant, and she was aware of Yvonne Rainer's work in the USA (see p. 29). The most direct influence was received from other forms of radical art, like theatre and performance art, developing in this country. Release technique was undoubtedly highly influential, but it is primarily an attitude to the body. It did not necessarily provide dancers with a vocabulary or style to be copied. Nor did many British choreographers who found the technique useful elect to adopt its image basis when making work.

However, perhaps the most important consideration to bear in mind when comparing British and American traditions is that X6 made a point of looking to home. It was an organization that a group of British artists felt they needed for themselves at that time; the work was informed at its core by the particular backgrounds of these artists and their working colleagues, and by the radical political climate, including the women's movement, that sprang from 1970s Britain. New Dance attached particular importance to the notion of dance as means of self-realization and of establishing relationships with the social realities of the day. It is interesting that the pages of *New Dance* magazine are peppered with warnings against getting 'trapped in an avant-garde backwater'[75]. (The Collective explains this today as warnings against the avant-garde that ignores social context: 'while wanting to take the art form of dance forward, we wanted to be a different *kind* of avant-garde.'[76]) As Early emphasized in 1986, in a definition that might be considered representative of X6 philosophy, New Dance was about liberation.

The end of X6

X6 Dance Space was forced to close in September 1980, like other artists' studios and workshop spaces at Butlers Wharf, vacated to make way for docklands property developers to move in. The Arts Council registered dismay, convinced, by this time, of the value of the work that was being done there.[77] But it seems that the Collective was coming to a natural end as well: 'We needed the Collective at first as a means of support and power and of understanding how to work with others, and by then, I was able to stand on my own two feet . . . but, by the end, the structure of the Collective was getting in the way of our personal ambitions . . . it's fundamentally inefficient' (Claid). Lansley recalls the context of the X6 closure, that, within the women's movement certainly, there was a trend away from collectives by this time – 'a frustration that collectives kept individuals down'. However, in the most positive sense, the Collective members felt that they were now ready 'to go out there individually and change the world. We were looking forward to taking our knowledge and experience out into the established dance scenes, mainstream and independent.'[78]

Before the 1980 closure, a number of the artists who had been at one time closely associated with the Space were voicing frustrations of another kind. Some indeed had already stopped frequenting X6, having found their own feet as independent dancers. Betsy Gregory, for instance, who had

84

discovered after making a few pieces that she no longer wanted to be a choreographer, was 'sick of discussions going over the same political ground . . . and wanted to go back to studying technique more formally'.[79] Craig Givens was tired of the 'turgid discussions' and 'preaching a message' and what he felt as 'the spontaneous performance, anti-technique philosophy' and 'wanted to be involved in work of a tighter and more defined nature'. Givens had developed his career as a designer, danced with Cycles, and performed his own solo show at X6 in 1979, with works by himself, Gregory, Early, Duprès and Spink. He turned down an invitation to join the X6 Collective in its later years.

It was the 'unfinished' nature of much of the work shown at X6 that had kept some choreographers outside the X6 fraternity, like Rosemary Butcher – 'people didn't work long enough at things'.[80] Kate Flatt, while recognizing the significance of X6 as a creative base for artists outside the major companies, now expresses strong reservations about the political emphasis at X6 (she herself tended to remain on the outskirts of that activity): 'a lot of work got dissipated amongst the political activity at X6 . . . too much was collective expression, too little was developed by individuals . . . we could have concentrated more on making better dance. As it was, what we made was often very low in its expectations of itself.'[81] Anna Furse, on the other hand, was wholly sympathetic with the political aims of the Collective, yet became frustrated with the rough presentation of much of the work shown at the Space, what she calls 'feeble publicity', the late starts to shows, the continuing lack of facilities, etc. She feels that all this was symptomatic of a general lack of self-ambition at X6, a result of the self being subsumed under group power, or of a belief that personal ambition and professionalism somehow meant colluding with the establishment. Lansley herself has described her solo work during this period as 'transitory in the sense that it was improvisational and relatively unstructured',[82] while it was 'nevertheless a very important period for me'. And she has admitted that the 'de-structuring process' at X6 could interfere with production.[83]

It seems possible, then, that after a certain point the focus on the individual and collective community in the process of radical self-appraisal – 'artists finding themselves' – limited the usefulness of X6 to the broader New Dance community. There was now a generation of other New Dance artists who had needed X6 to give them a start, but who, after a certain point, no longer found it a support for their artistic ambitions.

Before the closure of X6, the Collective set in motion the foundation of Chisenhale Dance Space in the East End of London, another artist-run space. However, from the start, it was decided that Chisenhale had to function in many important respects differently from X6. There were delays. A floor was laid in November 1981, and the space did not officially open as a public performance space until December 1984. Chisenhale has always had a much larger collective membership than X6, an administrator, and a more public programme, including a close involvement with the local community that X6 never made a priority.

Early has since made community dance the main focus of his work and based himself at Chisenhale. He founded the community dance company Green Candle in 1984. Until May 1988, Prestidge was also based at Chisenhale, as a community dance worker. In 1989, she moved to Stoke-on-Trent, and has been teaching and working independently there in dance. From 1981–88, Claid was Artistic Director of Extemporary Dance Theatre. She changed its programme policy away from repertory in the 'contemporary' mode (the look of LCDT or Rambert transposed to a middle-scale company) to New Dance repertory and seasonal projects, and reflected her X6 experience in the working methods and movement style of the company. Lansley continued an independent career as a choreographer in the 1980s and directed movement for several theatre productions. From 1987–89 she was Artistic Director of English New Dance Theatre, based in Newcastle-upon-Tyne.[84] Duprès continued her career as a solo artist and teacher, and danced with Siobhan Davies and Dancers in 1981 and Second Stride between 1982 and 1986. Since 1987, she has taught at Oberlin College and Regis College in the USA. Sarah Green, who stresses that she was always far more interested in social issues than dance, ended up totally disillusioned with dance, having hoped 'that art could change the world';[85] she left art behind and, after working for a period with the mentally ill, joined the women's movement at Greenham Common.

The general consensus now of those who used to frequent X6 is that what happened there was of undeniable and lasting value, whatever their reservations about the work shown there and the underlying philosophy, and whatever they chose to select and reject from the X6 experience. Undoubtedly, an organization like X6, with its interest in process and discussion and time-indulgent consideration for the person participating in art, could hardly have existed in the more pressured, market-led 1980s. It was a 1970s phenomenon. Yet, in the very nature of the X6 organization lies an important legacy to the New Dance of the 1980s, however osmotically this might have been received, however little recognized: a fundamental clearing process had been initiated to encourage 'thinking' dancers and to undermine the myths that surround the more traditional genres of dance. *New Dance* magazine continued to be instrumental in transmitting these ideas. Since X6, there has been an awareness amongst many New, independent or contemporary dancers, whatever they have chosen to call themselves, that personal politics are a part of dance, even if there has been less urgency to make these explicit to an audience.[86] Not least, X6 brought dance firmly in touch with the women's movement, the most significant social movement of the 1970s and 1980s. A new range of representations for women in dance was opened up; some women found new confidence to make their own work.

X6 was an educative force in broader terms too. It was an information centre and a London base where people could study alternative practice: conventional technique taught in a new way, contact improvisation and release work (methods highly influential into the 1980s). It was also a place where people could try out creative ideas, show their first work and, perhaps, fail. At a time when there were hardly any precedents, it gave artists the confidence to go out and make work independently and to form their own groups.

It seems clear now that a good deal of the late 1970s New Dance discussed here interlocks with what is considered the post-modern movement in dance, if we adopt a broad notion of what constitutes post-modern dance. It is also clear that this work continued to develop structures that had been introduced earlier – there are indeed good reasons for backdating the beginnings of New Dance. But X6 raised in the consciousness of British independent dancers that they were developing a tradition of their own: there was now a movement with its own label. Furthermore, the body of work presented at X6 broke new ground politically for British dance and helped to broaden definitions, wearing down resistance to dance pieces that did not have a developed dance or technical dance content.

Finally, X6 was the background to Chisenhale Dance Space, highly successful as a community dance centre and sympathetic venue in which beginning as well as experienced choreographers can present work. Chisenhale is still the only artist-run dance space in Britain.

CHAPTER 4

Sharings and Showcases
The dance festivals of the late seventies

By the late 1970s, enough dance activity was happening in Britain outside London Contemporary Dance Theatre and Ballet Rambert to generate a series of festivals, focal occasions to show this independent work and special forums for artists to exchange ideas. And there was much to celebrate. The three major dance festivals were ADMA (the festival of the Association of Dance and Mime Artists, see p. 60), Dance at Dartington and Dance Umbrella. Each was distinctive in its aims and flavour. Each had something different to say about dance in the late 1970s.

ADMA took place at the Drill Hall in Action Space (off Tottenham Court Road, London) in May–June 1977 and 1978. Dance at Dartington happened within the College, initially taking place during a weekend in June 1978, subsequently occupying an April–May position during the college's Easter vacation. Umbrella was essentially London-based to begin with, but it acquired an increasing regional commitment. The first festival took place in autumn 1978, the next in spring 1980, and thereafter Umbrella occurred regularly in the autumn. All three festivals were opportunities for artists to show specially created as well as recent work. Although Dance at Dartington and Dance Umbrella continued after the 1970s, it is their early life, from 1978–80, that is the focus of this chapter.

The ADMA festivals
The two ADMA festivals sprang directly from the ADMA organization. Artist-run, administered by a team of ADMA members, any performer or teacher was welcome to take part in these festivals, providing he/she was a member of ADMA: there was no selection process. Key principles were to give exposure to anyone who wanted it, for example artists working in isolation, and to acknowledge that people 'on the ground floor' were potentially as important as established performers.[1] The result was a celebration of the range and amount of new dance activity happening at the time, much of it unfunded work, and the most comprehensive view available of what was happening outside the main companies. There was also the opportunity to learn from the inside in classes and workshops, and to present work in a non-competitive, generous ambience. The collectively run Action Space

was a sympathetic venue: it had already acquired a reputation for showing radical, political theatre.

The 1977 festival was two weeks long and presented 33 performing groups or soloists (figures are for both dance and mime, see Appendix 5). Each day there were one or two performances, in the afternoon and evening, and one or two classes or workshops (one of these was a seminar, recorded in *New Dance* no. 3, entitled 'New Dance ... what is it?'). The festival day began at 10 a.m.

Demonstrating the growth of the independent dance movement, the festival expanded to three weeks in 1978 with 42 groups performing. A sample daily schedule was now two workshops/classes/seminars (again, a mid-morning start) and three performances, one lunchtime and two evening. There were affiliated events: Richard Alston and Dancers performing at Riverside Studios (one of his pieces, *Doublework* was also performed in a lunchtime at Action Space); Rosamund Shreeves' Chiswick Dance; and an exhibition of photographs by Chris Schwarz.

The ADMA Festivals were successful in bringing together many genres of work, contemporary and New Dance, dance with a performance art orientation, dance with film, and dance from other cultures, for instance, in 1977, Kathak, danced by Alpana Sengupta. Of course there was mime too: the 1977 festival included an early performance by Moving Picture Mime Show of *The Seven Samurai*. However, by far the largest proportion of work shown in both festivals was dance, only a small proportion mime. Classes were equally varied, ranging from improvisation and contact-release to ballet and contemporary dance, acrobatics and mime to folk dance and Natural Dance. (The Natural Dance Workshop specialized in encouraging non-trained people to explore their own movement potential, to 'discover the dancer and the artist inside themselves'.[2])

Most contributors were people working in London, the X6 fraternity and many more, but there were several regional representations in both festivals, like the Janet Smith Dance Group from Leeds, Cycles from the West Midlands, Laurie Booth, Libby Dempster, Arianna Economou and Linda Hartley, all students from Dartington College, and Helix from Cambridge. Not surprisingly, many of the contributors have long since left the British dance scene. In the 1978 festival, there were also several participants from abroad. ADMA's grant application to the Arts Council had suggested that the festival could well take off and become a major international event. Audiences numbered from between a handful to well over a hundred. There is a note in *New Dance* no. 7 that 1700 people attended the 1978 festival in some capacity.[3] *New Dance* gave the most comprehensive reviewing.

A non-selective festival was bound to include both interesting and much less interesting work, but it is hard to talk of standards, because it was accepted that the work shown could be raw and unpolished experiment, emphasizing process rather than product, and that, if it broke away from established norms, traditional criteria no longer applied to it. As the writer Sarah Rubidge has recalled, audiences were 'willing to work through this first stage of experimentation with the artists and accept that some of the results would need to be perceived with a different "eye" to that generally used in the context of dance performance'.[4] Audiences at that time seemed more willing in this respect than they were to be in the 1980s. An important point too is that the rapport between audience and performers was warm and intimate, as it was at the much smaller and geographically difficult X6 Space. Dancers performed to audiences who contained a high proportion of fellow contributors and people with whom they had danced in a class or workshop situation.

The Drill Hall was an appropriately informal venue. It was a large white open space with basic technical facilities, but pleasant, and audiences sat on chairs and benches and, if these overflowed, gym mats. Reviews of the 1977 festival in *New Dance* no. 3 mention appreciatively the close physical relationship between audience and performers that the space offered and the emphasis, in some pieces, on real people working in a real space, 'not some faceless denizens from a long-lost proscenium stage'.[5]

In this spirit too, several events transcended the traditional frameworks of dance performance, and several included an element of audience participation, much more typical of 1970s than of 1980s work. One such piece with a theatre orientation, and which many thought the high point of the 1977 festival, was *Halflife* by Tim Lamford and Julyen Hamilton (one-time students of the LSCD). The two choreographers/performers worked through male stereotypes in this piece, inspired by Jung's dream that he had killed Siegfried. This was a metaphor for man's need to find his own direction and to abandon the traditional image of the male hero. 'The dream showed that the attitude embodied by Siegfried, the hero, suited me. Therefore it had to be killed.'[6]

In *Halflife*, there was humorous subversion: the lover, who carries his lady and her large spider-plant up a ladder to a ledge high above the space, allows himself to be used as a footstool and then eats the carnation she holds in her lap; the hero, who appears carried corpse-like to the sounds of Siegfried's Funeral March (from Wagner's *Götterdämmerung*), and who then exits cheerfully; two towelled athletes who bend over each to extract a bright jaffa orange lodged high beneath his towel at the groin, and then exchange oranges to make peace. Finally, sliced oranges were handed around the audience.[7]

During the same festival, Fergus Early co-ordinated an all-night event *Ballet of the Night*, based loosely on the idea of Louis XIV's *Ballet Royale de la Nuit*. To mark each hour, Early appeared in a brief dance event, dressed in different bizarre regalia each time, and at 6 a.m. inside a black umbrella horse, with Morris bells on his legs.[8]

The X6 Collective members played a prominent role in the ADMA Festivals. In 1978, Duprès offered her first solo programme *Dance and Slide*. The same year, there was *X6 and Xtras, an Xtraordinary Evening*: this began with performances of Early's folk-based *Sergeant Early's Dream* and *Around Rolling*, a gymnastic dance by Mary Prestidge and Sarah Green, and later moved the audience into the small theatre downstairs for divertissements of song, dance and mime and a round of late-night jazz.

The two ADMA Festivals were instrumental in letting what was going on in Britain at the time be seen, and in providing a platform where risk and experiment would receive sympathetic support. There was the inherent danger of a community whose members were less than rigorous in their criticisms of each other, but the principle of a non-selective, all-embracing festival in the still early days of independent dance, a movement finding out what it had and what it was, was an eminently sensible one. The Arts Council offered a small grant of £1334 for the 1977 festival, and was moved to offer £2000 in 1978.

However, it appears that the second festival, much more ambitious than the first, suffered severe organizational setbacks. There was a string of last-minute cancellations of events. The *Time Out* dance critic Jan Murray, who had written encouragingly about the 1977 festival, reported to the Arts Council that eleven events were certainly dropped, and often without replacements.[9] Helen Crocker, writing from the inside as a festival co-ordinator, complained in *New Dance* about the irresponsibility of some participants, causing disorganized events and sometimes angry, bewildered audiences, a lack of 'festival spirit', and insufficient support in clarifying the non-selective policy of the festival to audiences.[10]

The Arts Council was not pleased. A report on the 1978 festival sent to all the Regional Arts Associations listed 18 groups as professional or interesting, and 17 as substandard, student or amateur.[11] (It is Arts Council policy only to fund professional work.) The Council also held the view that the Action Space Drill Hall was inadequate for acceptable professional presentation of performances.[12] On the other hand, some groups that appeared in the ADMA festivals had no pretensions to be other than amateur. The question of professional standards is a difficult one, seeing as styles were developing that did not require a traditional professional dance training and artists were not being funded at a professional level. *New Dance* published comments from enthusiastic workshop participants, and argued with the Council's lack of understanding of non-technically based dance work and lack of sympathy with work that had a pronounced content other than dance.[13]

A grant for a third open-door festival was never given. The 1978 ADMA Festival was the last.

Dance at Dartington

Mary Fulkerson was the mind behind the Dance at Dartington Festivals. She tells us that the original impetus came from two sources.[14] The first was the group of American guest teachers/choreographers who happened to be at Dartington College at the same time. Since her arrival there in 1973, Fulkerson had invited a line of American colleagues to teach with her on the full-time course, and she wanted to give them a wider introduction to the British and European dance scenes. The second reason was that, after teaching at X6, Fulkerson wanted to help the emerging New Dance community in Britain, to build a stronger relationship with what was going on outside Dartington, and to provide a once-a-year meeting-point for artists who might be working in isolation. Dartington College also wanted to celebrate the acceptance by the Council for National Academic Awards (CNAA) of its proposals for an extended study of movement within the BA degree in theatre.[15]

Fulkerson's idea was to have a dance festival for dancers and passionately involved 'non-professionals'. Thus, there were to be plenty of classes and workshops as well as performances, and it was a festival that would encourage experiment, true to Dartington's liberal tradition, 'predicated more toward development than achievement, more toward exploration than arrival'. The situation was to be relatively 'non-competitive, non-critical'.[16] The national press was invited to the early festivals but, probably to the advantage of the Dartington kind of festival, there was never the pressure for press coverage that was necessary to ADMA and Dance Umbrella. *New Dance* covered the festivals; Jan Murray wrote warmly about the 1978 and 1979 festivals in *Dance and Dancers*.[17]

Those who took part in Dance at Dartington were like an easy family, performers becoming students becoming audiences, like the ADMA festivals, but even less public, as the festivals were residential and the community of participants relatively stable. 'There were no stars,' wrote Claire Hayes of the 1978 festival (*New Dance* no. 7). 'Babies, and students, critics and performers, holders of purse strings and teachers alike – all came in the sunlight just people sharing a common love of dance, which was good, and a true celebration.'[18] It is significant that people returned year after year: by the 1980s, it was estimated that 40% of the participants had attended more than once.[19] Participants stayed in local bed and breakfast establishments or could camp (for fifty pence) by the River Dart. The Dartington situation is idyllic, glorious Devon countryside and the restored fourteenth-century Hall with its elegant courtyard, terraced garden and jousting green. As Murray commented, Dartington is the sort of place where 'virtually any activity would be enjoyable'.[20]

Another unusual feature of the festival was that its contributors were unpaid. Expenses, food and accommodation were covered, but otherwise they gave their services in the spirit of offering something to an emerging field of new, young choreographers and performers. Contributors were invited, although a principle was to be as non-judgemental as possible, and artists who initiated the offer of work were warmly received. There were small grants from South West Arts and the Dartington College Theatre Department. Costs for participants were kept to a minimum, and a few bursaries were offered each year to assist with travelling expenses. With minor modifications, these policies were retained until Fulkerson's departure from the College and the last festival in 1987.[21] Fulkerson directed and organized the festivals herself, with assistants. Steve Paxton, who graduated from being a guest teacher to teaching full-time at the College, 1978–80, helped administer in 1979 and 1980.

After the first weekend event of June 1978, festivals followed the pattern of beginning after the participants' arrival on the Wednesday and continuing until late Sunday afternoon. Starting at 9.00 or 9.30 a.m., participants could enjoy three or four classes daily (with a choice between two or three classes running simultaneously) and two or three performances (daytime and evening). Short lectures were also scheduled in some festivals. In 1978, for instance, Peter Brinson spoke on 'The Future of Dance in Britain', and Early on 'X6, the Magazine and ADMA'.[22] The 1980 festival introduced discussion sessions as an alternative to practical classes.

Festival numbers steadily increased. The first festivals publicized room for 50 participants and some additional observers. Murray reported that over 100 in total (contributors included) were eventually involved in the 1978 festival;[23] a number came on from the ADMA Festival that year. Evening concerts were open to the public. Numbers increased to over 200 in the 1980s.[24] The number of teachers and choreographers clamouring to show work increased correspondingly, although time obviously restricted the amount that could be presented. Whereas the 1978 festival featured 15 groups and soloists, numbers increased to over 30 by the late 1980s (see Appendix 6). There was a tradition of sharing many of the performances between several choreographers. The College opened up its studios and the Great Hall for classes. Its Dance School studio and intimate Barn Theatre were the performing spaces.

Dance at Dartington rapidly became cosmopolitan. By 1979, there were already participants from eight countries.[25] However, especially in its early years, the festival was strongly flavoured by Fulkerson's enthusiasms. Most of the American choreographers/teachers shared her interests in release, working from an image basis, and in contact improvisation. Several of them had been guest teachers in the Dartington Theatre Department and/or colleagues at the American universities (Illinois and Rochester) with which she had been associated: Nancy Topf, John Rolland, Marsha Paludan, Nancy Udow and, of course, Paxton.[26] Fulkerson herself performed and taught regularly at the festivals.

93

Other American contributors in the early festivals included the following: Katherine Litz (1978), once a member of the Humphrey-Weidman and Agnes de Mille companies, who brought a remarkable series of humorous solo vignettes, making her British debut at Dartington shortly before she died; Barbara Dilley (1979),[27] who had a background of working with Merce Cunningham, Yvonne Rainer and Grand Union and later co-directed the dance programme at the Buddhist Naropa Institute in Boulder, Colorado (Fulkerson had been on the summer faculty there); Lisa Kraus (1979) who performed and taught Trisha Brown repertory (she was a Brown company member) as well as her own work.

Then there were the British artists who had developed a strong link with the Theatre Department, sharing some of the Dartington premises for dance: Alston, now returned from the USA, Rosemary Butcher and Miranda Tufnell. (Tufnell's work used minimal movement and stillness, and explored 'the rhythmic and spatial connections within one's daily movement experience'.[28]) Dartington students like Laurie Booth and Arianna Economou, also contributed, later as ex-students.

Other British contributors in the early days included Kirstie Simson, a Laban Centre graduate who became an important independent dancer in the 1980s, Kate Flatt and Tim Lamford, Emilyn Claid, Maedée Duprès, Fergus Early and Mary Prestidge (the last four X6 Collective members), and Janet Smith. Pauline de Groot became a regular contributor from Holland.

There was minimal Graham-based input to these festivals,[29] although they included a number of classes and work in other technical dance styles by, for instance, Alston and Janet Smith. The latter introduced a weighty, relaxed style influenced by the approach of the American Erick Hawkins. However, the teaching and performing of set technical steps and the styles associated with these was never the emphasis. A certain kind of work and teaching rapidly became associated with the Dartington Festivals, gave them their particular ethos, and it revealed Fulkerson's and Paxton's particular interests and choices. It was work that celebrated an 'every-man/woman approach to movement, relaxed efficiency over a pedestrian stance',[30] and it often included improvisation, spoken text and the use of props.

A review of the 1979 festival in *New Dance* noted that the festival reflected these particular predilections of Fulkerson and Paxton, and expressed concern that it was not showing the range of work happening in England. And perhaps there was too much homogeneity of approach in the classwork, wrote *New Dance*, 'people started their fourth class of the day lying on their backs, visualising a centre line . . . '.[31] Fulkerson at this time was still finding out who it was that constituted New Dance in Britain. But a broadening of programme was already apparent by 1980. Furthermore, the British New Dance community realized the usefulness of the Dartington approach as one that imposed no style, and its philosophy of individual growth was warmly shared.[32] Many New Dancers were drawn at some point to take something from Dartington, and the trend continued from the late 1970s through into the 1980s. As for the festivals themselves, a need for this kind of event, a festival for dancers, was immediately recognized.

Dance Umbrella

Unlike for the ADMA and Dance at Dartington Festivals, the idea of the Dance Umbrella Festival came not from working artists, but from the Arts Council and from arts administrators. Jan Murray states in *Dance Umbrella: a short history* that the festival was a response 'to an obvious need: that of the new wave of dancemakers for proper presentation and management, and of a fast-growing dance audience for exposure to important contemporary work by foreign and UK artists'.[33] The idea stemmed from an Arts Council advisor's casual suggestion in 1977 that a showcase festival for British work along the lines of the New York Dance Umbrellas would be a good idea, a festival with a central body taking care of all administrative matters, such as liaison with venues, technical back-up, publicity and press contacts. But the idea that there should be some kind of festival might also have been prompted by the ADMA precedent.[34] The same year, 1977, Val Bourne, then assistant to the Arts Council's Assistant Dance Director, Jane Nicholas, and Nicholas Hooton, administrator of Riverside Studios, prepared a paper on a prospective festival at Riverside. Arts Council money was later approved for a first festival to take place in autumn 1978. At that time, Ruth Glick was festival co-ordinator, working in tandem with Bourne (by then the Greater London Arts Association's first dance officer) and an Umbrella committee. Later, Umbrella was established as a charitable company and, in November 1980, Bourne became its founding director with Fiona Dick as administrator. As well as running a series of annual festivals, Umbrella has functioned as a management service, from April 1980–1989,[35] and as an information service which, amongst other things, published (from December 1980) a Dance and Mime Newsheet. It has also organized conferences and seminars, the first in December 1979, the Dance Artists in Education conference in Birmingham.

If Umbrella was conceived primarily as a festival for British work, another important characteristic was its presentation of foreign groups and, especially in the early years, groups from the USA. The report that Umbrella prepared on its 1978 festival indicates that the purpose of its commitment to foreign work was twofold: 'to present for the contemporary dance audience some of the current influences and trends in dance in the USA, but perhaps more importantly to expose the English dance scene itself to comparison and contrast with what is happening in New York, where contemporary dance has been established for a longer period of time'. An early title for the festival, Dance Exchange, reflects this aspect.[36] There had been no consolidated approach to bringing over foreign groups before this. In the late 1970s, the ICA had held a short international season, Dance Theatre '77, (presenting Penta Theatre from Holland, Margaret Beals from the USA, and Moving Being from Cardiff), Riverside Studios introduced Trisha Brown and Lucinda Childs for brief seasons in 1979, and X6 had its own series of foreign visitors. But these were *ad hoc* ventures.

From the point of view of British work, Umbrella was conceived as a selective, showcase festival. The home contributors to the 1978 festival were invited on the grounds that they received substantial subsidy from the Arts Council or from a Regional Arts Association, the idea of Umbrella having originated from the Arts Council.[37] It was acknowledged that Umbrella needed to be still more selective after 1978.[38] Home contributors to the 1980 festival were no longer selected as all those who received funding, instead as 'all those British artists considered to have reached a standard of professionalism'.[39]

From the outset, Umbrella worked on building audiences (beyond a narrow group of dance aficionados) and presenting artists 'professionally' in 'decent theatres' with seating capacities of 200–400 people.[40] Initial press coverage was poor, but from the beginning it was better for Umbrella than for either the ADMA or Dartington Festivals. Umbrella also held a broad view of the kind of small-scale dance that could be presented, not only New or post-modern dance, but contemporary dance whose link to the Graham-based LCDT and Rambert work might be patently obvious, even work by young choreographers from The Royal Ballet. The festival covered 'the spectrum of contemporary dance . . . the breadth of dance activity outside of the main companies'.[41] At a Dance Umbrella Directors' Meeting after the second festival (22 July 1980), this breadth of vision came up for discussion. Should the festival now be slightly modified, should it become a 'post-modern Festival', or should it become a 'safer, middle-of-the-road Festival'?[42] It was decided to hold on to the existing wide-ranging selection.

The statistics for the first two Umbrella Festivals are as follows. The 1978 festival was three weeks long, presenting 15 British groups and soloists officially, 3 more in an ICA Dance Platform, and 5 from New York, including John Jones as guest teacher and choreographer. There were 40 performances: 27 British, 13 American, including 3 daytime performances by education companies for schools (see Appendix 7). Umbrella was primarily a London-based festival using two venues, the ICA and Riverside Studios, but there were also a few related performances at the Arnolfini Gallery in Bristol. Audience capacity for the London venues was estimated as 67.5% for evening shows and the audience figure for the entire festival as almost 7500.[43] (Figures account for paying and non-paying audience.)

96

14. *Halflife*, created by Julyen Hamilton and Tim Lamford. Hamilton and Lamford are seen here performing the piece in the Drill Hall at Action Space as part of the 1977 ADMA Festival. (Photograph: Geoff White)

15. Workshop led by Steve Paxton in the Great Hall at Dartington during the 1978 Dance at Dartington Festival. Paxton is seated on the steps, second from left.

16. Maedée Duprès in Rosemary Butcher's *Uneven Time* (1978), part of Duprès' solo show *Dance and Slide*. The 1978 Dance Umbrella included a performance of this solo show. (Photograph: Geoff White, whose slides were used in *Dance and Slide*)

Umbrella '80 was six weeks long, with an extra week after a two-week break, presenting 16 British groups and soloists, Janet Smith appearing in two capacities as a soloist and with Robert North and Dancers, 8 American, with Paxton appearing either with David Moss (a musician) or with Lisa Nelson, 1 from Canada and 2 from Holland. There were 59 London performances that year, 33 British, 18 American, 8 by the artists from other countries. Some critics felt that this was an overload of performances and that the festival was still not selective enough.[44] Paxton and de Groot were foreign visitors who had also contributed to Dartington Festivals. Now, there was a greater spread of London venues involved: the ICA, The Place Theatre, Riverside Studios, the Shaw Theatre (as part of the Camden Festival) and, offering an alternative to the traditional performance format, the Whitechapel Art Gallery. Two more regional venues were involved, the Plymouth Arts Centre and Sherman Theatre, Cardiff, as well as the Arnolfini Gallery again in Bristol. In London, audience capacity reached 78%, and the figure for the entire festival was just over 11 000.[45]

Both festivals included repeat performances for some artists, two alternative programmes for some others, and late as well as early evening shows. Unlike ADMA and Dartington, Umbrella was an evening-based festival.

Both Umbrella festivals ran extra events, seminars on dance education and administration, film seasons, classes and workshops. A 1980 meeting established a national dance lobby, calling for increased funding for dance in several specific areas and greater media coverage. The Dance and Mime Action Group (DAMAG) was formed, which in 1982 became the National Organisation for Dance and Mime (NODM).[46] Eleven workshops/classes were held in 1978, five in 1980. Umbrella regretted the low number in 1980.[47] However, there was never the intention to hold the same proportion of classes as at the ADMA and Dartington Festivals.

It is interesting that by 1980, Umbrella had reached the size of its festivals through the 1980s in terms of the number of participating groups/soloists and performances (the two bigger festivals in 1981 and 1982 were an exception), although there was further regional expansion during the 1980s, leading eventually to independent, regionally-based festivals. By 1980 too, Umbrella had proved its success with audiences and, to the artists involved, the usefulness of festival exposure and specialist administrative support.

However, in terms of presenting British New Dance work, the early Umbrellas were conservative.[48] A glance at the line-up of artists/groups selected for 1978 and 1980 reveals that the majority of British contributions stemmed directly from the traditions of the big established companies, in terms of both the nature of the work presented and the mixed repertory programming. EMMA, Extemporary Dance Company, Basic Space Dance Theatre, and the black company MAAS Movers were all primarily repertory companies. Only the following could be considered as New Dance from those first two Umbrellas: the Rosemary Butcher Dance Company, Cycles Dance Company, Fergus Early, Maedée Duprès, Jacky Lansley, Tamara McLorg (her *Solo* billed as a 'marriage of words, movement and music'), Ian Spink (part of the 1978 ICA Dance Platform), Dancework (a duo whose work developed from Cunningham principles) and the Tim Head/Miranda Tufnell/Dennis Greenwood collaboration (explorations with light and shadow, film, props and movement in the Whitechapel Art Gallery). Richard Alston and Dancers appeared in both these festivals, but I would no longer categorize Alston's work at this time as New Dance or post-modern dance. And it could be significant that, in 1978, most of the one-only performance spots were allocated to this New Dance wing: Spink in the ICA Platform, and solo performances by Duprès, Early and McLorg. Of course, the argument might have been that these British performers received other exposure outside the Umbrella, but they would not have appeared elsewhere in such high profile circumstances.

My own recollections are that, for several years, American work dominated the Umbrella festivals, if only because it seemed so fresh and positive in concept and performance, and so clearly breaking new ground in comparison with most British work on display.[49] That too was the view of many critics at the time. British entries were generally criticized, for their 'flatulent stodginess',[50] 'sloppy technique' and 'shortage of original work'.[51] There was, for instance, Douglas Dunn, an ex-Cunningham dancer, who opened the 1978 festival with *Gestures in Red*, a rigorous solo investigation in silence of certain basic movement premises like moving backwards, scudding on his back at the beginning, or exploring possibilities while remaining fixed to one spot. Or Sara Rudner in her *As Is As Solo*, another rigorous marathon in a more soft, slippery, loose-jointed style that betrayed her long experience of working with Twyla Tharp. And in 1980, David Gordon and Valda Setterfield, from the Cunningham and Judson stables, brought their zany, ironic juxtapositions of slides, text, chairs and movement. Umbrella's American guests were more established names than those who appeared at X6 Dance Space. Paxton and Lisa Nelson were unusual in appearing in both contexts.

Not surprisingly, an antagonism developed within ADMA towards the Umbrella Festival. Umbrella was seen as a rival, given comparatively generous funding, intimately connected from the start with the Arts Council, and it survived. Umbrella could also have been seen as a poor representation of British New Dance in those early years. It was all too easy to get the impression that foreign contributors were being introduced as models. The Americans, after all, had a longer tradition of post-modern work and more experience of working professionally than most British independent dancers. It is perhaps significant that, in the minutes of the Umbrella Directors' meeting (22 July 1980), the American term 'post-modern' is used rather than New Dance. And, although there was good reason to make the most of an input that was briefly available, with the exception of Alston, it was only the Americans who were invited to teach classes and workshops. It could have seemed like one-way instruction. *New Dance* wanted the 1978 Umbrella committee to 'ensure that some British groups and individuals got reciprocal red carpet treatment in New York',[52] but this was never attempted in the 1970s.

Bourne has argued that, to sustain and build public audiences for the festival, Umbrella needed to select work that was more professionally presented than that of many British groups at the time[53] (see p. 83). It was as if Umbrella was looking to the 1980s, when the notion of 'product' seemed to become increasingly important and audiences less willing to accept failure, however interesting the experiment.

However, there are questions to raise other than that of standard of presentation. Perhaps many New Dancers at the time were best speaking to themselves, to a small group of enthusiastic dance watchers, many of them dancers? Umbrella wanted to show work to its greatest advantage in 'decent theatres' and, according to Bourne, the majority of British independents also wanted to show their work in good spaces. But was some work inherently better suited to the more informal surroundings of Action Space and Dartington? There have been numerous occasions when exciting work at Dartington transferred very badly to central London venues. And then, as Sarah Rubidge has suggested, did the Arts Council need to be persuaded of the validity of New Dance – 'and the best way to do that was to present the less radical and/or relatively sophisticated work?' But she also suggests, could the Umbrella Festival have been 'just the vehicle for persuading the Arts Council that experimentation is the life-blood of the art form and that, by their very nature, experiments are not always successful'?[54]

A result of Umbrella's selections in 1978 and 1980 was that a certain kind of British New Dance work was kept at a very low profile. This was the 'political' work and work with a performance art orientation and minimal step content. It is Early's view that, for a while, public taste was defined by 'dancey' and often abstract work,[55] which was also the tenor of much of the visiting American work at the time. Bourne today admits her personal preference for that kind of work in the late 1970s.

In the 1980s, indeed from 1981, British New Dance was more broadly represented in Umbrella festivals – Bourne feels that it was better presented by this time – and the performance art, political, theatrical kind of work that was largely ignored in the late 1970s came through more strongly in programmes. In many of the 1980s festivals too, British work stood up well next to foreign contributions, which came increasingly from Europe (the main flavour of the 1989 festival, for instance, was French dance). After a drop in audience figures in the early 1980s, audiences continued to increase:

101

21 000 for London in 1989. Umbrella had become 'the world's largest con-temporary dance festival',[56] and, by the late 1980s, the only surviving dance festival from the 1970s.

Looking back, Bourne insists that Umbrella was never conceived as a replacement for ADMA although, by virtue of its timing, it appeared to take over after the second and last ADMA Festival. Indeed, minutes of the Arts Council meeting that agreed funding for the first Umbrella Festival (9 November 1977) report that November dates were being considered for it specifically to complement both the May ADMA Festival and the January/February mime festival at the Cockpit Theatre. Bourne also argues that there was a need in the 1970s for both kinds of festival, ADMA and Umbrella, open and non-selective, as well as selective and showcase. But this dual need, as we have seen, was not satisfied.

The three festivals discussed provide a fascinating insight into the tensions within dance outside the large companies in Britain at the end of the 1970s. This was the time when a rumbling and lively experimental movement was just getting organized. There was the determination to celebrate a home profile, whilst work from abroad, especially from the USA, might have looked like an imposed model, another wave of cultural imperialism of a post-modern kind after the Graham import of the previous decade. There was also the tension between what New Dance artists and middlewomen, skilled administrators close to the Arts Council, saw as appropriate for the development of an audience for the new kinds of dance.

One outcome of these tensions was the early demise of the ADMA Festival, which most British experimental dance artists considered to be their prime performance platform. The failure of the ADMA Festival presages the ethos of the 1980s when increasingly, for their survival, artists had to weigh what they wanted for themselves against external demands. A much more market-led era was about to begin.

In the 1980s, and continuing into the 1990s, Chisenhale Dance Space in the East End of London and the central London Place Theatre (since the first 'Spring Loaded' season in 1987) have partly filled the ADMA Festival gap, committed to presenting the range of independent dance experiment in Britain, including the less established groups.[57] However, with the end of Dance at Dartington in 1987, a phenomenon of the 1970s died. The open-door, artist-initiated dance festival, with its easy, informal inter-change between artist and audience, class and performance: this was now a thing of the past. And so, it seemed were those generous, egalitarian ideals of the 1970s.

PART 2

CHAPTER 5

Richard Alston

The early career 1968–77: a summary

In 1989, as Artistic Director of Rambert Dance Company, Richard Alston summarized his early career prior to his study trip to New York (1975–77) as simply 'trying to find out what to do ... and wanting to work through ideas that hadn't yet been explored in Britain'.[1] Certainly, the range of his artistic ideas in his early period was considerable (see pp. 26–28, 48–49). Some pieces, out of Cunningham and Judson Dance Theater traditions, were open-ended in construction, perhaps containing some element of in-determinacy in performance, or were pedestrian in movement style. Others were more traditional in structure or in evoking a distinctive situation or mood. One, *Thunder* (1972), a gesture to Twyla Tharp, used popular culture as a source. The common feature was Alston's determination to find alternatives to the narratives, emotional expression and symbolism that characterized the post-Graham work around him.

Alston's visit to America was the turning point in his career. After that visit, his line of development and aesthetic became more focused. By then, Alston says,[2] he had developed a dance language, rich and individual enough presumably to merit the term 'language', and committed himself to establishing a relationship with the dance heritage, to a position that acknowledged the past as well as it looked to the future.

The work for London Contemporary Dance Theatre

Inexperienced and relatively unfocused as he was in his early 'sorting out' period, Alston's voice had been immediately recognized by the Artistic Director of LCDT, Robert Cohan. During this period, alongside his in-dependent work, which culminated in the formation of Strider, he made a series of works for the LCDT repertory. *Cold* (1971) was an alternative look at *Giselle*, comparing the obsessions of the nightly dancing of Wilis and daily ballet class, with a glance at female co-operatives, and set to fragments of the original Adolphe Adam score.[3] The other three works were all related to each other: the dance material from *Combines* (1972) was reworked in *Lay-out* (1973), which, with a change of score in 1974, became *Blue Schubert Fragments*. Several other Alston pieces were transfer-red to LCDT from workshop performances at The Place, or from Strider:

Something to Do (transferred in 1970), *Nowhere Slowly* (1971), *Tiger Balm* (1972), and *Headlong* (1975).

Combines was the most radical of these pieces, and extraordinary in the context of the LCDT repertoire. Pre-Strider, it was Alston's most ambitious piece to date, using several media, and including film and slides by Sally Potter (the title *Blue Schubert Fragments* was 'found' from one of the film reels).[4] Lasting 50 minutes, it was also Alston's longest work from this period.

Alston has mentioned the aim of collage and the influence of Rauschenberg's *Combines* (hence the title), their assemblage construction and mixture of urbane, everyday objects and painterly strokes. Likewise, the Alston/Potter *Combines* mixed the everyday and vernacular, social dancing, portraits of the dancers in forties street clothes and pedestrian activity next to stylized 'art' dance, popular songs sung by Mildred Bailey, Ella Fitzgerald and Frances Langford next to Schubert and Bach. The structure in time was a series of episodes, live dance alternating and sometimes overlapping with film or slides shown on one, two or three screens simultaneously.

Potter and Alston have also mentioned the influence of Gertrude Stein, borrowing her use of repetition to suspend time into a continuous present, to isolate the moment to be observed. Such formal emphasis represents the other intensely analytical aspect of *Combines*. Alston brought dance structure strongly into the foreground. A solo for Siobhan Davies, for instance, was repeated ten times in all: other members of the cast, instructed to pick up her dance material by learning it during the performance itself, demonstrated its structural processes. The conventions of theatre were invoked by being both used and dismantled: the on-stage experience set against filmed scenes of backstage, performance set against film of 'warming up' and rehearsal in a studio, the dancers as performers set against the dancers as people in portrait and group photographs. Potter brought to the work her background in 'structural film' (see p. 29). She emphasized her own editing procedures with various structural procedures, like the immediate repetition of sequences, or mathematical cutting that brought a visual pulse or rhythmic pattern to the foreground.

With *Combines*, I am reminded of Sally Banes' category 'analytical postmodern dance' (see pp. 4–5), a kind of work that was happening in the USA at precisely the same time. In this respect, *Combines* followed on from a piece like *Shiftwork* (1971) (see p. 28).

America, 1975–1977

In America, Alston attended class at the Cunningham studio and with the ex-Cunningham dancer Valda Setterfield.[5] He also began an intensive study of ballet under Alfredo Corvino, a former teacher with the Ballets Russes de Monte Carlo. He took advantage of the wide range of dance performances in New York: ballet – he was especially interested in the Ashton works that he saw there, and some Bournonville divertissements performed by New York City Ballet – Fred Astaire films, as well as work by post-modern choreographers/dancers such as Steve Paxton, Trisha Brown, Lucinda Childs, Sara Rudner, Douglas Dunn and Twyla Tharp. Concentrating on study and, like many American choreographers he saw, exploring his own dancing as a source of movement ideas, he made few pieces during this period. His major programme presented at the Cunningham studio *UnAmerican Activities* (1976) was largely retrospective. Collecting together material from several works made since 1970, he formed a Cunningham-style event; he performed himself, alongside dancers he had known in England, Siobhan Davies, Eva Karczag, Christopher Banner and Sally Hess.

The mature career from 1977

Background: professional associations

When he returned to England, Alston experienced a burst of creative energy. The outcomes of this were *Rainbow Bandit* (the 1977 version) for LCDT, the choreography for English National Opera's *The Seven Deadly Sins* (1978), and the formation of Richard Alston and Dancers, a small *ad hoc* group that performed four programmes of his works between 1978 and 1980. Meanwhile, believing strongly that a choreographer should also teach, he opened up regular Cunningham-based technique classes at Action Space, attracting a good number of students and drawing from these classes the dancers for his group. It was thus that he discovered Ian Spink and Michele Smith, both of whom had recently arrived from Australia, and Maedée Duprès and Julyen Hamilton, while he 'borrowed' Tom Jobe and Davies from LCDT.

Teaching was a means of subsidizing his work at this time. Alston preferred not to be beholden to any public funding body when he launched his new group.[6] However, there is no doubt that, by the time he returned from America, he was recognized as the leading figure of the new generation of British contemporary dance choreographers. His group took part in both the 1978 and 1980 Dance Umbrella Festivals.

Alston remained on the edges of the New Dance activity that had sprung up during his absence from London, tending to be a spectator rather than a participant. However, he did perform a solo version of his *Connecting Passages* as part of a five-day season at the Acme Gallery (1978), which included New Dance presentations, and his group appeared at the 1978 ADMA Festival, at Action Space, and as a related activity at Riverside Studios. Maintaining his connection with Mary Fulkerson (see p. 37), he was a regular contributor to Dance at Dartington Festivals, from their inception in 1978, until well into the 1980s. He also choreographed for Duprès' solo shows.[7] But, with his work increasingly demonstrating a rapport with dance tradition (it was now very different in artistic stance from *Combines*), Alston's style of work was becoming further and further removed from what most New Dancers were trying to do.

In 1979, Alston's involvement with Ballet Rambert began. At that time, the company was under the direction of John Chesworth. Since it had become a contemporary dance company in 1966, Rambert had developed its own style of expressionism, different from that of LCDT, strongly flavoured by the work of Christopher Bruce and Glen Tetley. Alston's first work for Rambert *Bell High* was premiered in 1980, and, later that year, he became Resident Choreographer.

The move to Rambert was a logical step for Alston. It happened at a time when he was increasingly enriching his dance language with elements of classical ballet vocabulary, and the basis of Rambert schooling had remained classical. In fact, he had always been interested in ballet: it was early experiences of watching ballet that had originally stirred him to take up dance as a career. His combined interest in Cunningham and ballet is not illogical. The fast footwork and the rhythmic energy (largely produced by steps), the articulateness in the torso and emphasis on flow and efficiency with physical energy are all common stylistic characteristics. *Bell High* was suffused with the spirit of Bournonville, which Alston remembered from his visit to the 1979 Bournonville Centenary celebrations in Copenhagen.[8]

It is possible to see now that the balletic turn in his work reached its peak in 1982 and 1983, when he created, using pointe work, *The Prince of the Pagodas* for the Royal Danish Ballet and, the next year, *Midsummer* for The Royal Ballet. For a while then, he chose to see himself as a classical, European choreographer: 'I'm working in Europe, I'm interested in European traditions and finally I just didn't see myself making a stand here for modern dance.'[9] Several writers at this time proposed a special link between Alston and Ashton.[10]

The connection with Ballet Rambert offered several other important opportunities to Alston: the chance to work with a regular, large ensemble of dancers with their own rehearsal space, to come to terms with the proscenium setting, and to make work for regular repeated viewing within a repertory system. Not least, there was the attraction of Rambert's live orchestra of up to twenty players, the Mercury Ensemble, and of having regular stage design for his pieces. Such a working situation is totally different from that of a freelance choreographer making small-scale work for occasional performance.

During the early 1980s, Alston continued to work freelance outside the major companies. His connection as guest choreographer with Second Stride from 1982 is especially important (see p. 132), although it was brief.

It ended in 1983, by which time, he says, Second Stride interests, increasingly theatre-based, and his own, increasingly balletic, no longer seemed compatible.

In 1986, Alston assumed the Artistic Directorship of Ballet Rambert, since when he has worked solely with this group of dancers. The position demands that order of commitment. It is an important fact that running a large established company like Rambert contains its own share of problems that directly affect artistic activity: the need to keep financially afloat, to attract audiences, to encourage private sponsorship, whilst being thoroughly committed to artistic standards, keeping repertory vital and promoting challenging collaborative projects. So far, Rambert's success under Alston has been exemplary. The company's Diamond Jubilee season in 1986 won them the Olivier Award for the 'most outstanding achievement in dance', the first season under Alston's directorship and, in 1989, Rambert received the first Prudential Award for the Arts. The backbone of the repertory has been Alston's own creations for the company. However, pouring a big proportion of his creative energy into direction has meant that Alston now makes less work of his own than he did in the past.

Now, under Alston, Rambert has left behind its commitment to expressionism and embraced wholeheartedly its Director's very different artistic ethos. But there is no question that it is still a contemporary dance company, and Alston's own style has swung back in full recognition of this. In 1987, he changed the company's name to Rambert Dance Company to represent more accurately the nature of the work.

The integration of music and design

Following his period of study in America, by which time he had developed his own dance language, Alston set about integrating the other resources that are customarily a part of dance in the theatre. He felt ready to be prompted into new directions by music and design. On a television South Bank Show about his work (1982), he admits too that, after the first ten years, his choreography, by itself, had 'got too subtle, inbred, for its own good'.[11] Most notably, Alston began to use music as his fundamental source of inspiration and, in the manner of tradition, responded to its structures and moods. *Home Ground* (1978), a solo for Maedée Duprès, to a series of keyboard Lessons by Purcell, was his first piece to use music in this way. Before this, he had tended to use silence or music co-existing in the Cage/Cunningham sense as a backdrop to his choreography. In his early career, much as he loved music, he was afraid of using it badly: he had found that using musical phrase structure and rhythms tended to interfere with his dance phrasing and to produce results which he considered banal.[12]

From the early 1980s, he has stressed the fundamental role of music as a starting point for his work, much as Balanchine did, and his programme notes, like those of Balanchine, tend to refer to music above all other considerations. Musical choices have ranged between classical and popular, live music and taped scores, music of past and present. There has been a shift towards the use of contemporary scores in his work. His criterion for choice is that music should be 'physical', containing breath within it – he has chosen several vocal scores for this quality – or that it should have what he calls 'rhythmic tension'.[13] However, he has used scores with contrasting passages of boneless, limpid rhythm, for instance, the slow movement of *Apollo Distraught* (1982) and outer movements of *Mythologies* (1985/89). There is, too, the pragmatic consideration of the available orchestral forces. It is pertinent that Alston has often chosen British composers, in 1978, Purcell (for *Home Ground* and *Breaking Ground*), in the 1980s, Britten, Tippett, and Vaughan Williams, and of the new generation, John Marc Gowans, Oliver Knussen, Peter Maxwell Davies, Nigel Osborne and Simon Waters. He has used the music of Osborne more than that of any other composer, four pieces in all: *Apollo Distraught*, *Wildlife* (1984), *Mythologies*, and *Zansa* (1986). With Osborne he has also taught courses for choreographers and composers, at the Dartington College of Arts Summer School (1986) and the International Dance Course for Professional Choreographers and Composers at the University of Surrey (1988).

Alston has spoken of collaboration as his favourite working situation, and 'laying yourself open to an artist whose work you admire' as an important liberating experience for him. The models he cites are various: Diaghilev's enterprise, the Graham/Noguchi and Stravinsky/Balanchine collaborations, and Cunningham's work with Robert Rauschenberg and Jasper Johns. During his Rambert years, collaboration has been possible on several occasions, and so far, perhaps not surprisingly, he has turned to British artists, to the composers Gowans and Osborne and to the visual artists Howard Hodgkin, John Hoyland, John Hubbard, Allen Jones and Richard Smith. The *Wildlife* collaboration turned out to be seminal to his career. Incorporating a new score by Osborne and a series of moveable kites by Smith intruding upon the dancing space, it prompted a major shift in the nature of Alston's movement vocabulary. Peter Mumford, the lighting designer, has been a regular collaborator; he has also designed sets for several pieces and directed *Strong Language* for television (in 1988).

The subject of the dances

Some of Alston's pieces, like *Doublework* (1978) and *Dutiful Ducks* (1982, revised 1986), have stressed the 'here and now' of place and time. Their main subject is dance and dancers. However, the hints of situation or of an illusory 'world' in which a dance seems to take place have featured with increasing frequency in his work. In this respect, it is possible to draw a line through from early works such as *Windhover* (1972) and *Tiger Balm* (1972). Often, the title and set give the key to the situation, but it is important to emphasize how much remains unspecific: there is minimal use of body language or gesture to express meaning. *Midsummer* is simply a riotous, sunny landscape (by Hubbard) containing dancing of a complementary youthful spirit, or *Wildlife*, a place where some imaginary flora and fauna may be found. In some pieces, the situation clearly changes, although the identity of the protagonists is still kept remote. In *Zansa*, a society in blue, abstracted in unitards, dances for its life. It is augmented by a group of bright white and yellow intruders who merge forces as if to combat some higher order of energy. Finally, all parties are floored.

Apollo Distraught was a dance realization of the abstract conceit of Apollonian/Dionysian conflict. Alston recalls that the imagery sprang directly from the music, itself an exploration of the tension between 'a contained, proportional form and a rather explosive content'.[14] A dominant female figure (Catherine Becque) seeks repose and strives to tame the exuberance of her female followers. They scud and storm around her, forcing asunder any stable configuration that they make. In a central adagio of lifts and balances, three quiet, mysterious male figures demonstrate the possibility of sustained repose. Many writers have suggested that Becque is a female Apollo in this piece and the men three Muses, in other words, that there is a reversal of the sex roles in Balanchine's *Apollo* (1928), but Alston has always preferred not to establish any specific character identity.

Only a few of Alston's pieces are based on a more specific narrative, his settings, for instance, of Stravinsky's *The Rite of Spring* (1981), to the composer's piano duet version (1911/12) of the score, and *Pulcinella* (1987), and of Osborne's *Mythologies* (1985). Alston admits that he has never found narrative easy to handle. It is significant that, in *Pulcinella*, he simplified Massine's story for the original 1920 ballet and, within phrases of dance, rhythmicized the mime that communicates story (Commedia gestures, or others familiar to any traveller in Italy today). He then left himself plenty of time towards the end of the piece for the dance to blossom and for the reconciliations of lovers to be celebrated. 'I will *not* waste good music on telling stories',[15] he said in interview to Barbara Newman.

In *Mythologies*, Alston worked through the Tsimshian North American Indian myth *The Story of Asdiwal*, Claude Lévi-Strauss' structural study of which had been the starting point for Osborne's score. Feeling that his choreography had been overwhelmed with factual detail relating to the hero Asdiwal's various adventures and travels, Alston made a second, much abstracted version of the piece in 1989. He drew upon the imagery behind the story but eliminated narrative detail.[16] The second *Mythologies* still has a central male figure, but there are no longer any named characters or literal gestures. The piece is now principally a contemplation of physical qualities, the body in contact with changing land surface, temperatures, expanses of space, experiencing different speeds, energy and fatigue. This is not narrative in the traditional western sense, except for the framework theme of a person setting out on travels and coming back to rest – frozen in Mumford's blinding icy landscape. There is no notion of the progress of time as a constant, nor of narrative propulsion, only the few abrupt shifts forward into a new period and place suggested by the dawn of a new episode. Taking ideas from Osborne's musical structure more readily than he did in 1985, Alston seems to have isolated for meditation the sensual qualities from the story that interested him.

Unusually, the story behind *Night Music* (1981) was devised for the benefit of Alston's designer, the painter Howard Hodgkin. Alston recalls that, only when he had formulated a scenario involving Mozart and personalities from his life, with dancers as actual characters, could Hodgkin start work on the set and costumes. Alston developed the story from his music, selections from Mozart's *Divertimenti* and *Notturni*, that had been written for the house parties of his friend Gottfried von Jacquin. The dance concerns an imaginary party in Vienna at the von Jacquin household, and the confrontations, sometimes uneasy, between the guests (including Mozart). The story suited well Hodgkin's penchant for suggested conversation and interaction in social situations. But the choreography is such that any narrative is subtly underplayed, subsumed into a series of dances, and there is no programme indication of story or character to the audience.

A few of Alston's pieces derive their meaning from their reference to another, popular dance/music culture. Alston has spoken of his admiration for Twyla Tharp's settings of the most complex dance structures against easily accessible music: he recalls his enthusiasm for her *Deuce Coupe II* (1975) to Beach Boys music for the Joffrey Ballet. The recipe is a useful one for audience appeal. *Strong Language* (1987) – a development from the 1985 *Cutter* for Extemporary Dance Theatre – is set to a tape and synthesizer score by John Marc Gowans, and uses some of the characteristics of contemporary disco dancing. *Rhapsody in Blue* (1988), to the solo piano version of Gershwin's eponymous work and his Preludes for piano, looks back to the world of Astaire and exhibition ballroom dancing. Both these pieces are dressed by fashion designers, Katherine Hamnett and Victor Edelstein respectively. And *Java*, which appeared in two versions, the first (1983) for Second Stride, the second (1985) an expanded version for Rambert, glances back to the forties and fifties. This was the period during which *Java*'s music, by the black American group The Ink Spots, achieved a considerable popularity. Alston's first piece of this kind was *Thunder* (1972).

17. *Combines* (1972), choreography by Richard Alston, danced by members of London Contemporary Dance Theatre. (Photograph: Eleni Leoussi)

18. Rehearsal of *Doublework* (Richard Alston and Dancers, 1978), choreography by Richard Alston. The picture shows the end of the final duet, danced by Alston and Siobhan Davies. (Photograph: David Buckland)

19. BELOW: Michael Clark and Ikky Maas in *Rainbow Ripples* (Ballet Rambert, 1980), choreography by Richard Alston, design by David Buckland. (Photograph: David Buckland)

20. RIGHT ABOVE: Catherine Becque in *Apollo Distraught* (Ballet Rambert, 1982), choreography by Richard Alston. (Photograph: David Buckland)

21. RIGHT BELOW: *Zansa* (Ballet Rambert, 1986), choreography by Richard Alston. The picture is taken from the 'Mbira' section. Dancers, from left to right: Sara Matthews, Ben Craft, Amanda Britton, Bruce Michelson. (Photograph: Catherine Ashmore)

The most sophisticated of these pieces that absorb popular culture is *Java*, with its multiple references to social dancing, showbiz, and the format of soloist and backing group in the 'microphone dances' (Alston's term). Slipped in too are a few well-known 'moments' from the ballet, like Giselle and Albrecht rocking back and forth in *ballottés* and Aurora's wrist flicks, as well as the odd quiet nod to other choreographers, like Bruce, Balanchine, Ashton and Tudor. The notion of sly in-jokes had spread from the music: the 'whispering grass' (originally Maedée Duprès) who is advised 'Don't tell the trees ... the blabbering trees' is really about police informants, and the coffee and tea of Java Jive, 'I like coffee, I like tea' are euphemisms for drugs.[17] Dressed smartly by Jenny Henry in black trousers and a variety of white and sparkling jackets and waistcoats, *Java* is not primarily parody, nor a text of disparate references playing against each other. Alston has spiced his own style with a number of others that he is fond of, and integrated these other styles thoroughly. His idiom is rich enough to sustain them effortlessly. *Java* is smooth, feather-fingered, just like the songs.[18]

Rare aspects of subject matter in Alston's work are intimacy and emotion, and this could well connect with his tendency to shy away from narrative or, in the case of *Pulcinella*, to use the distance of cartoon Commedia characterizations. When he did admit these feelings in a series of rather 'pastoral' pieces of the early 1980s, *The Field of Mustard* (1980), *Landscape* (1980), *Night Music* and *Midsummer*, the results were often a touch sentimental. Several critics perceived this. Clement Crisp described the quality of *Midsummer* as 'a particular dewy, instressed English lyricism'.[19] There are two outstanding exceptions. One is the final duet in *Doublework* (1978), which Alston made for himself and Davies, a very passionate dancer. It is the most personal duet in this piece about duets, like the crux of the matter (see pp. 124–126). Then there is the concluding duet for two men in *Voices and Light Footsteps* (1984), in which the melancholic 'poet' figure[20] finally accepts the consoling embrace of his companion.

Generally, Alston's work is asexual in nature. He has pointed out that his *The Rite of Spring* focuses on violence in the elements, not on violence in sex.[21] It is significant too that he takes for granted androgyny (women dressed as men in *Java* and *Rhapsody in Blue*) and role reversal (in *Apollo Distraught*), without indulging any particular point about the sexual implications of what he has set up. Generally, the couple does not have as central a position as in traditional modern dance or ballet. Alston frequently favours trio combinations[22] or draws soloist couples back again into a community texture.

Alston's attitude to sexuality is open and flexible. *Apollo Distraught*, for example, gives women full-throttle power and independence and men the chance to be gentle, languid, even vulnerable to each other. However,

Alston's humanity is essentially more to do with dancers as individuals than as members of a sex.[23] The Rambert dancers give an unusually powerful sense of working together as an harmonious community, and they are co-operative and considerate towards each other.[24] The men lift the women, as is traditional. The particular lifts that Alston chooses demand this – after *Doublework*, that is, which included instances of women supporting men and the mutual sharing of weight within an abundance of lifts and supports. But Alston's doublework respects women physically and never denies the sense of person or personal strength. Furthermore, his dancers often emerge as strongly distinctive personalities. He has always emphasized the crucial role of dancers, their particular qualities, in determining what he makes for them.[25] Some become so thoroughly attuned to their material that they achieve a sort of self-realization through it: Catherine Becque in *Apollo Distraught*, for instance, Mary Evelyn in *Voices and Light Footsteps*, or Gary Lambert in *Dutiful Ducks* (when it was revived in 1986). To explain this 'distinctive personality' in terms of some aspect of character being imposed on the movement is to miss the point, but there is a sense of individuals revealing or indeed discovering something new about themselves through the character of the movement itself, and this can be intensely moving.

Movement

The belief in the power of movement and in its ability to propose its own structures, in dance about dancing, is fundamental to Alston. It is nowhere more evident than in his commitment to building and remoulding a language over the years, a base-line for the vocabulary that is specific to individual pieces. He has not felt the need to invent a personal vocabulary from scratch, as so many American modern dance choreographers have felt they must.[26] Instead, he has turned to existing codes and created a personal language by uniting what interests him from these various sources. As 'vocabulary' perhaps, the sources can still be identified (i.e. at the level of basic steps or shapes), but the nuances are his own.

Before he went to America, Alston's work incorporated elements from Cunningham's vocabulary and later release principles (see pp. 52–53). In the early *Nowhere Slowly* (1970), there were even touches of Graham class vocabulary, although contractions and extreme body tensions were absent. After America, Alston retained his 'release' interests, developed a much more certain and rich response to the Cunningham vocabulary and turned to classical ballet for another kind of resource.

The Cunningham code is still easy to spot in the use of the torso to twist, curve and tilt, in the precise 'steppiness', the intricate rhythms, the 'nervous directional changes'.[27] But there are major differences in the use of weight and momentum. In Cunningham's vocabulary, the weight is placed clearly up or down, and shape is fought for as a major component of the movement material alongside rhythmic demands. Alston allows for the play between fall and recovery,[28] dipping or plunging and rising up again, or simply giving body weight generously, fully, as the dancers do to their partners in *Doublework*. Giving into gravity has been a feature since Alston's earliest work, and stems, he says, from his T'ai Chi studies at the LSCD. In his style, there is also an element of letting natural momentum take its course, and sometimes even motion and risk at the expense of shape. The result is a more organic use of the body, and sympathetic reactions between body parts rather than the body isolations so often found in Cunningham's work. There are also subtle differences in rhythm. Fall and recovery lends itself naturally to lilting triple time rhythmic structures. In his technique class, for example, Alston might rephrase Cunningham's movements from duple to triple time to suit his different dynamic approach.[29]

Release principles undoubtedly connect with such 'sympathetic' nuances of style. They are also at the root of Alston's continuing concern for movement to be achieved with maximum ease and efficiency, the relaxed upper body, for instance, over the most precise and fleet footwork.[30]

The ballet vocabulary with which Alston infused his style when he began his association with Rambert could be seen in the increased footwork, intricate allegro, use of demi-pointe and crossed positions of the feet, in the new emphasis on jumps and turns and *batterie*, as well as in many steps and shapes taken directly from the classical language.[31] By the time of *Apollo Distraught*, niceties such as the diagonal alignments of *épaulement*,[32] with the head in opposition to the turned shoulder line, had entered the vocabulary, also the idiosyncratic Cecchetti attitude (which became a metaphor for momentary stability in *Apollo Distraught*), one arm raised curved, in front of the body, the face directed up towards the palm.

Alston created a series of self-consciously balletic pieces during the early 1980s, revealing his most concentrated attention to classical vocabulary. For Rambert, he made *Night Music*, *Fantasie* (1982) – a short duet to Mozart – and *Chicago Brass* (1983). For ballet dancers, he made *Midsummer* and *Prince of the Pagodas*, also two short works, *Crown Diamonds* for Rambert School students, and a male duet *Coursing* for the 1984 Dance Umbrella. In relation to other pieces, the language of these ballets was rather cramped and tentative.[33] It was as if Alston was undertaking a radical rebuilding of language here. The Rambert dancers did not look at their best in these circumstances.

Alston's work is stronger when he maintains the freedom and explosive potential of his contemporary language and uses these in conjunction with classical formality and precision. He does this, for instance, in *Apollo Distraught*, and in the crisp little solo for Michael Clark, *Dutiful Ducks*. (Clark was Alston's discovery, his facility in both contemporary and classical styles a great inspiration). Eventually, Alston made his peace with ballet. *Voices and Light Footsteps*[34] and *Pulcinella* absorb their references to Bournonville and Ashton into the liberated expressions of contemporary dance with complete confidence.

Alston's language experienced other infusions in the mid- and late 1980s. A strain of sharp, angular behaviour sprang from *Wildlife*, inspired then by the forms of Richard Smith's kites and certain stick-like characteristics of Balinese dance.[35] The style re-emerged in a group of works that were all, significantly, to new music, *Zansa*, *Dangerous Liaisons* (1985) and *Hymnos* (1988). *Pulau Dewata* (1989) borrows from the vocabulary of arm gestures and bent-kneed walks of Indonesian dance but, like the composer Claude Vivier, Alston integrated these oriental features into his own existing language. Alston has identified a link between *Pulau* and his earlier folk ritual-inspired works *The Rite of Spring* and *Dumka* (1979, for students of the LSCD).

Subtle points of style have emerged within Rambert since Alston assumed the Artistic Directorship. A fine tuning has given the company a sure sense of its own style that is rare in any group of dancers. Alston has been responsible for this fine tuning which, while prompted by his own work, has naturally affected performance of other repertoire. Across all the work now, for instance, there is a striking spaciousness of behaviour, a leanness of line that comes from confident extension as much as physique. Leanness is to do with easing the body outwards into space, lengthening, across and down the back, and up the back of the head (release principles at work again), carrying the physical sensation through to the extremities of fingertips and toes and shooting an imaginary line far beyond the body. There is a freedom to be open, across the front of the body or by stretching one side forward above the waist or at the hips, in the open-hipped attitude absorbed from Cunningham, or the *grand jeté* with the raised arm extending from the same side as the leading leg. This openness and length is crucial to the Rambert effect of devouring space in travelling sequences, a manner most unusual for British dancers.

Structure

Since he returned from the USA, Alston's dance material has been more dense, more convoluted in its structuring than it was before, with far fewer walking and running transitions.[36] A continuing issue has been that of 'legibility', searching for ways of maintaining the viewers' understanding of structure whilst challenging their perceptions. A piece like *Connecting Passages* (1977), his last work to be made in New York, is already testing to an extreme our capacity to grasp the structure of dance material through time. A video of the solo version for Eva Karczag[37] invites scrutiny of the present, of each distinct moment exquisitely performed, of the quality of motion, tiny multi-directional flurries, long, stretched balances, languid circlings. It invites no recognition of any longer-term shaping; a sense of the past is rapidly dissipated. It is the kind of work that Alston might well have called 'too subtle for its own good'.

Since the mid-1970s, he has explored various ways of engaging spectators with material that might be very complex, fast or small, understanding that this reads less easily than slow, large or simple movement. In an article in *Artscribe* (1979), discussing *Rainbow Bandit* and *Doublework*, Alston summarized his notions of dance perception:

> Because dance occurs in time it involves not only perception of the instant but also visual memory, and so the limit to what one perceives is not merely how much the eye can take in but how much of that information can be retained.[38]

In *Doublework*, accordingly, much of the material was deliberately paced slow, so that its many small, intimate moves could be adequately grasped.

Yet, if the urgent issue for Alston after his visit to America was to make material clear, he has always wanted to preserve the sense of challenge, indeed to increase it, believing now that audiences can absorb a greater density of dance information than they could in the 1970s. He has explored different tactics for shifting the balance between challenge and respite during the course of his pieces.

In these respects, one piece *Soda Lake* (1981) stands out as an unusual Alston work, perhaps the most spare and unpressured of all his 1980s pieces. It is the silent solo for Clark around Nigel Hall's two-element *Soda Lake* sculpture (1968), a solo in which stillness alternates with flurries of activity, little nuggets of movement repeated, varied and interspersed with once-seen material. The dance responds to the literal implications of the sculpture,[39] its suggestion of a vast space beyond itself (originally the Mojave desert), scurries implying some desert animal that might inhabit this territory, also its properties as a base or marking post. The dance also responds to the formal implications of the sculpture, exploring areas around and along the linear paths suggested, reaching up and tracing the light oval loop above, reflecting the frisson of the near contact of the thick pole to the floor. It is essential to the qualities of *Soda Lake* to be open, transparent, with a languid rate of evolution and spaces for stillness and sleep.

Phrasing and rhythm
At the most detailed level, Alston tackled the problem of legibility in dance by examining phrasing and rhythm. Phrasing provides useful markers or signposts: punctuation, and moments of relative climax and release of tension. (This is totally different from Cunningham's phrasing, which

downplays any sense of crisis and respite after crisis.) Alston's phrasing is also related strongly to the image of breath, with its ebb and flow pattern and rise and fall of energy. Some work has been structured on breath, a large proportion of *Doublework*, for example. The long opening sweep down the diagonal and back up it again is clearly structured into four breaths by the four impulses passed between partners (originally Maedée Duprès and Julyen Hamilton): each impulse sets off a breath or chain of motion for the pair.

Alston's material can alternatively use pulse and metre as a signposting framework and as a force for generating momentum. A pulse framework does not necessarily preclude breath rhythm. Rhythm relayed to his dancers by vocal sounds rather than counts allows a play with time equivalent to rubato in music, the possibility, for instance, of slightly elongating moments of suspension, like inhalation, and making up for lost time afterwards. But pulse, like breath, in Alston's work, also provides the framework for asymmetries: clearly articulated, shifting rhythmic patterns and syncopations make important contributions to the liveliness of the material.

Musical/choreographic structure

Once he began to integrate sound and dance structures, Alston considered these issues of phrasing and rhythm in direct relation to sound accompaniment. Dismayed by the vague attitude to rhythm that he found in so much contemporary dance around him in the 1970s, he was impressed, he says, by the clarity of the link between melody and dance phrases in nineteenth-century ballet. He found very revealing an article 'Grace and clarity' (1944) in which John Cage too had acclaimed that clarity.[40]

A few of Alston's pieces of the late 1970s and 1980s phrased movement in relation to text-sound compositions by the American composer Charles Amirkhanian. The brief concluding section to *Rainbow Bandit* becomes articulate through the tight knitting together of dance rhythms and motoric text (Amirkhanian's *Just*), after the rest of the dance has been performed entirely in silence. An example of this is the pattern of five runs and a leap set to the repeating phrase 'Chug chug chug chug chug Bandit Bomb'.

Rainbow Ripples (1980) begins with a reworking of the same score (and a reworking of the *Rainbow Bandit* dance material), while pursuing a similar tight relationship with sound. This beginning is followed by a section to a second Amirkhanian sound score *Heavy Aspirations* based on a wry lecture by the musicologist Zuri Slonimsky and using speech/breath rhythm. It begins

Borborygmous is a wonderful word, it –
It means a rumble produced in the elephant's stomach.

And a male dancer matches the speech rhythm in a patter of differently weighted steps and *jetés*, with particular accents on the words 'rumble' (a lift of the body and arms corresponding with the lift in the voice) and 'stomach' (a big open *jeté* forwards). After making us work, urging us to listen hard (to meaning as well as to sound), as much as to watch during this passage, the effect of the final George Hamilton Green rag is of disarming simplicity. Into its merry pulse and pretty timbres (xylophone and marimba) we can relax at last, tripped up by temporary switches of metre, but nevertheless enjoying, as Crisp observed, 'a final release of verbal and dynamic tension'.[41] Light-hearted in tone as it is, *Rainbow Ripples* is also a study in watching/listening perceptual patterns. Alston used one other Amirkhanian text-score in 1982, *Dutiful Ducks* for the Michael Clark solo, which he extended for male solo and three female dancers in 1986. The style of relationship between sound and movement is the same.

The sort of close, harmonious interaction between music and dance that Stravinsky suggested is Alston's aim. He often quotes Balanchine's motto: 'See the music, hear the dancing'.[42] Alston's musicality has been remarked upon frequently. The critic Alastair Macaulay, for instance, has noted how he reveals music by his choreography and encourages his audience to listen.[43] But what exactly makes this musicality is far from simple.

Certainly, the South Bank Show on Alston (1982)[44] made far too much of 'mickey-mousing' relationships between music and dance. Alston has stressed that he prefers to think first in terms of whole phrases rather than choreographing to musical moments,[45] which is presumably what Arlene Croce meant when she said that Alston hears sound as shape.[46] Thus the dance can be free to develop its own logic and continuity. *Landscape* to Vaughan Williams' *Phantasy Quintet* is a case in point:

> If they're waiting [the dancers] for a particular squeak on a violin, sometimes it might not come: and then they're thrown. If they're actually understanding the whole phrase and how their dance phrase is made with the rhythm, then they can be as lively as the musicians in the pit.[47]

In a lecture-demonstration on *Hymnos*,[48] Alston illustrated how, after rather literally 'painting' the clarinet line (as he did Amirkhanian's texts) as a starting point for Mark Baldwin's solo, the relationship between sound and movement became freer during the rehearsal process. He takes advantage of the tensions and resolutions that arise from lines pulling away from each other and back together again. Yet there is still the effect of complementary lines at work here. In another lecture-demonstration on *Mythologies*, Nigel Osborne noted a similar effect where two dance phrases, originally set tightly to two musical phrases (the same phrases played twice), had gradually speeded up so that there was time for the dancers to perform a third phrase within the same musical timespan. The moment is in the fast central 'paradigm' section of the music. Osborne said that he felt the effect of dance 'anticipating' the music in the final version.[49]

Most often, when Alston has started a section by 'painting a line', his ideas inspired by the music, he has then allowed dance material to progress independently. In *Dangerous Liaisons*, to an electronic score by Simon Waters, he borrows a musical pulse when one emerges from the texture and continues to work with it in the dance after it has dropped out of the music. Then he might pick up on selected features, marking a characteristic moment so that it stands out more, in *Voices and Light Footsteps*, for instance, a sharp little two-beat motif from the Monteverdi, or a long sobbing suspension. Or he might introduce a rhythmic echo, a pattern heard in the music 'heard' again some time later in the dance. Sometimes, there is simply a complementary energy, the obvious correspondence, for instance, between the rush crossings of dancers and fierce vibrations of brass and piano in *Zansa*.

An important aspect of Alston's 'musicality' is his independent rhythmic patterning, and the vitality achieved through counterpoint with music as contrast to complementary structures. Counterpoint is an effect achieved by crossing accents or metres. Thus, in the joyous ensemble conclusion of *Pulcinella*, the dance accents give the impression of striding exuberantly and boldly across the music, both dance and music holding to their own shifting metrical structures. A quiet section of *Strong Language* nicknamed 'Strumming' is organized in a dance count system of 3–3–2. The musical 8-count units fall in and out of this accent structure, the result a sensual pattern of gentle conflict and resolution that keeps the section buoyant.

Alston's point of view on music is always crystal clear, but there are perhaps two main reasons why he appears so musical: because he enhances the characteristic aspects of a composer's style, and because, through developing a range of tactics for using music and shifting between them skilfully and sensitively, he can refresh our perceptions. His work regularly re-energizes our will to listen as well as to watch.

Alston understands well how his use of music can affect legibility during the course of a work. Complementary structures operate in mutual clarification. Alston has expressed a wish to elucidate new music, but the reverse is also true: 'I've discovered', he says, 'that I can articulate difficult rhythmic phrases if the sound echoes them.' Furthermore, as Balanchine has so often demonstrated, the repetition of dance together with its music creates moments of particular clarity within a large form. It is as if the effect of repetition is doubled. It is vital to the coherence of a piece as long and as complex as *Zansa* to have such shared memories, some substantial, lasting through a whole melody or section, others as slight as a sustained wind timbre which comes to signal the arrival of the bright intruders in this piece. These shared memories provide a lull in the density of information to be absorbed.

The repetition of dance together with music also contributes to mood and subject matter. Twice, a menacing chorus rushes in from the wings to confront the soloists in the last movement of *Apollo*, each time to a furious series of string trills; it is insistent, determined to break any calm. Contrast the recurrences in *Night Music* which seem to echo qualities of pleasant stability or gentle resignation in Mozart's party piece *Notturni* and *Divertimenti*.

Large structure

After his return from America, Alston began to make pieces of substantial or symphonic proportions, using large forces, and a generous time-scale. *Rainbow Bandit* was the earliest of these, *Zansa* outstanding amongst more recent works. In his *Artscribe* article, Alston describes his pacing principles in *Rainbow Bandit*, contrasting these with his method in *Doublework*. The discussion provides a useful insight into the way Alston conceives of large scale structure and acknowledges our perceptual capacities and limitations:

> I decided to . . . first present the material in so dense a form that it could not easily be grasped, and then unravel and expose it, using the clarity of the rhythmic phrase to underline and make it plain.
>
> And so the dance was made in three large parts, the first, of an illogical complexity, the second something of a respite and the third [set to Amirkhanian's text-piece *Just*] a rescue job on the material of the first.

The first section of this piece, Alston aptly describes, as 'intentional chaos'. It is highly unstable, disturbing as a result, although that disturbance makes sense later. No sooner is an impression established than it is dissolved, or the viewer is distracted by something else.

> There are passages which quite deliberately overload the eye or alternatively confuse it by distracting the focus; these are then pulled sharply in for the odd moment of clarity, setting up a play between leading and misleading the attention.[50]

Alston admits that an audience might well fail to identify the repetition of movement from earlier in the piece, but is confident of unconscious absorption. He also realizes that the piece will be repeated regularly within the LCDT repertoire and therefore can be re-viewed to catch more detail in the manner of 're-reading a detective novel'. But it is interesting that Alston has moved away from presenting such a degree of initial confusion since *Rainbow Bandit*.

The formal pacing of *Doublework* reverses the pacing of *Rainbow Bandit*. It was made for a brief season of performances and, it appears, for easier first reading. Based around three core duets, for three couples who had already developed a close working relationship, *Doublework* was otherwise concerned with presenting material twice, using the second meaning of the title. Repeated material might well be turned around in space for a second viewing, a Cunningham device and characteristic of Alston's work since his early period, but Alston allows the material to be clearly registered. He keeps a generous amount of it slow. The form unfolds additively, new material presented, then repeated, perhaps alongside the next new strand of material, and so on, 'all of which makes for a dense texture, but with a continuity which is clear to follow'.[51]

Alston has been concerned to establish a clear macro-form or shape across the full span of his 'symphonic' pieces (I am identifying 'symphonic' pieces as a contrast with those constructed as a suite or string of self-contained dances). Often, shape stems from musical structure. Often it is hidden under considerable complexity. The 1977 *Rainbow Bandit* already had that shape – despite its tremendous complexity. But it is interesting to see how the 1978 *Doublework* was altered in 1982, refined to admit this aspect of Alston's vision. The 1982 Second Stride version is already shorter and contains fewer dance ideas than the original, and it is less rigid about following the scheme of showing everything twice. But this is a part of Alston's primary aim to give the piece a 'shape in time'. He has spoken of wanting to add an early sextet (using the full cast), to create a sense of balance between the first and second halves of the piece.[52] What he was doing in effect was establishing an extra moment of clarity or stability within the piece, and this becomes a reference point during the progress of the piece, especially when the parallel sextet occurs later. Interlocking with the existing structure supplied by three punctuating core duets, this new sense of two balanced halves (with the final most intimate duet in a special position, like a coda) reminds the viewer of the relationship of parts to a whole, gives the piece proportions, a 'shape in time'.

In the second *Doublework*, the central section of the piece, once restless, containing many abrupt interpolations, has been simplified; the ensuing sextet, enlarged from a mere moment in the original version, becomes emphasized as a passage of stability. Slowness prevails, and there is unison across all six dancers. There is also growth towards the stability of the sextet, in the preceding passages, an increased clarity of material through simpler repetition and unisons built up across more dancers. One piece of material has been removed. Then, a full parallel is established, between this point in the dance and the sextet at the end, now, a movement that is repeated, three dancers gently lifted from sitting on the floor by the other three.

It is significant that the music composed for the Second Stride *Doublework* by Jim Fulkerson (the original *Doublework* was silent) focuses plainly on the note C at these two points. The C continues through the

125

concluding duet. Otherwise, these are the only points when the note is emphasized. C is the tonal focus of the music: these points are the points of maximum stability in the music as well as the dance.

However, there is a fascinating twist to this analysis of the second *Doublework*, another formal layer suggested by the revisions, an additional or alternative view. With some of the restlessness removed before the first sextet, a much clearer sense of a three-movement structure emerges, a slow 'centre' to the work bounded by two faster 'movements'.

Similarly to *Doublework*, *Hymnos* contains two parallel points that divide the piece into two halves. The first part of this very raw quartet is set to the first six short musical movements of Maxwell Davies' astringent *Hymnos* for clarinet and piano,[53] the second part to the seventh, eighth and extended ninth movements. Matching the recurrence of a passage of slow, repeated notes on the clarinet, each part concludes with the same frieze for the four dancers and the same quiet entry into it. The central frieze is the first occasion of emphatic quiet. Part II can be perceived as an expansion of Part I. It contains the climax of the piece (the dancers crouch low and freeze as the music shrieks and roars) after a lesser squall in Part I, and it features more of the dancers for more of the time. In Part II, there are also echoes and reworkings of earlier material. Interestingly, the concluding move of the piece becomes strange partly because of this two part structure: the dancers step quietly out of their frieze up into fifth position *relevé*, and the clarinet steps up too. The special anxiety of this brief concluding action arises not only because the dancers end hovering on their toes, but also because we have been encouraged to 'relax' with the closure implications of the repeated frieze.

The *Dangerous Liaisons* choreography has the outline shape A–A′–B[54] that follows the structure of Simon Waters' tape score. Here, structural outline is confirmed by the chronological ordering of material to a much greater degree than in *Doublework* or *Hymnos*. But Alston has said that hardly anyone watching the dance would grasp this A–A′–B structure. The seams between different material and entries of dancers are frequently disguised, the repetitions constantly varied. This hectic and perilous piece seems to thrive on a tension between stability and confusion. It is quite possible that, as in *Rainbow Bandit*, the organization and shape register at a sub-conscious level and make the piece seem, at a deep level, coherent and 'tight'.

Alston used the word 'tight' when describing what he was aiming for in the second version of *Doublework*. It could be that he was simply expressing his notion of 'shape in time' in another way, but he has been known to use the description 'tight' in a rather different sense. Here, tightness is to do with holding or knitting a piece firmly together, by reworking the same material in different ways, overlapping sections, using variation, counterpoint and cross-references, or by preserving a thread through a piece, like the duet in *Rainbow Bandit* that appears in three segments, one for each section of the piece.[55] This is rather like organic symphonic or sonata thinking in music. Interestingly, the structure of the first movement of *The Brilliant and the Dark* (1983, for Second Stride) is strikingly close to the sonata-like organization of the first movement of Britten's cello sonata.

Dangerous Liaisons, with its network of references crossing sections, is a later and an especially fine example of symphonic-style structure. But *Zansa* is Alston's most ambitious piece of this kind: dense, complex, intricate, with a strong architectural framework. *Zansa* contains two musical works by Osborne, *Mbira* and *Zansa*. Alston's response to the 'Zansa' section is an expansion of ideas presented in 'Mbira', with additional ideas thrown into the melting-pot (although both music and dance for 'Zansa' were actually created before 'Mbira'). 'Zansa', in broad outline fast, slow, fast movements, is harder to read than 'Mbira', featuring more dancers, 13 instead of 6, and more complicated counterpoint. Its foundations shift almost inconspicuously, with some dance and musical sections overlapping, and likewise John Hoyland's cloths are introduced during sections, rather than brutally underlining major change elsewhere. In terms of pacing, Alston appears to rely on 'Mbira' as preparation, containing as it does the essence of 'Zansa' in material and mood.

Examples of how a recurring idea used for 'tightness' becomes inflected differently as it occurs in different contexts are the racing choral crossings that produce some of the most high energy moments in the 'Zansa' section.[56] There are four crossing phrases, each of them convoluted and presenting the dancers following on canonically behind each other. Each appearance of these phrases is different: the phrases are seen in pairs or separately, as a riot of counterpoint across all eight blue dancers or as one simple line of canon, and sometimes as a partial crossing. Finally, in the most turbulent last movement of 'Zansa', the crossing shoots out directly towards the audience, to striking effect, not only because of its direct approach, but because, for the first time, it breaks away from the familiar side-to-side pattern.

In this last movement of 'Zansa', the two tribes bond together with the same material. Alston uses material to reinforce drama between the tribes and then harmony, demonstrating their separateness at first, later, their joining forces.

Zansa is worlds apart from pieces like *Combines*, or even *Doublework* (first version). These earlier pieces stress heterogeneity rather than homogeneity, divergence rather than integration. They spread as flat constructions rather than shapes with the rise and fall of climax and resolution.

Alston has continued to make looser episodic pieces through the 1980s. He might wish to concentrate on an issue that demands this type of structure, like the popular reference in *Java* and *Strong Language*, which suits a cabaret-style string of numbers. Or there is a language to build, which demands to become the focus of attention. This was the case in *Wildlife*, which was, Osborne remembers, for both composer and choreographer, like a 'cauldron ... raw material with a freshness that couldn't possibly have been arrived at from a tighter, symphonically-controlled structure'.[57] *Wildlife* turned out formally crude, clearly sectional, with actual pauses between several sections. This worked well in this case in that it allowed time to enjoy the movement of the kites, to see their beauty and contemplate their contribution to this piece. Then, after this attention to a new kind of physical language, Alston says, he needed to make *Zansa*, 'to get at that material in a tighter form'.

Visual textures

Another aspect of Alston's work that has changed radically is his visual texture or stage picture. Several works of the early 1980s, the ballets in particular, look simple after *Rainbow Bandit*, or even after the earlier *Blue Schubert Fragments*, which opens with six dancers in counterpoint with each other. Alston felt that he had to rethink texture now that he was working regularly with a large ensemble under proscenium theatre conditions, simplifying, and duplicating dancers in unison lines and blocks to make their material clear.[58] And, for the more balletic works, he kept texture simple in order to concentrate on a vocabulary that was still unfamiliar to him – 'so that I could see it all the time'.

During this period, the early 1980s, Alston began to test out the potential of the group as a block formation within the proscenium frame,[59] treating it as an organism that has a life of its own, but that is sufficiently contained for a spectator to grasp what goes on within it. This is the essence of group usage in *Java*. The line-ups and unison ensembles are, of course, part of its popular reference but, with his big cast of twelve, Alston explores any number of sly ways of letting groups expand, contract, and dissolve into others, with counterpoint between two separate masses and, perhaps, against a soloist as well. There are several instances when Alston allows a touch of anarchy within the group. There are unisons, for instance, with the material performed with different facings. In the opening 'Your Feet's Too Big', the audience looks down two lines of women, three women in each line, all apparently dancing differently. But, in fact, they mirror their opposite numbers, upstage left to downstage right, middle right to middle left, and so on. Later, in 'It's Funny', with a soloist out front, and a line of men swaying just inside from the wings, a wedge of seven women centre stage dissolves into two tight lines, the front line shooting suddenly into an unruly frieze. The textures in *Java* seem to be constantly slipping from one to the next.

128

After *Java*, Alston brought back single person strands of counterpoint more boldly alongside his other textural devices. In *Dangerous Liaisons*, which seemed, when it appeared, like a consolidation of everything that he had learnt to date, Alston introduces his most wayward textures for a long time. There are only six dancers – two trios – but they are a hugely volatile ensemble, constantly splintering and reassembling into twos, fours, even six-part counterpoint in the 'Grand Slams' (nicknamed thus because all the dancers end their phrases together as an accent, in a closed position). In *Zansa*, using greater numbers, Alston complicates the stage picture even more, introducing chaotic textures at breakneck speed for tension, overloading the eye at the same time, or more quietly, creating the effect of blurring or disintegration after more stable, sculptural groupings. However, even here, there is never the long-term high loading of the eye that he introduced in *Rainbow Bandit*.

The emphasis in this discussion has been on dance structure and language. These seem to be the core concerns through Alston's work. It is according to these terms too that he has been most influential. There are several choreographers who similarly make dance language and structure a priority: first of all Siobhan Davies, most strongly influenced by Alston during the 1970s, also Ashley Page and Mary Evelyn. The same concerns too have governed Alston's repertory choices as an Artistic Director. There are pieces by the choreographers mentioned above, but also commissions and existing repertory from the Americans who celebrate dance about dancing and dance structures: Merce Cunningham and members of the post-Cunningham generation, David Gordon, Trisha Brown and Lucinda Childs.[60] And, committed to collaboration for his guest choreographers as much as for himself, Alston, whenever finances permit, encourages commissions from composers and fine artists.

Certainly, Alston can now call upon a wide-ranging background as a choreographer who has worked successfully in many different modes and with very different kinds of dancers. A summary of my favourite pieces underlines an impressive versatility. There are the pieces, full of vibrant movement ideas that seem to have jumped all existing codes, like *Soda Lake* and *Doublework*, the pieces in which formal control becomes drama, as a repressive force combatting explosive tendencies, in *Apollo Distraught*, *Dangerous Liaisons* and *Rainbow Bandit*, and a piece like *Java* in which fluent technique merges effortlessly with fun.

Alston has been 'labelled' in a variety of ways in recent years. He has been called a classicist by Alastair Macaulay.[61] Nigel Osborne feels that he is a modernist like himself.[62] The dance writer David Vaughan has proposed that he is Britain's first post-modernist, and that *Pulcinella*'s 'juxtaposition of baroque forms and modern harmonies' is 'a prototypical post-modernist exercise'.[63] I prefer to see Alston now as a modernist choreographer who subscribes first and foremost to that notion of dance about dancing, while using certain principles developed by 'classical' ballet choreographers. And today, he too chooses to see himself in this way.[64]

Alston might once have been called one of Britain's first post-modernists when, in the LSCD and Strider days, he was experimenting with Cunningham and post-Cunningham structures, and looking to the American post-moderns for an alternative to Graham-derived expressionism. In the late 1960s and early 1970s, he was already biased towards dance abstraction and determined to remove himself from a tradition alien to him. That radical post-modern direction was an entirely logical one to explore. Some of his work at that time seems to fit Sally Banes' category of 'analytic' post-modern dance, formalist work with a special reflexive stress (see p. 5). However, Alston had moved firmly away from that particular reflexive position by the late 1970s.

Then, if we look at the 1980s notion of post-modern dance as an art of self-conscious reference, only a few of Alston's more recent pieces seem to conform to that notion, and they do so only lightly. He sometimes refers specifically to a dance style beyond his own base-line language, for instance, in *Java*, *Strong Language*, and *Pulcinella*, but the emphasis here is on a new integrated language, much more than on reflexive enquiry or ironic play between codes. References occur as incidental, post-modern 'features', or as puns and in-jokes for cognoscenti. His 'reference' works still proclaim his foremost 'modernist' interest in dance about dancing.

Alston today prefers not to emphasize the divergence, radical juxtapositions, unresolved oppositions, 'flat' structures in time, conceptual issues that are all distinctive features of post-modernism. He stresses integration, even when he mixes periods and vocabularies as source material, tightness, unity, the hierarchy of climax and release, and *dénouement*. His post-modern explorations of the 1970s have led him to affirm the continuing values of modernism in his mature career.

CHAPTER 6

Siobhan Davies

Background: training and professional associations

Unusually amongst the choreographers discussed in this book, Siobhan (Sue)[1] Davies developed her career within one of the large established contemporary dance companies, LCDT. This was the only company for which she choreographed, until the 1980s, when she made work, on a 'part of the year' basis, for independent groups that she directed herself. A reason for this is that her first ambition was to be a dancer in LCDT, and only after that was fulfilled, did she begin to show an interest in choreography. Davies was accepted into LCDT as a performer and, it turned out, became one of the outstanding contemporary dancers of her generation. For a while, she developed parallel careers as a full-time dancer and choreographer, fittingly, for her home company.

Davies had come from studies at the Hammersmith College of Art and Building to join, in 1967, the first year of students on the full-time course at the LSCD. That same year, she was given a walk-on part in the first performances of the Contemporary Dance Group (which was renamed London Contemporary Dance Theatre in 1970), in Anna Mittelholzer's *Family of Man*. She was appointed an apprentice dancer with the company for its first London season at The Place Theatre in 1969, becoming a full member in 1971.[2]

Davies recalls how, as a student, she never took advantage of the choreography course offered at the School: she preferred to continue part-time art classes at St Martin's School of Art.[3] But once she began to choreograph, as a professional dancer, she never looked back. When she presented her first public piece *Relay* for LCDT in 1972,[4] critical favour was immediate, and within a few years, she had achieved recognition as a major force in British dance. Peter Williams added her name to the list of important female choreographers like de Valois, Andrée Howard and Nijinska;[5] Clement Crisp proclaimed her in 1977 'the most interesting and impressive young choreographer in the country'.[6] Davies became an Associate Choreographer of LCDT in 1974 and, in 1983, Resident Choreographer, part of a triumvirate directorship of the company. 1983 was also the year when she stopped performing.

The working connections that Davies had with the independent dance

131

scene in the 1970s were largely, though not entirely, a result of her association as a dancer with Richard Alston.[7] Davies and Alston had met as
students in the same year at the LSCD, both had an art school background
in common, and both found shared inspiration in ballet and the work of
Merce Cunningham: in 1970, they travelled together to see the Cunningham company in the south of France. Davies soon became a frequent
dancer in Alston's work, in his early pieces for workshops, in 1970 as a
member of his touring lecture-demonstration group, as well as performing
in his works for LCDT. It is interesting that in 1973 there was a plan,
although it never came to anything, for her to make some appearances with
Strider.[8] On sabbatical in New York in 1976, Davies performed in
Alston's *UnAmerican Activities*. Then, on his return from New York,
Davies became a member of Richard Alston and Dancers alongside her continuing LCDT commitments; she danced Anna to Julie Covington's singing
Anna in Alston's choreography for *The Seven Deadly Sins* (the English
National Opera production, 1978). Davies says that, while Robert Cohan
used her in mythical, archetypal roles within LCDT, Alston encouraged her
ability to perform abstract movement.

Davies' move out into the independent scene as a choreographer in the
1980s was prompted by several factors: the desire to make more work than
she could for LCDT, where she was restricted to approximately one piece
a year, to try out ideas that might have seemed too risky for LCDT or that
needed a less tight working schedule, to work with a different group of
dancers and to experience more intimate performance situations. First, in
1981, she formed Siobhan Davies and Dancers, and the following year,
with Ian Spink as co-director and Alston as guest choreographer, Second
Stride. Managed by Dance Umbrella, Second Stride was originally intended
as a one-off project, a joining of two groups as a chance for Davies and
Spink to share dancers and to make larger-scale work than they would have
been able to do independently. There was also the opportunity of a three-
week US tour, to include New York's first sight of British modern dance.[9]
However, with the success of this project and the eagerness of Alston and
Davies to continue making work beyond their Rambert and LCDT commitments, the group re-formed for a second year and preserved the creative
momentum to continue on after that as a regular part of the year event.

With Siobhan Davies and Dancers and Second Stride, Davies entered the
uncertain world of small-scale touring and Arts Council project funding.
However, these two companies were to receive regular and relatively sound
support, and grants of this kind were variously supplemented, by a GLAA
dance award in 1980 (Davies was one of the first choreographers to receive
such an award), and increasingly during the 1980s by help from arts trusts
and friends. While Davies undoubtedly has used the small company situations to make her most exploratory and most intimate work, it is interesting

that there have been successful overlaps between small and large company repertory: *Carnival* (1982) and *Rushes* (1982) transferred respectively to LCDT and Rambert Dance Company.

A major crossroads in Davies' career came in 1987 when the award of the first Fulbright Fellowship in Choreography enabled her to make a nine-month study trip to America. This marked a natural break with Second Stride – pursuing different interests, Spink became sole director of that company – but a less comfortable end of her long association with LCDT. Whether because of the context of the LCDT repertoire, with Cohan's highly theatrical, Graham-based work as its backbone, or the particular nature of her own work, Davies' works had long been seen as the cool, intellectual, even difficult contribution to the company's programmes. By 1987, the policy and dancing style of the company had become incompatible with Davies' interests.[10] She formed her own small Siobhan Davies Company in 1988, her first programme commissioned by Dance Umbrella, while the company received prestigious Digital Dance Awards in 1988, 1989 and 1990. She also moved over, as it were, to Alston's Rambert, becoming this company's Associate Choreographer in 1989. On her own admission, Davies had grown creatively tired during her last years with LCDT, and a number of critics were noting an aridity in her work at this time.[11] Post-Fulbright, a renewed energy has been widely recognized.

During the 1980s, Davies had several works televised. She made work specifically for the television medium, several short essays for the Dance-lines 1987 programme, and later two works devised for television as well as for theatre – *Wyoming* and *White Man Sleeps*, premiered by the Siobhan Davies Company in 1988, and broadcast and directed by Peter Mumford, in 1989. *Silent Partners* (1984), for Second Stride, was the subject of a London Weekend Television South Bank Show (1985).

The choreographic link between Alston and Davies in their respective careers has often been pointed out, but his influence might sometimes have been exaggerated. There are many important distinctions as well as similarities between their choreographic styles. Increasingly over the years, Davies has made explorations into areas that have held little interest for Alston. Yet they have always shared a central principle, of developing a rich language of movement, and devising a range of structures that arise from the dance medium itself rather than from theatricality, spectacle or stories.[12] She, as does he, remains determined to challenge audiences by providing complex work that demands concentration and encourages more than one viewing. In her own words, she wants 'to work out my own particular version of the language of dance, trying to make that as rich as I possibly can ... the most intricate language that I can get; yet, at the same time, trying to find the most legible way for that to be seen.'[13] This could just as well be Alston speaking. Thus, in the 1970s, her style, vocabulary, phrases and patterning in the stage space, became increasingly complex. Then, in later years, while taking on board other issues, she has regularly gone back to reconsider and enrich her movement language and to develop her own solutions to the challenge of 'symphonic' construction in dance (see p. 125).

The subject of the dances

Initially, Davies' choreographic task was to rid herself of the Graham-based class language in which she was trained, but which she believed would restrict her creatively. She began by improvising to jazz, a means, she perceived, of inviting new movement to emerge. Then, for *Relay* (1972), her first piece for the LCDT repertory, she constructed material from the movements and physical situations associated with sport: running, hurdling, boxing, wrestling, punting, swimming. It was a light-hearted trio, and the dancers manipulated three boxes, in ways that suggested Olympic medallists' plinths, or an umpire's chair, finally a boat. *Pilot* (1974) too contained touches of humour, the framework for dances a group of bored travellers waiting, shifting their suitcases round the stage and back to the starting corner for diversion. The next three works evoke moods, but are without any specific time or place. *The Calm* (1974) is built around a dynamic principle, peacefulness and agitation contrasted, and eventually the entire ensemble quietened. *Diary* (1975), the outcome of reflections upon movement during a company tour and holiday, is a simple series of dance episodes, the fact that there is no overarching structural principle determined by the irregular rehearsal schedule: episodes were conceived and made independently as time permitted.[14] In *Step at a Time* (1976), Davies contrasts precise motion and shape in solos and duets, the dancers in brightly coloured unitards, with swirling ensemble motion deliberately blurred by voluminous white all-in-ones. *Sphinx* (1977) contains direct reference to animal movement, within an abstract framework.

From 1978 onwards, Davies' work, looked at broadly, has developed in two concurrent directions. There are further essays in which pure dance values emerge most strongly, although titles provide a poetic context: *Celebration* (1979), her first piece for Ballet Rambert; *New Galileo* (1984), *and do they do* (1986), and *Red Steps* (1987) for LCDT; and *Embarque* (1988) and *Sounding* (1989) for Rambert Dance Company. Then there are works in which emotional states or progressions become more pronounced, and the dancers are costumed as people, in an approximation of street clothes. The latter kind of work has interested Davies far more than it has Alston. This is a major distinction in their work. Yet Davies' style is to keep narrative or 'plot' extremely simple, and there is no firm border-line between the two polarities of her output. In the later 1980s, the intense communication, sensuality and physical generosity between partners suggests

134

that her more abstract pieces have been informed by her experience of narrative. It is hard to decide whether formal or 'narrative' issues should be discussed first. Opening with 'narrative' should not imply that this is any more important than the other aspect of her work.

Narrative

The first of the 'narrative' works *Then You Can Only Sing* (1978) followed *Sphinx*, and is a sequence of statements by five women. Set to the words and music of Judyth Knight, it expresses aspects of individual personality and circumstance: loneliness, humour, uncertainty and confusion. Davies says that the relationship between the singing and dancing Anna in the 1978 *The Seven Deadly Sins* (see p. 107) had prompted her to introduce Knight as a singing counterpart on stage to each dancing character. Typically, Davies depicts ordinary people, their tribulations and everyday relationship to one another – no myths, no big generalizations about mankind.

Soon, Davies went ahead to develop character in more detail. *Something to Tell* (1980), like several of her later works, draws on literary source material. It sprang from her response to Chekhov, to what she perceives as his minimal plot development but extensive revelation of troubled personality.[15] The dance concerns a woman in loneliness and desolation, Davies herself and her partner (danced by Robert North) join in 'several conversations as in a play':[16] a series of solos, duets, and ensembles with six younger characters who might represent aspects of her past. The woman seems tense and despairing and in need of her partner's care but, after conversation, finds resignation and a certain peace. There is no action as such, no reason given for her behaviour, simply feelings 'to tell' in movement.

Bridge the Distance (1985), also for LCDT, is less of a continuous story, more a suite of distinct dances in which a fractious, clumsy and extravagant youthfulness contrasts with the serenity and balance that comes from maturity and experience. There are various couple dances, including an opening dance for all four couples and a nervy ballroom burlesque for a single pair, also a solo for an older man in a special gestural language that sets him apart from the others. There is nothing quite like this solo anywhere else in the dance repertoire. The gestures do not form a simple code like mime, although the classical gesture of beauty, the hand circling the face, is included. While we recognize gestures such as reaching out and holding back for what they must imply, others are hard to interpret in mime terms. What emerges from this language here is an abstracted representation of the protagonist's eloquence and knowledge and, by sheer wealth of movement ideas, a subtle communication of the lively undercurrents of the man's personality flowing beneath his composure. In the final section of *Bridge the Distance*, the two parties, young people and the older man, are set against each other; Davies demonstrates structurally the older man's greater understanding by placing him one phrase ahead of the group. Appropriately, *Bridge* is a work that indulges those qualities that Davies recognizes in mature dancers (here Patrick Harding-Irmer), qualities beyond technique: those of precision in shaping and timing and of presence, that are only gained through years of performing experience.

Bridge contains allusions to Thomas Mann's *Death in Venice* novella of 1912. A young boy briefly commands the attention of the older man. The costumes are Edwardian in style, and there is an allusion in the score, Benjamin Britten's third string quartet, in which he in turn quotes from his operatic setting of *Death in Venice*. At the point in the work where the key quotation occurs, Davies sets the brief but important unison for older man and boy (who could be likened to von Aschenbach and Tadzio in the novella). But it was never her intention to make very specific or frequent reference to the story, and the older man, in her mind, could just as easily have suggested the figure of Britten himself.[17] Again, *Bridge* is more about feeling than story. As in several of Davies' works too, the title contains multiple meanings: referring to the bridge on the violin, bridges in Venice, a structure that needs crossing in order to communicate, and the distance between old and young, experience and inexperience.

The special acting abilities and individuality of the Second Stride dancers and the intimate venues in which they performed encouraged Davies to make several 'character' pieces for this company. Indeed, Second Stride was instrumental in carrying forward her narrative interests. But *Carnival* (1982), her first character piece for this group, is atypical. Her only extended essay in humour, a setting of Saint-Saëns' work for two pianos and chamber orchestra *Carnaval des animaux* (1886), the work mixes references to the animals and other things depicted, to certain traits with which the different animals are anthropomorphized, and to the instruments for which the work is scored. Thus, 'The Swan', for many viewers the most memorable episode of the work, suggests images not only of the swan and the cellist, but even the swan-neck of the 'cello itself, whilst observing, through Philippe Giraudeau's performance, the dignity and grace of Saint-Saëns' setting.

In *Minor Characters* (1983), she used words again, the first time since *Then You Can Only Sing*, but on this occasion without music, simply a script by the American writer Barbara McLauren. Sally Owen and Betsy Gregory are on stage as speakers in this piece, and sometimes the dancers, too, engage in the dialogue and monologue. Davies is again exploring ordinary people – hence the title 'minor characters' (it came from a book by Joyce Johnson). It is in this piece that she explores the language of small hand and head gestures for the first time, the language that eventually led to the *Bridge the Distance* solo. Davies says that her Second Stride codirector, Spink, had demonstrated to her the power of small, non-technical movement, and she had been impressed by his integration of movement and speech: she had recently performed in his *New Tactics* (1983). Continuing her gestural explorations, Davies' next piece for Second Stride was *Silent Partners* (1984), the history of a man and a woman, she explained in the South Bank Show.[18] Each passes through a series of three relationships – Giraudeau with Lenny Westerdijk, Cathy Burge and Ikky Maas; Michele Smith with Juliet Fisher, Michael Popper and Maedée Duprès. Each takes what he or she 'learns' (movement ideas) from one encounter into the next. Finally, Giraudeau and Smith meet one another in a duet of heightened passion and tenderness. One of the most poignant, sensual images is the gesture 'learnt' from Smith's duet with Duprès: each dancer in turn traces the outline of the other's head, face, neck and chest with the hand. This is done gently, without actually touching, but the gesture is 'felt' by the partner, whose head bows and then drops back to reveal the fullness of the neck. In each duet in *Silent Partners*, we learn more about the characters involved. Davies also demonstrates in this piece that a regular, symmetrical formal proposition in dance can carry a constantly developing 'story'.

Davies named her characters for the first and only time in *The School for Lovers Danced* (1985). This is a condensed version of *Così fan Tutte* in dance, using some of the Mozart score and following in outline da Ponte's libretto. The theme of the two men, Guglielmo and Ferrando, absenting themselves and returning in disguise to woo afresh their fiancées Fiordiligi and Dorabella is preserved. Davies provides mime and dances to selected recitatives and arias appropriate to individual characters and scenes. This is by far her most literal piece, her most detailed excursion into plot. Ironically, perhaps because Davies restricted her choreographic flow by tying herself so closely to the music, the characters seem less developed than in other works, and by ending the story simply and early with the young men's success in their deception, the more interesting psychological developments are left out. *The School* contains some fascinating moments of quick-witted mime and movement, although ultimately it is unsuccessful and, continuing on from the gestural language developed in *Bridge the Distance*, it marks an extreme of literalism which Davies has since rejected.

Davies' most strongly narrative piece since *The School* is of quite a different nature, and turned away from this language of hand gestures. Post-Fulbright, for the Siobhan Davies Company, *Wyoming* (1988) begins with a series of five very different solos, individuals evoking various sensualities and emotions in response to a vast landscape and sky around them. Davies had been impressed by the expansiveness of the great plains of the American West and was also inspired by the descriptive writing of Gretel Ehrlich.[19] The dancer Scott Clark, for instance, is found sitting low on one hip, pondering perhaps, and then he rises, bouncing, skittering as if over sand – a little jump to the side, and the feet are drawn lightly together again –

137

or bounding lightly between all fours. Paul Douglas demonstrates his experience of the enormity of this landscape, standing or leaping wide, or merely impressing width and length with his back and arms stretched to their utmost against the ground surface. Lizie Saunderson introduces an element of anguish, a great heaviness into the floor – she rolls, as if burdened, into the weight of one thigh – and her arching up and back, her bird-like hoverings and sudden skipping flurries read like a series of small, sharp cries.

A while later, Clark confronts Saunderson and greets her. But she does not see him – she stands as if hypnotized. Shifting duo and trio ensembles relax the emotional tension. Then, with the second greeting, she is ready for him. The frozen stance melts into a bow to the floor and on into a celebration of sharing; statements from their previous solos are like messages passed between them to unite them. As in *Silent Partners*, the basic structure carrying the story is formal and in large part regular: fundamentally, in *Wyoming*, a series of solos leading to a duet.

The television version of the piece (directed by Peter Mumford) introduces more specific meanings. John Marc Gowans' score is supplemented here by quotations from Ehrlich's short story *Spring*, read by Julie Covington. There is reference to different weather conditions (the words transcribed here from the television piece):

> I was still cataloguing the different kinds of snow ...
> A Pacific storm blows in from the south like a jib-sail.

and to spring as a three-part affair:

> False spring, the vernal equinox, and the spring when flowers come and the grass grows.

The relationship between the woman, who is 'I' the speaker, and the man (Saunderson and Clark in the dance) is documented:

> One night he did come to my house ... my silence turned him away like a rolling wave.

At their second meeting, the man is named:

> Now when I dream of Joel, he is riding that horse. One night he rides to my house, all smiles and shyness. I let him in ...

Other Davies works evoke human situations in more general terms, time, place, individual character remaining unspecific, or perhaps one or two 'people' presented in an abstract situation next to undefined dance personalities. *Plain Song* (1981), for Siobhan Davies and Dancers and *Rushes* for Second Stride are of this semi-abstract kind. *Plain Song* presents a harmonious community of men and women (they are undifferentiated in costume – loose, stone-coloured tops and trousers), one of them, a woman (Davies), moved to make a personal utterance, and then eased gently back into the group. The atmosphere is almost devotional. *Rushes*, entirely different in quality, shows a community going out of control, a group of six shifting from relative composure, its members distinguished in solos and duets, to a state of unrule, a mob 'rushing' about the stage to 'rushing' cascades of notes on the piano. Once again, the title has more than one connotation. In neither of these pieces do individual characters develop.

The Run to Earth (1986) for LCDT has its 'people', a leading couple, and its anonymous crowd. The pair run to earth literally, repeatedly skidding and dashing themselves to the floor, to rest, cower or draw breath, or like hunted animals fleeing to the safety of the den. (The design too, by David Buckland and Russell Mills, lit by Mumford, 'runs to earth'. It shifts continuously throughout the piece, gradually crumpling to the floor.) There is also the cosmographical metaphor of a human, earthly partnership, alone and fearful, voyaging amid alien worlds and beings. The couple clutch and cling to one another – reaching desperately upwards, in lifts shooting high above the crowd – as often as they return to the ground. The crowd introduces quite a different semaphoric vocabulary, mainly cool and passionless, or they become, in a faster central section, mildly playful, like dancing angels.

Cover Him With Grass (1989) for the Siobhan Davies Company has a tape score by Kevin Volans evoking the sounds of Africa, hammering, worksongs, chanting, and the dancers bend sensually into its rhythms and 'work' with a pole as complement to its images. At one point, a man lies as if dead, and this is followed by a section in a very different language, suggesting perhaps a state of transcendence after earthly rituals. But the play between established context and abstraction emerges as a rather uncomfortable stylistic break in this piece.

Leaving aside *The School for Lovers Danced*, which contains some one-to-one visualizations of words and encourages the audience to keep looking for such parallels, it is clear that Davies generally prefers to bring out a sort of subterranean language of the body, which can be tremendously effective in the communication of feeling and rich in its power of suggestion and ambiguity. Her formal devices are often metaphors for the structuring of experience and character, for example, the duet plan in *Silent Partners*. Her habit of allocating characters specific material and then varying that material seems both to establish identity – 'that person's story'[20] – and to show the variety of the individual personality. The characteristic later sharing of material with other dancers often seems to suggest togetherness, harmony, resolution.[21]

It is typical, too, that Davies gets her power from presenting feeling as a turbulent undercurrent, feeling strictly restrained, even repressed, the emotional moment often marked by slowness, stillness and quiet, intimate circumstances. Davies says that she had recognized this potential in The Royal Ballet performances by Fonteyn and Beriosova that she had seen and admired years before. It is a restraint that some critics have had problems with, interpreting it as bleakness, austerity, dramatic uncertainty, even choreographic aridity.[22] In other words, these critics do not perceive the turbulence and the powerful effect achieved by holding it back. Alston, who does note Davies' peculiar power in intimacy and quietness, feels that a new undercurrent of passion was released into her choreography after she stopped performing.[23] Davies had displayed an unusual passion in performance, but had taken care, she says, to discipline her early works, rarely revealing this aspect in her choreographic personality.

Yet, it is important to remember that, for all her attentiveness to character, Davies never surrenders the richness of the dance language that she has built up over the years. Indeed, as shown below, she has discovered how those properties of dance, like rhythm, spatial forms within the body and across the stage, double- and ensemble work can inform and enhance narrative and make subtle its personalities, as much as they make an abstract contribution.

Movement

From her earliest works it was clear that Davies had an unusual gift for the original and powerful dance idea that would be woven into her broader, more characteristic vocabulary of moves. In the early work, vivid memories spring from the slow, creamy duets in *Diary* (1975) and in *Step at a Time* (1976): the striking two-body shapes that are passed through, given life by counterpull and physical intensity. There are also compelling ideas in the solos that Davies made for herself, like the one in *Sphinx*, where she dances an enigmatic creature crouching with a strangely vibrating leg like a tail. In her early career, she made many of her most interesting explorations on her own body. And in later works, the simplest idea can stand out, like Jeremy James' three knocks with the fist in his solo in *Sounding*. The knocks make a descending arc before him and let go into a broad swing of the arm down and up behind his body.

In the more generalized terms of her characteristic movement vocabulary, there are common denominators throughout Davies' work. First is her attitude to weight, allowing the body to fall, to yield to gravity as well as to resist it. This is never more emphatic than in *Sounding*, a piece that stresses the 'down' rather than the 'up' in great plunges and scoopings to the floor.

140

There is also a fluidity or organic flow between moves and a special length of line. These qualities were undoubtedly motivated by her own predilections as a performer.

Elsewhere, it is possible to see distinct changes in style at different stages of her career. At first, she stressed body design, line and shape in her work, which were stressed in other LCDT repertoire at the time. She has said that this was partly a response to criticism of the LCDT's dancers' technique in the early 1970s and the dancers' concomitant lack of confidence.[24] On the other hand, she did have at her disposal Linda Gibbs, a dancer of exceptional technical ability, and used her special precision to great effect in several early pieces. Already characteristic of her work during this period is a generosity and openness, and the full use of the body, including the torso, that she had experienced from Cohan's Graham-based style and, in a quite different way, Alston's work. As well as searching for her own images, she incorporated moves from these choreographers or moves that she would have learnt from class. (It is worth recognizing that Davies always used the Graham-style contraction far more sparingly than Cohan, but that the LCDT dancers tended, following their basic training, to interpret body curves in terms of contraction.)

Sphinx marks a turning point in the development of her vocabulary. As Davies was now exploring the qualities of animal movement, body design gave way in importance to motion, and the movement in this piece does not stretch out into space as much as in earlier work. Ripples that pass through the torso and hands used like paws tend to draw space inwards and to internalize the effect of the movement.

Then You Can Only Sing springs from what Davies learnt in *Sphinx*, but the motivation is emotional, the dance often passionate. This effect of passion is created by movements that involve swing and risk, by swirls and by bold, strong impulses as well as the surrendering to gravity before recovery and suspension. The activity now has strong emotive connotations, like abandonment, temper, working something out of the system, even ecstasy. As Davies pursued this new approach to vocabulary, we notice that, for a while, her focus turned increasingly to the upper body, away from the legs. There was less elevation. Davies now explored the vertical dimension in terms of going to and from the floor and discovered a great variety and fluency in her methods of achieving this.

In the 1980s, Davies' vocabulary shifted into yet other directions. There was, alongside her 'regular' vocabulary, the new richness of gesture introduced into her character pieces, and the 'speaking' full-body movements selected and directed to indicate personality and dynamics between personalities. But also, not wishing, she says, to be pigeon-holed as a slow and musing sort of choreographer, she accelerated her tempi and introduced more emphatic angles and points in body shapes. This sharpening process shows first in *Rushes* in its hectic bursts of activity and its attention to specific angles of the body, created by the elbow when raised emphatically, the knee in falls, and when the foot is trapped in the hand, or the ankle, when flexed feet become handles with which to move a dancer. At the same time, Davies began to check her speed and swirls of movement by the sharp contrast of sudden halts, frozen images becoming important as points of punctuation and as the motivic content of a piece, first in *Free Setting* (1981) and also in *Rushes*.

With *The Dancing Department* (1983), placed shape became a more important part of the vocabulary again, and it is clear that by *New Galileo* (1984) she had thoroughly integrated her earlier concern for shape and image into her freer movement language. Such integration was entirely appropriate to the content of this piece. The eight dancers in *New Galileo* are like a constantly shifting universe with sharp and imaginative images set up rapidly, briefly fixed, then shattered or exploded. Some of these images are like Davies motifs, recalling other pieces by the choreographer: the foot trapped in the hand, or the heel as handle. *Galileo* also contains more balletic reference than any other piece by her. There are clean ballet fifths amongst its placed positions, also an emphasis on lifting the weight up out of the ground, both in doublework and use of three-quarter pointe, and even Rose Adagio-like promenades in attitude.

In *and do they do* (1986), Davies introduced a new fleetness, calling for more rapid, detailed work of the feet and lower legs, neat, small jumps as well as major elevation and a faster torso than ever before. The LCDT dancers had problems with this style, unaccustomed to such demands of quick-footedness and fluency with weight. These problems were answered immediately upon Davies' 'moving over' to Rambert, in *Embarque* (1988), a far more enlightened work in every respect. *Embarque* uses to advantage the great power and beauty of the Rambert dancers by this stage of Alston's directorship, ready to charge through space, evoking the great American plains again, to give in boldly to weight, and yet, with their ballet and Cunningham training, fast and meticulous with small moves. *Embarque*, to Steve Reich's racing perpetuum mobile *Eight Lines*, contains the fastest and most intricate movement that she has ever made.

Yet, only a few months later, Davies made work of an entirely different nature for her own company. *Wyoming* and *White Man Sleeps* were the results of lengthy explorations into image-based work with her dancers.[25] In the USA, Davies had opted to do classes that were concerned with making personal movement choices from images and sensations, work allied to the tradition of release (see pp. 52–53). Using release concepts here as a starting point for choreographic ideas, she wanted to abandon certain habits and get behind the stylistic 'barrier' of traditional dance technique. On her return, she conducted workshops with her dancers based on similar principles – all

142

of them, with the exception of Scott Clark, new to this approach – before shaping their quality-imbued movement into structured movement and phrases. As much as *Embarque* is broad and far-reaching, *White Man Sleeps* explores small, private movements in the space close to the body and the frisson of almost touching and lightly touching:[26] Clark and Lauren Potter brush or pat a body part, the inside of an arm, the cheek, forehead, or spot near the ankle, and in contacting a partner, that touching seems to enclose the other person as if they become one. And the principal opening motif of the piece shows detailed motion, a small circling of the pelvis, a light jiggle of the shoulders, amongst other moves. Davies also devoted workshop sessions to 'liquid gesture' in preparation for this piece.

But perhaps *Wyoming* revealed most clearly that something new was happening in Davies' work. Here, the dancers had read Ehrlich's writings for themselves (several essays were used), and responded in workshop to their various images, for instance, the subtle textures of the ground and the idea of the skin adapting to different temperatures and weather conditions, becoming a snow skin or rain skin. And Davies rehearsed the piece with different 'quality' instructions: 'think only of small details' or, at another time, 'think only of sending yourself across a very large area.'[27] The story of the man and woman meeting that is spoken over the television version of *Wyoming* was the original inspiration for its equivalent moments in the dance. Clark, significantly given a major role in the first programme of Davies' new company, raises his arms high one after the other, using the flat surface of the inner arm as a greeting to Saunderson. A gesture that is very plain structurally is infused with a particular liveliness and made strange. At the end of their duet, when the woman seems to have found peace, she can literally let him lay her down, as if to sleep, and her back breathes deeply into his. Davies pinpoints the vibrancy of a particular sensation within a vast landscape. *Wyoming* is the kind of piece that leaves behind a trail of unforgettable physical memories and sensualities, and it is important that Davies gives time, sustainment, for deep consideration within the moment of performance. Choreographic structuring here, by contrast, seems to demand less attention.

Two years later, in 1990, Davies introduced a similar 'personal' approach to the Rambert dancers. Making *Signature*, she invited the dancers to contribute some of their own dance ideas. It was as if they were writing their own motifs, making their own marks. A woman (Catherine Quinn) is seen simply sinking and gently bouncing back with an easy play at the knees – it feels like the free-with-the-weight experience that you have when standing cushioned by deep water. Or she tosses her hand as lightly as if playing with a bubble of air. A private image behind the simplest movement makes it a sign, peculiar and interesting.

Later the same year, Davies incorporated real signs in *Different Trains*, which she made for her own company. Here, she used the hand language of the deaf to tell personal stories, enjoying its resonance through the whole person, and developing from it a full-body dance language.

Structure

Davies' movement has taken on new nuances over the years; the same applies to the manner in which she has put material together into phrases and larger structures. Her earlier works are relatively easy to read. The ideas unfold slowly: fast material is juxtaposed with simple running and walking transitions and constructed in short, repeating units; the more convoluted, non-repetitive passages are paced very slowly so that there is plenty of time to grasp their information. The later work makes greater demands on the audience's powers of perception. It attends to the detail as well as to the full scale of the body and shifts the eye more restlessly as the movement has become more wayward in orientation. It is rhythmically far more irregular, the phrases longer and denser, without the perceptual relaxation afforded by transitions.

Davies' change in approach is logical for a maturing choreographer interested in developing a sophisticated movement language. It is also something to do with the change in working process that she introduced in 1981 with her first two pieces for Siobhan Davies and Dancers, *Standing Waves* and *Plain Song*. She tells us that, in making these works, before setting dance to music or determining structure, she made a series of distinct phrases in silence on each of the performers involved. *Plain Song* had seven phrases for its seven performers, the material in each of these phrases deliberately complex and containing no repetition. Her procedure then was to mould or vary this material as the basis of her work, taking parts of the phrases, sometimes reshuffling the order of the material in them, changing their orientation in relation to the stage (a device that Cunningham introduced and that has been used by many choreographers since), perhaps taking a movement upwards or downwards, into a lift or to the floor. The density of material generated in the original phrases could thus be maintained through the work as a whole. Once Davies had discovered this density, she found that she could recreate it alongside the developing structure of a piece, without making phrases first. And she continued to use her technique of shuffling or reordering movement ideas to make new phrases.

In her earlier work, Davies had already begun to use variation technique. In *Step at a Time*, for instance, Gibbs' opening crouch and rise with arms extended is later performed standing on her partner's knees, or it becomes part of a duet, when the outstretched hands are held. Since then, Davies has used the technique extensively, and with much more sophistication. It is a strong unifying device, the element of repetition helping to make a complex language comprehensible, and it has rich potential. As Paul Clayden (a dancer with Siobhan Davies and Dancers and Second Stride) once observed, Davies is able to make a twenty-minute dance out of a handful of ideas.[28]

Notably, as she moved towards greater complexity, the nature of Davies' duets changed. They became more contrapuntal – already, in *Something to Tell*, in the central duet for Davies and North, each dancer has his or her own strand of material. This is a true conversation, and the term 'conversation' is one that Davies herself often uses about her favourite duet form. Each dancer in turn makes a statement, sometimes one taking over abruptly and forcefully, like interrupting, and there is the occasional brief unison, like a moment of agreement. Later, the dancers move simultaneously, but still, despite moments of contact, with their independent material. Finally, they dance in unison, a metaphor for communion and shared experience. Davies has continued to explore this democratic contrapuntal duet form since then in both abstract and narrative works, and in still more complex manner. The two dancers often might function tangentially to each other, weaving a counterpoint of fascinating spatial and rhythmic implications, setting up lines of tension across space, perhaps crossing lines, and releasing them, breathing independently or matching up for the brief moment of in-breath before exhalation. Unisons and lifts become moments of sudden excitement, unusually powerful by contrast with counterpoint. As Davies once said, duets like these are much more than the sum of their component parts: 'like the matching of two sounds one against each other . . . it makes for third, fourth and fifth sounds'.[29]

It is logical, too, that Davies was able to present her large structures with more subtlety and variety as her career progressed. Her earliest works are clearly episodic, dances following dances with simple cross-references between sections. In *Step at a Time*, she found a simple way of forging links by opening a new section with the move that concluded the previous one. In some later works, she has kept her frameworks simple – *Carnival*, a string of episodes, and indeed *Wyoming*, with its series of solos, then a duet and trio, culminating in a duet. But in many others she has experimented with more fluid and irregular structures: a more uneven pacing of the large-scale events, 'false' sections, a dance, perhaps, that does not develop as one might expect because it is overtaken by another, dancers overlapping from a previous section or breaking into the next. There is in all the later work, from the 1980s onwards, a subtle web of repetitions, variations, and a weaving together of material that knits the parts of a work together. Davies, in other words, has developed her own answers to 'symphonic' construction in dance (see p. 125).

Her finest symphonic pieces of the 1980s and 1990s demonstrate a very secure handling of large form. This is crucial to the intelligibility of a work that is as challenging to 'read' on the surface as *Embarque*. Fundamentally, this piece can be analysed as a series of five accumulations with numbers increasing from one or two dancers to six or eight and then dropping ready to start the process again. It is useful to feel that big structure. Two major peaks involving all eight dancers (three couples and two extra women) occur half way through and at the end of the dance, and are marked by exuberant cavalcades of dancers in canon threading around each other in a path around the stage. In a sense, the final cavalcade, by referring backwards, balances the centrepoint of the dance, creating another layer of big structure. But there is also a feeling of curtailment: the second peak grows much faster than the first, which evolved from a substantial section for all eight dancers, and follows a quick sorting out into the original pairings of dancers after some partner-swapping. The final halt is sudden (one couple left onstage); Davies has chosen to leave the spectator breathless, excited, to end the dance on a decisive upnote. The effect at the end of *Sounding* is not dissimilar, with its accelerating accumulation of full cast into a sudden frieze.

Spatial aspects

One of the most distinctive components of Davies' work throughout her career has been her use of the stage space and the grouping of dancers in that space. There has always been a striking feeling for territory and spatial implications in her work. It is significant that, in *Relay*, as well as using sport to suggest vocabulary, she saw it as a useful guide to the spacing of her performers. A little later, specific channels for action became characteristic, a favourite being the long strip of space using the side to side dimension of the stage. Thus, for much of the time, the quiet couple in *The Calm* occupy a channel upstage as background to faster dancers. Thus, too, *Step at a Time* begins with Gibbs moving in a shaft of light across the apron, then returning with a partner while Davies takes up Gibbs' opening crossing again in the distance. The much admired sculptural duet made for Cathy Lewis and Namron in *Diary* is another example of such a journey in a line across the stage.

She chose less obvious spatial devices for later works. In *Ley Line* (1979), as the title suggests, the stage is traversed by a series of imaginary lines. Davies uses these for entries and makes their points of intersection determine the area in which the various solos, duets and groups take place. She uses this device again in *Rushes*, but this time with an imaginary graph as the framework for meetings.

Davies developed her own characteristic ways of breaking up or focusing the dancing space, by placing dancers as onlookers or obstacles, static or moving, around which movement has to take place. Thus, she could enhance her statement in *The Run to Earth*, which seems to be about its leading pair of dancers coming to terms with each other and with their unpredictable, unreasoning environment. At the beginning of the work, the

22. Siobhan Davies in the solo that she created for herself in *Sphinx* (London Contemporary Dance Theatre, 1977). (Photograph: David Buckland)

23. ABOVE: Charlotte Kirkpatrick in her solo from *Then You Can Only Sing* (London Contemporary Dance Theatre, 1978), choreography by Siobhan Davies. (Photograph: David Buckland)

24. RIGHT ABOVE: A moment from the end of *Silent Partners* (Second Stride, 1984), choreography by Siobhan Davies, design by David Buckland, lighting by Peter Mumford. In the foreground: Philippe Giraudeau, Michele Smith. (Photograph: David Buckland)

25. RIGHT BELOW: *New Galileo* (London Contemporary Dance Theatre, 1984), choreography by Siobhan Davies. Dancers in the middle- and foreground, from left to right: Michael Small, Linda Gibbs, Lauren Potter, Patrick Harding-Irmer. (Photograph: David Buckland)

26. The final moment from *Wyoming* (Siobhan Davies Company, 1988), choreography by Siobhan Davies. Dancers: Scott Clark, Lizie Saunderson. (Photograph: David Buckland)

established structural relationships with the music in this piece, especially at the calm ending, when it was appropriate for there to be some unity between the rhythms of music and dance.

Then You Can Only Sing was the first occasion for Davies to make a point of fitting her dance rhythms to the sound (the commissioned music by Judyth Knight). Since this piece, she has used both commissioned and existing music. Her choices have been catholic and more enlightened than in the 1970s: mainly twentieth-century music, but also reaching back to medieval music, and Bach and Mozart. She has used the music of Britten four times: in *If My Complaints Could Passions Move* (1980), for LSCD; *Something to Tell*; *Mazurka Elegiaca* (1982) for Linda Gibbs' solo show *Leaving Places*; and *Bridge the Distance* (1985). She commissioned scores from Michael Finnissy for *Free Setting* and *Rushes*. From the mid-1980s, Davies has turned consistently to new music, demonstrating strong inclinations towards minimalism: she has set scores by John Adams (*New Galileo*, *Red Steps* and, for English National Ballet, *Dancing Ledge* (1990)), Brian Eno (*The Run to Earth*), Steve Reich (*Embarque* and *Different Trains*) and a commissioned score by Michael Nyman (*and do they do*). But she has also used several scores of a different style by the South African-born composer Kevin Volans, setting existing scores for *White Man Sleeps* and *Cover Him With Grass*, and commissioning music for *Signature*.

Since *Then You Can Only Sing*, Davies has continued to respond to musical structure, but in varying degrees of detail, either broadly, contacting the music structurally at cue points, or more precisely, responding to melodic organization and phrasing, pulse and metre, or, occasionally, to rhythmic patterns and contrapuntal structures. Davies is not inclined towards the closest of these relationships between music and dance. Looking back on *The Dancing Department*, she worries that her approach was too academic, her choreography too constrained by adherence to the music, even though this was by no means a consistent, precise visualization of the rhythmic patterns and contrapuntal ingenuities of Bach's *The Musical Offering*. She is happier with her solution to Satie's piano music in *Plain Song*, where her pre-determined phrases encouraged play against the music as well as suggesting passages of detailed unity. And in 'The Swan' from *Carnival*, she gained nuance from repeating images in different relationships to the musical phrasing (as well as turning them round in space). There has remained an urge to let movement speak in rhythms unhampered by external forces. It is significant that, for *Silent Partners*, Davies chose silence. There is only a tiny bloom of saxophone solo at the end. She was concentrating on a new approach to narrative. 'Think protective . . . think dependent' was the kind of instruction that she gave her dancers. She felt in the end, that the 'natural' length of moves discovered would have been removed had the choreography been attached to music.[32] And for similar reasons,

153

parts of Patrick Harding-Irmer's solo in *Bridge the Distance* were created in silence, to find their own timing, and only linked with the music later.[33]

Time and time again, Davies has settled for the freer relationship between music and dance. An interesting example is *Sounding*, in which Davies originally worked tightly to the gong accents in Giacinto Scelsi's score *Okanagon*. The wonderfully weighty impulses into reverberation – 'the heartbeat of the earth' was Scelsi's description of his score – were a direct inspiration for movement. But the dance eventually found its own freedoms. Of course, music that has no pronounced regular pulse, the kind that Davies most often chooses, lends itself naturally to such freedoms. Time and again too, Davies sets up bold changes in movement tempo and dynamics, even sudden halts into stillness, that are in no way suggested by the music. The most extreme examples of this are in *Red Steps* which, counterpointing any musical implications (Adams' *Shaker Loops*), contains many passages of very slow motion or still poses, sometimes with nothing else happening on stage.

Yet there are occasions when Davies has allowed herself to be guided, successfully, by detailed musical structures. Britten has given her a phrasing framework ideally suited to dance statement and conversation while, at the same time, allowing freedom for breath rhythm. A fine example of this occurs in the 'Cello Suite no. 3 (the score for *Something to Tell*), the recitative-like passage at the beginning of the passacaglia, with its phrases alternating high and low registers. This provides a perfect complement to the conversational beginning of the Davies/North duet, and Davies recalls enjoying the freedom to respond on the spur of the moment to different live performances of the score. And in *and do they do* and *Embarque*, to scores with obsessive motoric drive, she has used musical metre to reinforce and give added vigour to her dance impulse. In both these works, Davies responds to the separate musical layers, sometimes to one at a time, sometimes, with dance counterpoint, to more than one simultaneously: to the rapid motoric undercurrent – fleet allegro; to a sustained melody – slow, broad full body gestures. However, rarely does she paint a rhythmic and melodic line in detail. Usually, the dance provides all kinds of lively syncopations and cross-patterns. It is interesting too that in *Embarque* (to Reich's *Eight Lines*), Davies follows the overriding principle of accumulation, a series of waves, taken from the music, but has chosen not to make all the dance waves happen at the same time as those in the music.

Design and lighting

The minimal design element in Davies' early work distinguished it from most other LCDT repertoire at this time. She used no decor at all, only lighting by Charter (alias Robert Cohan) and simple costumes: white tracksuits for *Relay*, T-shirts and jeans for *Pilot* and then, as lycra became available, catsuits or leotards with close-fitting trousers. These choices were of course appropriate to Davies' concern with shape at this time. In *Step at a Time*, she makes a point of the sleek, sharp image, through its contrast with more fuzzy impressions – billowing suits, worn for ensemble interludes, and projections on gauze at the beginning and end of the piece (by Michael Creevy), ghostly suggestions of a figure in high-flying trajectory.

When Davies began to introduce narrative, it was logical that she should make design more prominent, in order to humanize her characters and to make their situation more specific. *Then You Can Only Sing* was the first piece to break the mould, with the women wearing skirts. It was this piece that prompted Antony McDonald to approach Davies with the idea of a collaboration,[34] a meeting that resulted in *Something to Tell*, her first piece with a set. His costumes, dresses, trousers and shirts have the style of street clothing and differentiate the dancers, and his striking Venetian blind set with doorway suggests an exterior passage upstage and an interior where conversations take place. McDonald's designs reflect his experience of working in drama, which was probably the reason why he was drawn to Davies once she had turned to narrative. His style, as in Ian Spink's work,[35] is to introduce props and to encroach into the dancing space with his design, thereby creating new territories. Something of this is seen in Davies' *Minor Characters*, where he evokes a room, with suspended mirrors, table and chairs.

Davies has worked most frequently with her photographer husband David Buckland (design) and Peter Mumford (lighting). In her collaborations with Buckland, the connections between choreography and design are of a different kind. For *Free Setting*, Buckland hung three transparent screens printed with blown-up photographs of a single woman, a couple and a trio respectively. The images are both a reminder of previous images in the choreography and a taste of future connections, and they encourage the viewer to perceive more acutely the sculptural forms in the dance. Freezing into pictures is part of the choreographic content. Furthermore, the photographs lend structure to the dancing space, invading it for the opening of the piece, when they are hung low, partially masking the dancing. Mumford highlights the sudden freeze content by abrupt lighting changes.

In *Rushes*, the relationship between photo-image and choreography is clearer still and extends to 'narrative' content. The backdrop unfolds to show three couples in the same 'portrait' that has been created on stage. The portrait is a leitmotif of the dance piece, returned whole or in part, facing different directions, finally disintegrated. But the backdrop also establishes a social context for the piece, showing the dancers in everyday clothes. Then it changes, a complement to the choreographic change from a group of six dancing individuals to a faceless mob. Moved by a motor, banners descend to cover the original drop, a public, abstract statement covering what was once a private social image. Finally, the portrait is removed entirely, leaving only the banners. Buckland was inspired by Alexander Rodchenko's poster art, its stark shapes and colours:[36] black, red, grey are the colours of the *Rushes* design and costumes.

Silent Partners is the culmination of this series of photo-designs, and the most fascinating of all the Davies–Buckland collaborations in its interdependence of photo-image and live personality. Buckland here provides a landscape of individuals and couples, a family of presences. They are captured in ordinary clothes, in suits, bathing costumes, dresses. In manner, they suggest tenderness, aggression or sexuality, although some of their encounters are ambiguous. A wall of celluloid hangs down, leaving a corridor in front of these presences, while the landscape perspective extends far beyond the rear of the stage. It is thus that Buckland, in spatial terms, indicates the progression in time which is such a crucial concept underlying the choreography. Both the corridor and backdrop refer to another time more or less distant. With the exception of the focal couple of the piece, all the dancing protagonists move from stage to corridor, flowing into the backdrop, adding to the landscape and becoming the past. In another sense, the figures in the landscape are not so unrelated to those in the foreground. A couple of the photographed poses strongly resemble those danced; others reflect the moods of the choreography. The figures are immediate in narrative implications, while their dress provides a context for the stage metaphor.

Very different in kind is the Buckland–Mumford collaboration *New Galileo*. This is one of Davies' simplest designs, and one of the most effective. The set here creates the actual spatial and temporal framework for the choreography. A pair of light beams hangs overhead, close together at the beginning, the gap between them increasing surreptitiously throughout. Thus, they delineate spaces of changing shape and size and make an assertive framework for the ambitious, insatiable movement of the dancers. However, the light beams also create a time limit, as the piece reaches its logical conclusion when the bars can separate no further. Davies maintains that she was experimenting with speed and space in this piece, so the expanding set is appropriate to her conception.[37] Three photographed video images suspended at the back carry the idea of time and space further: one of dancer Jonathan Lunn standing in a pose from the piece, with a studio clock behind him; another of Europa, the second of Jupiter's Galilean satellites; the last of birds in flight, the *Three Red Birds* by Georges Braque.

Buckland's most recent contributions have contained more anthropological or topographical allusions: on floor cloths for *Wyoming* and *White Man Sleeps*, and screens, again unfurled during performance, for *Cover Him With Grass*, and on a huge cylinder of light for *Dancing Ledge*. Davies has also collaborated with the painter Hugh O'Donnell, for *Red*

Steps and *Drawn Breath*. But recently, it is Mumford who has provided her with her most powerful environment, for *Sounding*. The stage space is made mysterious and contained by a gauze front curtain. Then, during the second half of the piece, it is crossed dramatically by lighting, diagonal and orange bands bisecting front- and back-cloths in opposite directions and a third band linking their two lower points across the diagonal of the floor. The floor diagonal emphasizes a characteristic direction in Jeremy James' 'knocking' solo, as well as being the line of the final frieze. Typically, Davies' designer has integrated his contribution with the choreography.

Some post-modern aspects

Sometimes, Davies' collaborators have added layers of meaning to her choreography that reach, in a post-modern sense, outside the 'world' of the dance. Buckland's front cloth to *Bridge the Distance* is an example, visible during the interval for audience perusal. Apart from the images of Venice that it contains, it draws attention to the workings and features behind and outside the world which Davies' characters inhabit. There is a quotation from the musical score of Britten's third quartet (in the movement subtitled 'La Serenissima', his own quotation from his opera *Death in Venice*). The cloth also presents samples of costume material and the real names of the performers in the piece. Elsewhere, there is the conjoined image of a dancer's face and a violin. On more than one occasion in the dance, Davies presents the visual pun of one dancer holding another like an instrument, a metaphor perhaps for her second idea of revealing the spirit of the music. But this is fleeting, and in no way disturbs the fundamental unity of her subject matter – the choreography is basically about a certain set of people – and our identification of each performer as a character. Davies, unlike Buckland, does not venture outside the 'world' of the dance.[38]

In another way, Mumford's television version of *White Man Sleeps* introduces a forceful layer outside the conventions of the dance, a regular reference back to the string quartet players[39] who accompany the dance, close-ups of the mechanics of their playing as well as long shots. Although Mumford sometimes overlays the dance with shots of the players, musicians and dancers seem to belong in distinct worlds, the musicians distanced through the use of monochrome black and white.

It is only in two works that Davies seems to have taken a split perspective inside her own contribution. Significantly, these are both works that use text, the first *Minor Characters* for Second Stride, the second an untitled work for Dance-lines 1987 using an unpublished short story, *The Letter Scene* by Susan Sontag.

The framework of *Minor Characters* is suggested at the start by the two speakers, Sally Owen and Betsy Gregory. They are reporting on their fantasy of eight 'minor characters' seen around a dinner table, memories from their past. After that framework has been established, there is a constantly shifting relationship between speaker and dancer (character). If a convention is established, it is only to be broken and another introduced. Sometimes there is identification, the same relationship between dancer and singer as in *Then You Can Only Sing*, and Davies recalls her interest in the alter ego Anna, Julie Covington, to herself as the dancing Annie, in the Brecht/Weill *The Seven Deadly Sins*. At other times, the speaker shifts to 'I' as the innermost thoughts of another 'I', the speaking dancer:

Speaker: (I'm going to slide my hand all over you: then you'll be in my hand.)
Dancer: Would you like something to drink?

to speaker as commentator, the dancer as third person:

Speaker: Doesn't she remind you of someone?

even to 'I', speaker as focus, with the dancers this time as commentators, Owen and Gregory seated on chairs in a confrontation egged on and shadowed by two dancers. This shifting relationship draws attention to itself, emphasizes the artifice of a theatrical device. It provides a mild sense of alienation perhaps, in the Brechtian sense. It also provokes a strange ambiguity. Are these characters self-standing, or are they possessed, an integral part of the speaker? The closer the speaker moves towards the dancer, the more intense that bond or entrapment feels.

In broad terms, the dance set to *The Letter Scene* and filmed inside the unfurnished Chiswick House in London, seems to be about distance between people, geographical distance, and memories, distance in time. But the choice of Sontag – selections, in fact, from her text – is significant. Her writing is fragmentary, non-linear, shifting between stories; it is in the style that she applauds in her critical writings. The two dancers, Michael Popper and Sally Owen, are accordingly differently inflected as the piece progresses. It is as if they become Tatiana and Eugene Onegin of the Pushkin story, which is referred to in Sontag's text. Or Owen shifts to being the unnamed woman who meets an unnamed man (Popper) in the Piazza del Popolo in Rome. Or they are merely anonymous as we hear meditations on the business of writing and receiving letters. Sometimes, images from the text are reflected in movement:

'That rush of warmth: she [Tatiana] wants to declare something.' (Owen rushes towards a wall and spreads herself over it.)

'The first time I saw you [in the Piazza del Popolo] you had a white scarf knotted at the throat.' (Owen's hands seem to outline this item of clothing.)

At other times, abstract movement seems to acquire meaning from the text.

158

Yet this television piece and *Minor Characters* are unusual works in Davies' career.[40] Normally she maintains the identity of single dancer with single character. Both works stem from her Second Stride period. Perhaps she was lightly influenced again by Spink and the bravado with which his dancers shift between roles and situations (see p. 202).

Davies and Spink are the first to recognize that there are fundamental differences between their approaches. Davies, Spink says, 'draws on an emotional core for her choreography ... I like to break the continuity in a performance – bring in surprises, use theatrical devices.' Spink, Davies says, is 'more anarchic than I am ... his pieces are full of strange resolutions or unresolved elements. I work more from the inside, as a performer.'[41]

Davies would seem, then, to be a modernist at heart, maintaining within her choreography a coherent 'world', abstract and stylized as that might be. It is a world that can be developed and added to, but, with rare exceptions, is maintained unbroken. She is modernist too in her insistence on the integrity of movement language and structures. These were the focus of her attention in her early career, and they became complex, challenging to read, even in her most 'narrative' pieces of the 1980s. Thus, Davies answers to the Graham-derived expressionism that dominated her training and performing experience with LCDT during the 1970s. In all these respects, Davies has much in common with Richard Alston. But her modernist style is entirely distinctive and, to compare her with him, her expression is notably more passionate than his in the more personal branch of her work.

Certainly, post-modern and New Dance techniques and inclinations have touched her work: release work, dance with text and, as we have seen in two pieces, a sense of artifice, the unity of performer and character broken. But they have come to her late, in the 1980s, some years after they had been introduced for post-modern and New Dance ends by other choreographers, and they have not swerved her violently off her main course.

At one level, Davies appears to have shifted boldly into new directions at various stages in her career. This is perhaps most obvious after 1981, when she began a dual choreographic career experimenting in small independent groups as well as working regularly with the large companies LCDT and Rambert Dance Company. But, at another level, it is clear that she has always absorbed ideas, whether about dance language or theatre, to reaffirm what is, in her personal terms, a modernist impulse.

CHAPTER 7

Rosemary Butcher

The dance context of Butcher's work

Rosemary Butcher has always been a solitary figure in British dance. Her influence on younger choreographers and dancers has been widely acknowledged – Miranda Tufnell once called Butcher a 'founder-person'[1] – and many of her dancers have themselves figured prominently as choreographers. But the line of work that Butcher has pursued, quietly and without compromise, has always been distinct from that of her contemporaries. And now, in the 1990s, perhaps more than ever before, her aesthetic counters current trends, minimalist simplicity against noisy, strongly coloured theatre and a barrage of symbols and ironies. 'The voice of the people,' Butcher observes, calls for other kinds of refreshment.[2]

In the 1970s, Butcher found no models or mentors in Britain useful to her. Her relationship with the centre of the New Dance movement in the late 1970s, the X6 Dance Space, was tenuous (see Chapter 3). She was invited to join in the activities there, and took part in the celebration *By River and Wharf* that marked the opening of X6 in 1976, but only on rare occasions was her work performed at the space itself, and then only as a small part of someone else's programme. Certain principles she shared with other New Dance choreographers. She invited her dancers to make a creative contribution to her work. She was interested in a relaxed body attitude, more natural, more pedestrian than that of the pulled-up technical dancer (and clothed accordingly in casual trousers and tops), and thus, while she had no formal training in release, she linked herself with the release tradition. However, her fundamental intentions were of quite a different order from those at the centre of the New Dance movement. Reactions to her work reveal as much about the context, in which she fits uneasily, as about the work itself. True to the spirit of the times, *Spare Rib* writers Maureen Hanscombe and Norma Pitfield interpreted her work politically, perceiving in it a stance they considered to be a breakthrough:

> Dance in our culture is permeated with stereotypes of role and situation ... Narratives are rooted in notions of true love triumphant or tragically thwarted ... Women are always delineated in a reactionary way, objectified and glamorised. The aesthetic of dance mostly depends upon traditional ideas of beauty demanding specific body types ... Rosemary Butcher and her small company realise

160

... a struggle to be freed of such bonds ... The exploration of bodies and of space conducted by a group wearing everyday comfortable clothing is an experience with which we can all readily empathise. It tells us more about our own bodies and our own space.[3]

Now, it is true that Butcher's work asserts an unstereotypical view of men and women that was unusual in British dance in the 1970s. It is true too that it accepts that everyman/woman movement, body shape and clothing can be interesting, and that it uses the body in an efficient, unforced manner. But Butcher maintains that any political stance was incidental, never her main intention. While her work can be seen to counter the values of traditional dance, she herself has always laid positive stress on other issues, reduced movement as a means of reactivating the spectator's attention after a plethora of full-blown technical dance styles, the reduction of the personal and of performance presence which would be refreshing after the habitual high emotion and role playing of expressionist contemporary dance. Far from emphasizing 'empathy' with the audience, Butcher encourages its objective distance.

In a seminar on definitions of New Dance at the 1977 ADMA Festival, Butcher's views were typically idiosyncratic. While others present, amongst them Emilyn Claid, Jacky Lansley and Kate Flatt, were concerned that New Dance should 'relate to the social context', Butcher insisted that she was simply searching for 'pure abstract form'.[4]

Background to the Rosemary Butcher Dance Company

That Butcher was out on a limb can be partly explained by the fact that her dance background differed markedly from that of other New Dance choreographers and, indeed, from that of any other of her contemporaries. She went to Dartington College of Arts in 1965, becoming the first student on a new full-time course there, studying choreography and improvisation with Ruth Foster and Graham technique with Flora Cushman. She attended extra vacation courses in Graham technique at the new London School of Contemporary Dance alongside such students as Richard Alston and Siobhan Davies. A year in the USA (1968–69) offered her a broad training in American modern dance. At the University of Maryland, she learnt Doris Humphrey technique from Dorothy Madden – it proved of lasting value, its characteristic fall and rebound and breath rhythm were later adapted, tuned down in her own dance style – and she took a course at the Cunningham studio in New York.

It was Butcher's return to New York in 1970–72 that marked the crucial turning point in her career, showing the way to her subsequent development as a choreographer. It was then that she became involved with the non-technical, 'minimalist' and improvisatory work of American post-modernists. She watched a wide range of their work, studying with Judson Dance Theater alumnae Elaine Summers and Yvonne Rainer, and in the workshops of Anna Halprin, the West Coast pioneer of a non-technical, improvisatory approach to dance. She performed with Summers' Intermedia Dance Foundation,[5] taking part in several outdoor events, in Central Park, for instance, and outside the Seagram and Ford Foundation Buildings. Butcher perceived that all around her choreographers were working closely with artists from other disciplines, expanding their own disciplines and choosing to show their work in galleries and outdoor spaces, outside the usual dance venues. This, she has said, encouraged her to be alive to new contexts for dance.

Butcher's experience in New York was unique for an English dancer and choreographer at the time. She might well have been the first British dancer to enter into this kind of activity, quite a different experience from the Graham School training received by English dancers sent over by Robin Howard in the mid-1960s. The regular British pilgrimages to study Cunningham and post-Cunningham work in New York commenced several years later. Back visiting Dartington in 1975, with her foundation in American post-modern work, Butcher could readily acclimatize to the contact improvisation (see p. 71) that Steve Paxton was teaching there. Awarded a Royal Society of Arts Scholarship, she returned to New York briefly in 1978. Several athletic works sprang from this visit, her 'sneaker period', deriving from what she had seen and experienced in New York. This was also a period when she was deeply impressed by the work of Lucinda Childs.

Butcher was a choreographic late-starter, for several years concentrating on assimilating the ideas of others. When she did begin to create, she immediately favoured a simple, highly economical movement vocabulary and a straightforward, untheatrical manner of performance. Thus, her first piece *Uneven Time* (1974), made for Scottish Theatre Ballet's Moveable Workshop, consisted of the simplest elements: walking and running in lines and circles, and everyday gestures like passing fingers through the hair, feeling the texture of a surface, or plucking an imaginary object from the floor.[6]

History of the Rosemary Butcher Dance Company

The Rosemary Butcher Dance Company was formed in 1975, and gave its first performance in March 1976, at London's Serpentine Gallery. The company has existed ever since and, with the exception of 1988, it has presented new works each year. The nature of the programmes has changed from a series of short works to one substantial work. Butcher's choreographic output is rather smaller than those of Alston, Davies or Spink.

Soon after the inception of Butcher's company, an audience of steady admirers emerged. The company appeared regularly in Dance Umbrella festivals, from the first in 1978, to 1985, and likewise regularly at Dance at Dartington Festivals, all of them, from 1978, except the last in 1987. But Butcher did not take part in either of the ADMA Festivals, except for the 1977 seminar on New Dance.[7]

However, the circumstances of the company have often been precarious. From the start of the company, critics and funding advisors[8] were divided in their opinions. There were strong supporters, but others found the work dull, over-extended, too austere to be interesting. One critic made the remarkable observation in 1977 that Butcher's work was 'punk dance'.[9] Years later, in 1989, the *Financial Times* critic Clement Crisp was to confirm his long-held opinion:

> Miss Butcher's six dancers – 4f, 2m – trudge glumly about ... have the theatrical vivacity of automata, wearing that scrubbed and innocent look I associate with amateurs striving in a Good Cause ... For the converted only.[10]

On the other hand, John Percival, who had been an enthusiast in the early days, worried that in her slower middle period, the early 1980s, she was 'a spent force', but was then pleased to be proved wrong once he saw the bracing *Flying Lines* (1985).[11]

There has always been a history of funding uncertainty. The company has relied mainly on small and intermittent Arts Council project grants. Early on, in 1979–80, there was a major input, a grant of £7000 for six months' work that enabled the company to tour extensively in Britain. These were the years when the newly opened Riverside Studios invited Butcher to bring her company into residence and when the company had its first foreign engagements (in Paris and Florence).[12] Then, for several years in the early 1980s, the company received no Arts Council grant aid other than small personal bursaries to Butcher herself, or awards for design or music. But Butcher was given a GLAA Dance Award in 1985. Project-based funding and the lack of certainty of receiving any funds whatsoever always poses difficulties for forward-planning and keeping a company of dancers together. Certainly, Butcher's work has suffered from occasional production miscalculations and unlucky collaborations. Additionally, her work seems to be by nature more fragile than most, specific in its contextual demands and easily destroyed by the smallest problem of presentation or unsympathetic location.

In a major effort to bring Butcher's contribution firmly into the public eye, a retrospective of her work was produced in May 1986, ten years after her company's first performances, and the first to be held by a British New Dance choreographer. Production values were excellent. With the early duets *Landings* (1976) and *Space Between* (1977) shown alongside work of the 1980s, work of larger proportions and involving collaborations with fine artists (installations) and composers, Butcher at last achieved wide critical recognition. It was as if the work made new sense grouped in this context. Butcher decided to end her relationship with the Umbrella festivals that year and to stage her showings independently, preferably in art gallery venues. Around this time too, Butcher's programmes and publicity began to be meticulously designed in a style appropriate to her work. The status of the company reached a new peak for three years (1986–88), and received the best Arts Council funding ever (£18 000 in 1987/88 increasing to £25 000 in 1989/90). It was chosen for The British are Coming Festival in Copenhagen (1987), and in February 1988, gave a performance in the Queen Elizabeth Hall, its largest ever London venue, to a capacity audience.

Butcher's dancing group has frequently changed its composition, partly because it functions on an irregular project basis, partly because many of her dancers have moved on to choreograph themselves. The fact of an *ad hoc* sporadic company has affected the extent to which Butcher could use or develop her particular working process or indeed see the niceties of her style emerge in performance. Just when she received her six months' grant, for instance (1978), she had to recommence work with a virtually new company of dancers. Julyen Hamilton and Maedée Duprès had just left to work with Richard Alston's new group (Duprès returned for Butcher's retrospective), and likewise Miranda Tufnell and Dennis Greenwood to make their own work. Her works, physically simple as they might appear to be, demand fine, experienced dancers and can be extraordinarily diminished in their absence. In fact, a major reason for the sudden cutback in Butcher's Arts Council funding in 1979 was the insufficient experience of her performers at that time. On many occasions, Butcher has coped with changes in the number of dancers performing in a piece. *Touch the Earth* (1987), for instance, which used one of Butcher's largest casts, began with a cast of eight which increased to nine for Queen Elizabeth Hall and BBC television performances, but dwindled to five when the work was taken on tour.

Dancers who have been in the company for two years or more include Gaby Agis, Maedée Duprès, Julyen Hamilton, Helen Rowsell, Caroline Pegg, Jonathan Burrows, Wendy Thomas, Miranda Tufnell, and the most long-standing, Dennis Greenwood (1977 to present) and Sue MacLennan (1976–88). For other briefer periods, the following dancer/choreographers have been company members: Laurie Booth, Eva Karczag, Yolande Snaith, Kirstie Simson and Janet Smith. Many of Butcher's dancers over the years have been trained at the LSCD, but gradually more have been drawn from further afield, and several (including Burrows, who dances with The Royal Ballet), have come to Butcher with considerable professional experience behind them. Butcher occasionally performs herself, usually solos within large group pieces.

164

Teaching

Teaching is an important adjunct to Butcher's choreographic activity. She has said that she needs a certain level of financial stability in order to operate creatively. Drawing on material from 'contact' and her own work, she has maintained a more considerable teaching programme for herself than most New Dance choreographers. She has also come to know many of her dancers through her improvisation workshops. To some, it seemed that she offered a pleasurable antidote to the high drama and tension of the Graham-based movement in which they had been trained.

There have been regular commitments in colleges and schools, including full-time lectureships at Dunfermline College (1973–74) and at Dartington College with Mary Fulkerson (1980–81), and for many years she continued her association with Riverside Studios in running regular workshops there. She has also worked as an advisory teacher to the Inner London Education Authority and, since the demise of this body in April 1990, as Dance Co-ordinator at the Holborn Centre for the Performing Arts.

Early works

In the mid-1970s, Butcher's movement was more athletic than in much of her later work, more expansive, with traces of technical dancing in step combinations and in the use of raised legs and clearly pointed or flexed feet. A recording of the duet from *Pause and Loss* (1976)[13] shows the dancers boldly swinging their arms and legs and dropping to the floor. There is a forceful attack, an indulgent approach to gravity and an extravagant separation of the legs in a repeated ground-hugging lunge in second position.

Landings (1976) was described in the 1986 retrospective programme as 'a duet based on the physicality of movement. The concern of the dance is gravity: each dancer is responsible for the other's weight; neither of them must let the other fall.' Performed in 1986 by Jonathan Burrows (taking Julyen Hamilton's part) and Maedée Duprès, the duet celebrates the extremes of physical power – competitive attack and playful swerves of direction as opposed to gentle, detailed gestures of contact – and abandon, letting the weight drop into a partner's support, back to back, front to front, and with many other variations. Both the material and the dynamics of performance are richly varied. *Space Between* (1977) was inspired by Japanese notions of personal space and based on a more reduced language, rounded arms tracing arcs in close containment around the body. The central section, with Burrows and Duprès side by side, shows mutual respect, each allowing the other his or her own territory. Yet this is also a partnership of great harmony and tenderness, and eventually, their movements begin to interlock. While different in tone, both *Landings* and *Space Between* come across as statements about two people. Butcher elected to

165

restrain such personal content soon after this, and to leave behind the lifting and supporting of doublework.

Around the time of these duets Butcher was making pieces that stressed real as opposed to theatrical space and time; some exposed structural devices or stressed the following of rules, a factual approach that detracted from personality. In *Suggestion and Action*, performed at the Acme Gallery, 1978, Butcher called out live instructions for Duprès and Hamilton to follow, thereby elucidating the dance processes. Audience members were also invited to read out instructions, as they felt inclined.[14] Encouraging such analytical attention to the workings of a dance recalls the tactics of American choreographers such as Lucinda Childs and Trisha Brown, as well as Sally Banes' category 'analytic' post-modern dance (see pp. 4–5).

Perhaps because of her background in the visual arts and her awareness of the systematic procedures of minimalist sculpture, Andrea Hill, writing in *Artscribe*, was particularly alive to the implications of these works. She writes that Butcher's *Uneven Time* (1978), for Duprès' first solo show *Dance and Slide*, required 'a transfer of energy from the dancer (moving in front of a fixed slide) to the slides themselves (which clicked by while the dancer froze in place)'. Static images of Duprès dancing 'succeeded each other so quickly as to produce an illusion of recreated movement'.[15] In other words, Butcher was playing in the spaces between stillness and movement, live and captured image. *Catch 5, Catch 6* (1978) was built on rules. Hill records what she was told of its structure:

> A large rectangle and a small square are drawn out on the floor in masking tape, and behaviour-rules are given to the dancers for movements accomplished in each area. In addition, each dancer is given a set of movement instructions plus an accompanying rhythm, also rules on how this sequence may be shortened or lengthened, improvised upon, performed with another person.[16]

Butcher says that she welcomed viewers' recognition that some kind of game was going on in this piece, and their involvement in it, even if the rules were not recoverable and not mentioned in the programme.

The development of a movement language

Since the 1970s, it is the reduced movement language that has predominated in Butcher's work. Although she settled on a different gamut of movement ideas for each piece, it would be fair to make the generalization that she pared her movement down in size and dynamics after the 1970s. She now confined her language largely to arm and upper body movement and simple walking and running, the movement often slowly and deliberately stated, with a restrained use of fall and recovery. (She admits that her collaborations with the artist Heinz-Dieter Pietsch slowed her

down for a while in the early 1980s.) Upper body movement increased in detail, revealing sequential flow or gentle subversions of action through the joints of back and limbs. Butcher might show the arm and chest unfurled to full expanse (frequently, for instance, in the running piece *Flying Lines*), but important too are such details as the crease of a wrist or elbow; the subtlest correspondence between dancers, linear, dynamic, or in point of motivation within the body, the minutest variation of a gesture. In her highly restricted context of quiet motion, a fall to the floor or a sudden run becomes high drama. Certainly, the language over the years has become more clearly Butcher's own. Then, in *d1* (1989), she introduced a new kind of allegro component into her work, developing from her 'sneaker period' athletic vocabulary, but now, for the first time, using change of weight for precise rhythmic effect in simple stepping and skipping patterns.

A concentration through a performer's body makes it possible for the spectator of a Butcher dance to gain a real sense of the smallest movement as a refreshing experience, to enjoy a deep, quiet pleasure from the most spare motional trace. The curling of bodies around each other, the melting into the floor in *Spaces 4* (1981), can have a peculiar poignancy, quite as effective as the more positive excitements whipped up by the rapid running circles in *Flying Lines* and exuberant skipping in *d1*.

Choreographic collaboration with performers

Butcher's choreographic process encourages a creative contribution from her performers, and she has evolved it gradually. In her earliest work, she demonstrated set sequences. Occasionally, as in *Pause and Loss* and *Catch 5, Catch 6* (1978), she gave the dancers rules which determined how these might be presented.[17] Thus, the order of events might change from performance to performance.

However, Butcher soon developed a method that avoided any form of personal demonstration, encouraging the dancers to find their own movement solutions according to the instructions and suggestions that she gave them. As she wrote in *New Dance* no. 1, 'the dancers have the responsibility of discovering their own movement and energy level within the outer structure of the dance'.[18] With Butcher's verbal language to guide the dancers, the early duets for Duprès and Hamilton were made this way. While these duets were fixed for performance, Butcher gradually allowed the realization of her movement instructions to take place anew within the performance itself. This happened first in *White Field* (1977), later in pieces like *Spaces 4* (1981), *The Site* (1983) and *Imprints* (1983). The limitations that she gave her dancers were clear, but she invited them to make new movement and new orders of movement for each showing, rather in the manner of retelling a story or making a speech from memory, leaving the fundamental content the same, but changing the syntax and vocabulary.

It has often been said by way of justification that decision-making in performance engenders a particular excitement, tension or wit from dancers.
Some work thrives on precisely this. Indeed, Butcher maintained in the
mid-1980s that, for some pieces, the more they became set and standardized
between performances, the less interesting they became. She would then
prefer to leave them alone and pass on to something else. But Butcher also
likes to draw on the possibilities that her dancers might propose, ideas that
she might not have thought of herself but which she then makes her own
by shaping, moulding or extending. Rather like playwright Mike Leigh
(Butcher cites his example), she encourages a creative discussion between
choreographer and performer, and finds that the dancers then have a special
commitment to their material. Yet, in the end, it is her eye that is the guide
and the images that she selects in the first place are crucial to the final effect.
Butcher admits that, under certain conditions, with performers less experienced in her methods, shortage of time, or simply if the work is fast or
complex, this creativity in rehearsal or performance is necessarily reduced.
Since the mid-1980s, she has preferred to keep her works almost totally
fixed for performance.

Butcher's choreographic method has had interesting implications for her
dancers and for the relationship between choreographer and dancer. In the
1970s, dancers like Duprès, MacLennan and Agis (who was taught by
Butcher when she was at school) found that Butcher taught them improvisation techniques that they could not learn elsewhere, and they welcomed this
opportunity for creative involvement. Butcher revealed a new dimension of
dance experience. In the 1980s, working with dancers who had a
background in improvisation, she did not see her role as that of an initiating
teacher so much, rather as of a controlling agent over what readily emerged.
The method has posed problems. It falls somewhere between two kinds of
working practice. In the 1970s, when collective working was widespread
and the idea of simply functioning as a dancer was queried, Butcher says
she was questioned as to whether she alone should be credited with the creation of a piece. Sometimes the dancers sought collective acknowledgement.
And the method provoked them on occasion to evade her control; Butcher
describes periods of virtual company 'mutiny'. Now, all her dancers emphasize how strictly she controls their activities and the very different nature
of their own choreography has demonstrated beyond doubt the individuality of Butcher's style.[19]

Structure
From her early work onwards, Butcher has tended to favour the Cunningham and post-Cunningham kind of non-climactic, non-developmental,
open-ended structure. The effect is a focus on the present rather than on the
process of progressing to a future. Even the motoric rhythms of Butcher's

27. *Passage North East* (1976), choreography by Rosemary Butcher, performed outside the Arnolfini Gallery, Bristol by the Rosemary Butcher Dance Company.

28. *Catch 5, Catch 6* (1978), choreography by Rosemary Butcher, performed by the Rosemary Butcher Dance Company. (Photograph: Chris Harris)

29. LEFT ABOVE: *Spaces 4* (Rosemary Butcher Dance Company, 1981), choreography by Rosemary Butcher, installation by Heinz-Dieter Pietsch. Dancers, from left to right: Beverley Sandwith, Dennis Greenwood, Sue MacLennan. (Photograph: Chris Harris)

30. LEFT BELOW: *The Site* (Rosemary Butcher Dance Company, 1983), choreography by Rosemary Butcher, installation by Heinz-Dieter Pietsch. Dancers, from left to right: Dennis Greenwood, Gaby Agis, Helen Rowsell. (Photograph: Chris Harris)

31. ABOVE: Rehearsal of *Touch the Earth* (Rosemary Butcher Dance Company, 1987), choreography by Rosemary Butcher, installation by Heinz-Dieter Pietsch. Dancers, from left to right: Jonathan Burrows, Caroline Pegg, Maedée Duprès. (Photograph: Peter Anderson)

171

minimalist musical scores seem to emphasize circularity rather than progression. And often in Butcher's work of the 1980s there has been no rhythmic drive at all, either within dance or musical accompaniment, at the most the odd fragment of pulsed activity.

Sometimes Butcher uses the structure of a series of fleeting 'one-off' movement ideas, 'things stopping and starting'. Or she subjects ideas to multi-repetition and then interrupts the sequence (Yvonne Rainer's idea of 'a "chunky" continuity'[20]). Or, she says, she adds ideas to each other and subtracts them like layering in a painting. This is not the same as the developmental, organic structural concept of theme and variation, the gradual metamorphosis of an original idea.

Yet there are exceptions to these structural 'rules'. The most recent Butcher works, those of largest proportions, *Touch the Earth* and *d2–3d* (1990), do seem to contain moments of climax. Partly prompted by her collaborators, Butcher feels, there are passages in these works that stand out as special high points of energy.

The structures of specific pieces are discussed below.

Spatial aspects: settings and installations

Since Butcher's early works, it has been obvious that the spatial aspects of dance are of greatest importance to her; rhythmic content is relatively unenlivened (in this respect, *d1* is an exception). She has called her work 'a kinetic sculptural experience',[21] and the eye is drawn to body designs, group arrangements, the lining up of body parts across dancers, or the imaginary forms traced around the body. Floor patterns are likewise a strong feature, often as geometrical units, straight lines, right angles, arcs and circles.[22] Sometimes, the spatial emphasis is such that the dancing group is seen as a distribution in space or as particles clustering and reclustering, not as a group of individuals with an identity of their own. This reflects her concern to keep the personal quiet. Butcher's titles give the clue, often suggesting a shape, an area or territory, or the crossing of space.

It is hardly surprising then that Butcher sees her work as closely allied to the visual arts, and the movement always in relation to its surroundings,

> because of its feel for dimension, and the relationship of people to objects and objects to people and people to people. It's a juxtaposition of moving people with the architecture around, which in fact makes the movement very alive and puts the dancers into a perspective.[23]

And visual artists, she finds, often respond more readily than dance audiences: 'They don't question someone sitting still for five minutes – they see it as part of the environment.'[24]

At times, Butcher has referred directly to the visual arts for information, to a Ben Nicholson relief (*Six Circles*, 1933) as a starting point for *Uneven Time*, or to Paul Klee's cryptic works for *Empty Signals* (1977). Most strikingly, *Pause and Loss* derived its title and content from two works by Bridget Riley, both of them crossed by a blur or fading out of the repeated dots that make up the rest of the painting. Butcher turned the blur into the diagonal of her dance, a line where dancers paused or where material became lost behind other dancers.

Setting is important to the particular nature of Butcher's work. She chooses to avoid the proscenium frame if possible, and she has explored a variety of alternative solutions, some open-air. The disappearance of the individual or withdrawal of personality has been most evident in the group work presented out of doors. A series of performances, for instance, in 1977, sponsored by the Greater London Council Parks Department found the Rosemary Butcher Dance Company dancing outside the Economist Building in St James's, the new London Museum in the Barbican, on the National Theatre Terrace and in Paternoster Square. The work could be seen from different viewpoints, and Butcher adapted existing pieces to her different circumstances. These were situations in which the movement was diminished or could even be lost, 'never-ending', she says, dominated by the surrounding architecture or assertive pattern of paving stones, or temporarily blurred by straggling passers-by. In *Passage North East* (1976), made specifically for the area outside the Arnolfini Gallery in Bristol, Butcher deliberately explored this issue. She contrasted distant and immediate views of her dancers, the piece beginning on the far side of the harbour as seen from the Arnolfini, involving a boat journey across the water and achieving completion in a dance close up to the spectators.[25]

Butcher has also explored a variety of indoor settings. While Riverside Studios was a regular venue for many years, she has also used art gallery spaces where viewers surround the dance, again removing her work from the proscenium arch context. *Multiple Event* (1976) used two adjacent galleries in the Arnolfini (another regular venue), the performers passing between them and picking up on what was going on in the room that they entered. In 1987, after a gap of several years, Butcher returned to the gallery setting, presenting *Touch the Earth* at the Whitechapel Art Gallery. A tour of 16 galleries (and 6 other venues) followed.

In the 1980s, Butcher's work demonstrated a tighter spatial framework and concentrated the choreography more clearly in consequence. Prompted by Riverside's then director David Gothard, who introduced her to fine artists of similar 'minimalist' persuasion, she removed the boundary outside the dance and introduced installations as an internal reference or focus for the choreography. The first two pieces of this kind were built around structures by Jon Groom: *Five-Sided Figure* (1980) and *Shell: Force Fields and Spaces* (1981), both geometric structures bounded by screens, in the first a five-sided floor, in the second an oval floor bisected and segmented in various ways. Butcher made reference to the spatial content of these structures, matching, adding to or setting counterpoint against their lines and curves. In *Five-Sided Figure*, Groom's angular space gave way to flowing, rounded movements. Inspired by the limiting installation, Butcher's dance took off on its own terms. In *Shell*, the movement was concerned with demonstrating the spirals suggested by Groom's title, also with articulating the radii, circles and segments of circles that appeared under the different lightings.

While Groom led his collaborations and, Butcher feels, had a somewhat static image of dancers completing his 'picture', the next collaborations with Heinz-Dieter Pietsch were closer and more flexible. Pietsch customarily involved himself with numerous rehearsals, bringing objects into the dancing space and watching the results. In *Spaces 4*, for instance, he improvised with polystyrene as he watched the three dancers in motion. He then made the final stage objects in white wood, the torn, rough corners of four implied squares, standing on the floor. Pietsch captured the lightness and neutrality of the movement in his work.[26] Opportunities for spatial connection between installation and dance were used, the dancers making corners themselves, matching a rough edge or giving substance to invisible boundaries.

A number of collaborations with Pietsch followed. For *Traces* (1982), he projected a series of linear light patterns onto a backcloth, relating them to the level of dance movement and to floor patterns, and sometimes enveloping the dancers. The installation for *The Site* (1983) was a low-lying, open rectangle of ragged paper pulp lit by neon lights, its rough texture complemented by the sensation of feet and hands rubbing with friction against the floor. For *Imprints* (1983), Pietsch created two fibre glass, plastic resin screens bounded by steel and concrete. They formed a barrier with a gateway between them, an area within which the dancers could leave an impression. Then, for *Touch the Earth* (1987), he made another pair of screens from steel, paper and resin and, for the first time, props, metal rods that could be carried during the dance.

While Pietsch has been Butcher's most frequent collaborator, she has also worked with the visual artist Peter Noble (for *Flying Lines*), Ron Haselden (for *After the Crying and the Shouting* (1989)), and architects Zaha Hadid and John Lyall (for the *d1–3d* triptych).

Work with film and television
Just once, Butcher has integrated dance with film, extending the live indoor event into an outdoor environment. Jane Rigby's film for *Night Mooring*

Stones (1984) showed a series of Scottish landscapes, hillsides and stretches of sand, some of them peopled by dancers, different images projected on three screens simultaneously. Sometimes the dance movement in the film echoed the live movement. However, since the 1970s, Butcher has been interested in making film herself,[27] using the expanded temporal and spatial possibilities that it offers. She was excited by the editing potential discovered when she worked with Anna Ridley on a production of *Spaces 4* for Channel 4 television (1985). The result was a compilation from several performances, including, for instance, two beginnings and two endings.

Certainly, film would fulfil Butcher's continuing desire to show dance outdoors, while allowing the possibility of detailed viewing in close shots. The outside experience she still finds special. She says that she set her dancers running up and downhill on Hampstead Heath in a rehearsal for *Flying Lines*, in order for them to understand that particular sensation (and publicity photographs were taken at the time). Typically, as the televising of *Touch the Earth* was being discussed, she spoke of her ideal of shooting on a vast stretch of sand.

The move to meaning

Butcher's use of installations and film has signified a gradual move away from abstraction to meaning and a sense of situation. Butcher's instructions to her dancers illustrate the change well. She used to give dancers abstract instructions relating to the numbering of movement sequences or to the spatial patterns to be followed. In making *Spaces 4*, she referred mainly to space and physical relationship. She recalls, for instance, 'moving another person on, matching in rhythm, lining up, referring to the edges, right angling, walking in a circle within a room'. In later work, her instructions carried suggestions of human situations: for *The Site*, (based on images of an archaeological 'dig' and the remnants of an early history),

> dragging, post-holing (making a landmark), scraping away, pinning yourself to the ground in a prehistoric shape, under-pinning, tunnelling, invading someone else's territory, interfering with others at work on the site.

and for *Touch the Earth* (which suggested a community bonding together, marking out their territory, labouring on their land),

> touching the earth, moving the earth, making a boundary or barrier, stepping over into someone else's territory, measuring the ground.

Touch the Earth is perhaps Butcher's strongest suggestion of human presence and interaction. In a *Time Out* preview before the work was presented at the Queen Elizabeth Hall, Butcher explained how her intentions had shifted from a *tabula rasa* to work that embraces meaning. Inspired by artists like Trisha Brown, Steve Paxton and Lucinda Childs,

> I started . . . creating simple dances that denied all outside references and erased all emotions. But gradually I've come to learn that whenever two people are put together on a stage it means *something*. It doesn't matter how abstract your ideas are, people will see it as they see it. Finally, I can't control that . . . I don't fight that any longer.[28]

The images given to dancers are vital in inducing a singular impression, and they are the basis of her layered constructions. However. while they illustrate a change in Butcher's working process, it is crucial to recognize that they are distilled and abstracted in realization. They are starting points, and may well make little sense to a spectator, or disappear entirely as a work is refined. They never build into a story-line. Nor do they suggest anything as defined and oppositional as a patchwork of radical juxtapositions: the result is wholeness rather than fragmentation. Critic Judith Mackrell felt the presence of imaginary objects in *Flying Lines*, in the movement itself beneath Noble's kite-like installation. She spoke of 'patterns that suggested the strings of kites nearly tangling as the dancers wove dangerously close to each other . . . the dancers whipped their arms like flags or streamers taut in the wind'.[29] (This dance had involved research into kite-flying technology and techniques.) *Flying Lines* could also be seen in the more general terms of human flight and aspiration, the tension between being grounded and being airborne, with the flying image released as the dancers run in celebratory circles and lines forwards and backwards.[30] The title of another piece *The Site* is telling, but the images given the dancers were perhaps most important as guides to creating an atmosphere of great desolation, three lonely figures toiling obsessively over an alien land surface and occasionally making an appeal towards the sky.

Some recent programme notes have suggested literal meanings that are barely recognizable within the choreography, let alone the source of any important semantic resonance. This kind of information roots the spectator's imagination and encourages looking for illustration within a piece. In this respect, the programme for *After the Crying and the Shouting* seemed misleading, heavily indicating the two themes of destruction that inspired the piece, the devastation of World War I (the title is based on a passage from T. S. Eliot's *The Waste Land* (1922)) and the ecological destruction of our planet today. But the work itself evoked a thoroughly generalized brooding atmosphere, with more than a touch of sentimentality, perhaps because most of the performers were new to Butcher's work and because of the rather pretty installation of small twinkling lights by Ron Haselden.[31]

Certain themes recur in Butcher's work, the theme of incompletion and denial, for instance, in the very reduced nature of the work. Leaving an impression is often suggested, and it is confirmed by titles like *Imprints*, *Traces* or *Six Tracks* (1980). Landscape, often the country, is a constant preoccupation, linking her directly with an English pastoral tradition, while the human element that it contains can spring either from the present time or from deep in the past. These are themes that link Butcher with Pietsch.[32] They are, perhaps, also the clue to her feeling of kinship with the sculptor Richard Long. He undoubtedly shares her interests in country and previous civilizations and her belief in the power of the simplest materials and shapes.[33] It is not abstract minimalism that preoccupies these visual artists.

Collaborations with composers

As part of her theatrical expansion, Butcher began to use sound accompaniment regularly (many of the earlier pieces were silent), commissioning scores from Malcolm Clarke, Jim Fulkerson and Jane Wells. At first, she responded broadly to the speed, dynamics and mood of the music rather than to specific rhythms. However, she began to use musical structure more positively in her collaborations with Michael Nyman, *Flying Lines* and *Touch the Earth*.

In *Flying Lines*, for instance, there is a genuine interplay between dance and musical structures. Sectional divisions were shared, and within these divisions Nyman improvised on the piano according to a basic melodic and harmonic framework.[34] While the dancers float in and out of time with each other's steps, occasionally, fleetingly, they might contact the musical pulse as well. Then, in some slow passages, they seem to shift from complementing the motoric style of the accompaniment to 'singing' or 'ringing out' with the high, sustained melody line. On other occasions, it is they who are heard pulsing with their feet whilst a musical vibration lingers on. When live performance was possible, Nyman could choose whether to go with or against the pulse of the dancers.

Touch the Earth

Touch the Earth, which has received the widest acclaim of any Butcher work to date, was striking for its use of the full depth of Whitechapel's long gallery, with a chamber group of two sopranos and amplified violin and viola hocketing and phrasing in haunting high registers across the space. The collaborators worked from a variety of images. Butcher had noted the arrangement of bunched posts marking out the lagoon in Venice, and she then began to read about the experience of the American Indians, their loss of territory and way of life, their working implements and their teepees (also constructed around a group of stakes). Her source was the book of

177

photographs and writings *Touch the Earth* compiled by T. C. McLuhan.[35]
Nyman was interested in the notion of processions and their constant tempo, also in Goethe's description in his *Letters from Italy* (1786) of gondoliers singing antiphonally to each other across the Venetian lagoon.[36]
Pietsch wanted to evoke ancient farming implements, using modern materials (the metal rods that the dancers carry). The programme noted that the Chernobyl disaster provided a modern parallel to the plight of the Indians. However, although fundamental premises were shared – distance, loss, an era past – the artists worked independently, and these starting points were as usual distilled, sometimes consumed, as they worked their materials.

The dancers, eight in all, are seen gently claiming their territory, different areas, within or outside a central circle of sand, or close to the walls or screens at the back. They place their implements, share them, lay them down, bow and open respectfully to earth or sky. There is an overriding feeling of sadness and loss, and a need for mutual support, lonely sculptural poses and rhythmic meetings in brief lilting shuffles or running patterns.

The overlapping of dance and musical episodes, and of entries and exits, creates a more continuous, fluid experience than *Flying Lines* and, unusually, the work seems cumulative in effect. Fragmentary bondings build to a passionate interchange between groups, the entire cast, who race forwards and back into the far distance. The lilting steps seem finally to blend in with the musical phrasing. We are left with the resigned statement of individual isolation within a community.

Touch the Earth is also an example of a work that suffered badly when production circumstances changed. Overamplified, strained sound production at the Queen Elizabeth Hall (otherwise a very sympathetic space) undermined the serenity of the choreography. Shot for BBC television in an empty tobacco warehouse, the piece fought against its grim, claustrophobic background. There was no compensation for the sensuality of the live event with the sound echoing all around, and the sunny spaciousness of the Whitechapel Art Gallery and the Queen Elizabeth Hall was missed. One can imagine the altered impact when the work later appeared in galleries amidst paintings and statues that could not be cleared.[37]

The d1–3d triptych

Butcher's 1989–90 project brought together her abstract and poetic interests in a new manner of stimulating interaction. It was also her most richly textured and exuberant statement to date, and presented her strongest group of dancers for a long time.

Responding to her own qualms about 'relevance' at the turn of the 1990s, Butcher plunged into a most affirmative year-long tripartite project of forceful dance, her collaborators an architect, Zaha Hadid (later superseded

by John Lyall), and the composer Jim Fulkerson. According to publicity information, an exploration of the 'relationship between ourselves and the ur-
ban environment', the dance was made to function in a variety of locations
– indoors, outdoors, behind glass – with evolution an integral element. *d1*
began in the huge, pillared, window-backed Royal Festival Hall ballroom
over Hadid's white tape line drawings, before being shown at arts centres
and galleries around the country (finally at the Liverpool Tate Gallery). It
soon accrued a new section incorporating Lyall's slides, and demonstrated
its adaptability to different spaces. The performers strayed out into infinite
space at the Royal Festival Hall as they left the centre of the dance, for
Butcher 'like the figures she used to watch walking in Italian piazzas'.[38]
Then at Reading's 21 South Street Arts Centre, which housed the regional
premiere of *d1*, the white walls contained the performers sharply like a
games court.[39] The second stage of the project, *d2* (which began with *d1*),
was shown in Christ Church, Spitalfields, East London. The nave had been
converted into an arena for dance, with the audience seated on two sides
– there is no front to the piece – high catwalks were constructed down each
side aisle, and slides were projected all round the space. The final stage of
the project *3d* at the Tramway Theatre in Glasgow featured a scaffolding
installation that was now central to the dance. Dancers moved up and down
a ramp at the back and across an eighteen-foot high bridge that extended
out over the dance in the space below.

Lauren Potter swings down the long diagonal at the start of the original
d1, with a buoyant, purposeful swing of the arms forward and back. Later,
there is a gradual acceleration and patterns for all four performers (each
in training shoes, T-shirts and trousers): two pairs from the sides, for instance, making a right-angled turn to dash between each other, or to approach each other and bounce off back again. This section runs like a
highly sophisticated piece of machinery which can assemble its four components in many ways, 1–3, 2–2, or 4, scattering them or making them
compact, slowing them into walking or standing, or forcing lots of fast,
stuttering steps into the timespan of that never-changing double-arm
swing. And this machinery can cope with cross-rhythms hiccupping against
the minimalist tape score as well as with rhythmic harmony. But the *d1*
machinery also emits feeling. The bouncing four-square convoy has a
triumphant air, and performers in a duet hang outwards from each other
as if to express a deep dependence. Butcher has allowed the dancers to
discover the drama in their movement phrases, and to reflect what they find
in their physical temper and faces. The more gestural second section is
dressed in white against projected abstract shapes, lines and grids, with
dashes of dangerous red, and later, calm washes of deep blue. At Reading,
the games court seemed to have evolved into something more like a
theatrical poetic space.

d2 introduces a high level component: six dancers in white up on the cat-walks, very slowly raising and lowering their arms, who eventually reflect in skeletal fashion the gestures seen below. In this second stage of the piece, Butcher adds further ideas, and reworks and intertwines material from the two existing sections, vestiges of skips amongst eloquent gestures, all breaking into a final accumulation of energy. These ideas were further extended in *3d*.

The excitement in *d1–3d* lies in the capacity to set up an impression, dissolve it and return it, a sort of vibration between impersonal and personal; between the abstract shape or trace of the arm and the resonant gesture, between the measuring of space in relation to time and the capacity for travelling to communicate feeling. There is playfulness, joy, as a dancer sweeps across the diagonal to catch up with a colleague progressing more slowly down a short border. The piece also teaches us about relativity, how, if matters are kept the same for long enough, the simplest change can be startling and wonderful: a run becomes a desperate race; a long gallop after motion on the spot creates an impression of vast space – suddenly the eye has to dart; an individual riff threatens anarchy. By virtue of their reduced nature, structural progressions project themselves into the foreground of the viewer's attention. But it is crucial that, in this triptych, Butcher's rigorous analysis of space and time (in some early pieces, her primary concern) reveals itself in lively dialogue with her more recent interests in feeling.

The admission of feeling is a very positive aspect in Butcher's work. On those occasions when geometrical and logical systems were of overriding importance and human 'presence' as far as possible eliminated (e.g. in *Shell*), there was a tendency for statements to dry up, to exhaust themselves a while before the end of a piece. The celebration of a more poetic, human content has stimulated her imagination and greatly enriched pieces like *Touch the Earth* and the *d1–3d* triptych. But feeling is nevertheless highly restrained, cool, and the means are still small, far smaller, for instance, than those of Richard Alston and Siobhan Davies.

Like Alston and Davies, Butcher retains strong formal interests and, significantly, she sees herself today as a modernist. She readily admits her debt to the first generation of American post-modern choreographers. It was they who provided her with a major inspirational influence in her early career while she remained on the edge of the New Dance movement in Britain. And her work has been touched occasionally by the reflexive, analytic post-modern developments in America. But Butcher prefers now to clarify her position in relation to the tradition of modernism, and especially in relation to modernist architecture[40] and visual arts. She shares in their celebration of the essential qualities of the art medium. Perhaps too, she wants to avoid the term 'post-modernism' now that it has acquired meanings so alien to her own work.

Butcher has derived more from minimalism over the years than we might have hoped. In a bold counter to the theatrical trend of 1990, she demonstrates that less can still be more – as the modernist architect Mies van der Rohe once said.[41] Certainly, opposing Robert Venturi's post-modern reply to van der Rohe,[42] Butcher's work proclaims that less is not necessarily a bore.

CHAPTER 8

Ian Spink

Background: training and professional associations

The Australian choreographer Ian Spink arrived in Britain in the late 1970s and has stayed ever since. Originally, he came to Britain as a participant on the 1977 International Course for Choreographers and Composers at the University of Surrey. He soon established a reputation as an anarchic spirit, a choreographer with a talent for dance as theatre, and a bizarre, interesting sense of humour.

Spink began his career as a ballet dancer, training at the Australian Ballet School and dancing professionally in the Australian Ballet (1969–74).[1] Then he became interested in contemporary dance, taking classes in Graham technique and joining the Dance Company of New South Wales in 1975 when it came under the direction of the Dutch contemporary dance choreographer Jaap Flier. Meanwhile, he developed his career as a choreographer. Beginning in 1969, pieces for Australian Ballet workshop programmes led to commissions from several major companies during the 1970s, among them Australian Dance Theatre, the Queensland Ballet and Dance Company of New South Wales. He won the Australian National Choreographic Competition in 1973 and 1976.

Touring as an observer with the Merce Cunningham Dance Company during its visit to Australia in 1976 was a seminal experience for Spink but, at about this time, he also came into contact with post-Cunningham work. The American post-modern choreographer Remy Charlip was commission-ed to create a dance *Wooloomooloo Cuddle* (1976) for the Dance Company of New South Wales. Spink also met Russell Dumas and Nanette Hassall, both of whom had worked with Strider in England and with various American post-modern choreographers.

Spink has said that he was not ready at first for these post-modern ideas. However, his own work shifted during this period from the modes of ballet or Glen Tetley – abstract and narrative works reflecting his early perform-ing and training experiences – towards Cunningham and post-Cunningham thinking. While he was with the New South Wales company, he created a Cunningham-style 'event', and pieces that introduced a minor element of in-determinacy in performance, *New Work I*, *New Work II* and *Cut Lunge* (all 1976). The last work that Spink made in Australia, *Two Numbers* (1977), looks forward most clearly to his future development: an example of theatrical collage, political statement, dance with meaning.

The 1977 International Course at Surrey, directed by Robert Cohan, proved an occasion for Spink to meet several of the people who were soon to play a part in his British career. These included the dancers Siobhan Davies, Tim Lamford and Beverley Sandwith, also the composer Jane Wells. Michele Smith, who accompanied Spink from Australia, was another participant on the course.

The X6 Dance Space offered Spink a sympathetic venue for performance and a platform for advanced ideas about dance – importantly so, since he was by now fully committed to work that broke away from traditional patterns. But his ties with the Space were ultimately short-lived: he no longer wished to practise what he calls 'confrontational politics' in his own work.[2] In 1977, he came across the work of Pina Bausch for the first time when he saw her *Bluebeard* performed at the Berlin Festival. The next year he saw Mary Fulkerson in performance at the first Dartington Festival. Both were important experiences. During these early years in Britain, he also took Richard Alston's Cunningham technique classes and danced in his choreography, with Richard Alston and Dancers, and in the Brecht/Weill *The Seven Deadly Sins* (1978) (see p. 107).

Spink was quick to show his work in London, first at an ICA Dance Platform in 1977, where he performed a work-in-progress alongside Michele Smith and Tim Lamford, whose own anarchic creative processes he had found stimulating (see p. 90). By 1978, he had formed the Ian Spink Group and, from then on, he was to receive Arts Council project funding, except for the financial year 1979/80 when he was cut from the list of project clients.[3]

The year 1981 was a turning point in Spink's career. It was the year when he met his collaborator, the theatre designer Antony McDonald (their first collaboration, *Some Fugues*), and when he had his first experience of directing theatre – *War Crimes*, with Tim Albery. From now on, theatrical enterprise and the collaborative process became standard. Spink has since worked regularly with McDonald and with lighting designer Peter Mumford; also on several occasions with Albery and the composers Orlando Gough and David Owen. At the same time, Spink entered into a more complex kind of dance theatre, longer works incorporating text and props and now regularly stressing character and reference. McDonald recalls that he met Spink at a point when he was 'aching to broaden his frame'.[4] Second Stride, from 1982 the focus of Spink's dance activity, encouraged this artistic expansion. This new company immediately brought him wider foreign and national recognition and a larger group of dancers as he merged his own company with that of his co-director Siobhan Davies. Second Stride also attracted a higher level of Arts Council funding for his work, generous amounts indeed compared with those received by most other project-funded groups during the 1980s (£45 000 for Second Stride in 1985/86).

In 1988, Spink became sole director of Second Stride, with McDonald as new Associate Director, Davies, after the period of her Fulbright Fellowship, having decided to work independently. The same year, a Time Out/01 for London Award for Spink's *Weighing the Heart* (1987) and a short season of appearances at Sadler's Wells Theatre (Second Stride's first performance in Britain in a venue of that size) thrust the group again into the limelight. In 1988, Second Stride also began an association with the Towngate Theatre in Basildon, gaining a full-time administrator for the first time and using the theatre as a rehearsal base. Both *Dancing and Shouting* (1988) and *Heaven Ablaze in his Breast* (1989) were premiered at the Towngate. *Heaven Ablaze* then enjoyed two performances at the Queen Elizabeth Hall as part of Dance Umbrella '89. Second Stride also won Digital Dance Awards in 1988 and 1989, and *Weighing the Heart* was nominated for an Olivier Award. Programme-length dance theatre initiatives now characterize the work of this company.

Spink has always been active beyond his own groups. Many companies and solo dancers have offered him commissions, for instance, Werkcentrum Dans in Holland, Basic Space Dance Theatre in Scotland, Extemporary Dance Theatre, Ballet Rambert and, during a return visit to Australia 1979–80, Australian Dance Theatre. For a while, he continued to make abstract as well as dance theatre pieces for other companies, while concentrating on dance theatre with Second Stride. He has also taken on challenges beyond the narrow field of dance, choreographing for and co-directing plays, choreographing for opera, and most recently conceiving work for television. Increasingly since the mid-1980s he has divided his time between Second Stride dance theatre and these other interests, sometimes taking the Second Stride dancers with him into his opera activity. He has freely allowed these various experiences to inform each other.

The development of a movement language
During the late 1970s, concentrating on developing a movement vocabulary in a series of abstract pieces, Spink established certain stylistic principles that have underpinned his work ever since. He was always ready to incorporate pedestrian and gestural movement, but at the same time he developed his own style of dance vocabulary, a complex fusion and expansion of other styles: 'Cunningham-five-times-removed-modern with little bits from ballet that interest me'.[5] Pieces have been differently inflected over the years, but across them we see the footwork from ballet, Cunningham's freedom in the use of the torso, also the easy fall and recovery, the sense of swing and breath rhythms that were stimulated by his work with Alston.

184

There is also a kind of risk and a deliberate awkwardness peculiar to Spink's vocabulary. Betsy Gregory recalls from her performing experience the subversion of any obvious physical logic, and the sensation of 'tumbling' and 'lurching around' in his work: 'you're never quite on your leg . . . always pushing yourself into an uncomfortable place'.[6] Spink also developed a rich vocabulary for dancers working in contact, finding any number of ways for them to tumble and flow around each other in duets and trios, women supporting both women and men, as much as men supporting women (as in *Canta* (1981)). Surprisingly, Spink has had no direct personal experience of contact improvisation (see p. 71).

Dance structure

Spink's characteristic method since the late 1970s has been to devise long, complex, winding dance phrases out of his vocabulary, phrases that can be freely turned around in space in the manner of Cunningham. 'Flat' organization is a notable feature. Spink avoids the sense of climax and resolution, and punctuation is concealed. Steve Goff, now a Second Stride dancer, aptly describes this as 'something of a movement continuum within which the phrasing is always twisting and turning, renewing and discovering itself, and giving an impression of limitless breath'.[7]

Likewise, more broadly, Spink avoids traditional 'symphonic' dance structures (see p. 125), the urgency of development and organic progression towards climax. For a while, well into the 1980s, Spink's primary structuring principles were immediate repetition (or repetition at a short distance) and change or disruption, and the results tended to be open-ended rather than reaching neat closure. *Some Fugues* (1981), for instance, is a series of dances that stops in the middle of nowhere, like its music. Finding the fugue structure sympathetic to his choreographic inclinations, Spink selected five sections from Bach's *The Art of Fugue*, concluding with the unfinished 'Contrapunctus 19'. The first and last of the dances follow the musical repetitions with both devotion and imagination. The first includes a typical touch of absurdity, 'free climbing sections'[8] up and over a quartet of chairs between statements of the fugue subject. The second dance achieves its 'flat' continuity from the relaying of one convoluted strand of material, each soloist taking over from where the previous one left off. Eventually the strand repeats, but without any punctuation to signal the repeat, and across a different sequence of dancers.

Canta Spink has likened to wallpaper, 'big patterns repeating . . . the kind of piece that could keep going'.[9] It takes the notion of a level dynamic to an extreme, and David Cunningham's tape loop score underlines this effect. As the American critic Deborah Jowitt noted, 'Many things happen; nothing changes'.[10] *Canta* seems to focus firmly on the present: the dynamic continuum precludes the sense of progression towards a future.

Yet the movement ideas are varied and brilliant enough to sustain the attention, offered in solo strands and close contact duets or trios, and many ideas are repeated in series.

Since the late 1980s, Spink's dances have relied far less on repetition structures. But they manifest a similar 'flatness', phrases winding around and back on themselves in space, networks of vocabulary re-assembled in different ways. Now, the dances are part of much larger theatrical structures.

Gesture in the early 'abstract' works

A notable feature of Spink's early 'abstract' works is their sudden switches to gesture or implied meaning. There are many instances of these swerves in direction, as if Spink cannot restrain a theatrical impulse. The effect is usually strange and gently humorous: for instance, the sudden 'bursts of naturalistic gesture'[11] in *Three Dances* (1979) set to music by John Cage, like pointing, banging the palm against the forehead, or scrabbling with hands like paws.

Sometimes, a whole section of a work lapses into gesture. The third fugue in *Some Fugues* stands out markedly from the other fugues as an improvised, gestural quintet around a line of chairs. *There Is No Other Woman* (1982), Spink's first work for Second Stride, likewise contains an 'odd' section of brief, child-like encounters and mysterious relationships.

Kondalilla (1980) is a work that starts out as abstract dance and is gradually taken over by another world, nature engulfing the proceedings, dancers 'bursting into bloom'[12] as they draw tatters of material from their overalls. The concept came from the Australian composer Carl Vine, whose taped mix included bird calls recorded at Kondalilla Falls in Australia. At the back of Spink's mind too was Ionesco's play *Rhinoceros* (1960) in which the various characters become rhinoceros, and a typically wry image: 'I had this vision of people who've eaten too much brown rice and begin to sprout branches and flowers'.[13] The manner of treatment is again abrupt: a fresh bloom emerges suddenly out of nowhere and catches the eye.

Early theatrical works

Similar disruptions occur in the group of far more specifically theatrical works that Spink created during this early period. These pieces introduce the technique of radical juxtaposition of imagery, and progress by sudden shifts of gear, jolting the viewer into new situations. Spink had used the technique as early as *Two Numbers* (1977) in Australia. Here he juxtaposed material from the ballet *Coppélia* (1870) with references to the horrors of the suppression of the Paris Commune, an event that occurred within the year after the premiere of this ballet. The piece was intended as an angry

186

statement about the gap between the romantic ideals of ballet and harsh reality. Sometimes the two situations alternated; sometimes they merged. Dr Coppélius' dolls were the corpses of Communards. An enthusiastic critic, Brian Hoad, recalls that Coppélia's mazurka was transformed into a 'heartbroken farewell to victims of all tyrannies, a funeral march for the death of innocent ideals'.[14] This is politics of the 'confrontational' kind that Spink ceased to practise in his later work. *Goanna*, produced in Britain in 1978, is one of the last examples of this type of work, its subject matter the classic Australian male, likened to the large Australian lizard of the title, macho and indolent next to his female victims.

Spink's talent for making a statement with minimal means was ex-emplified by *26 Solos* (1978), a piece that he says was influenced by seeing Mary Fulkerson's solo *Dark Coming* at the Dance at Dartington Festival that year.[15] Both works are theatre pieces exploring qualities of magic and the bizarre. The set for *26 Solos* is sparse – chairs, a table, potted palms. Three women enter and depart, one by one, later overlapping, but still maintaining personal separation. They are elegant in black, dressed by Spink's regular designer at the time, Craig Givens. Betsy Gregory is a pas-sionate personality in a wide-brimmed hat, Eleanor Brickhill sinewy in tur-ban and culottes, Michele Smith very cool with a half-veil. Sometimes they enter to do something ordinary in a plain, deliberate manner, like sitting on a chair or taking off gloves or high-heeled shoes. By contrast, other activities are extraordinary, a sudden flurry of dancing or a burst of big, barging movement. Or, more extraordinary, Brickhill acquires a moustache; Smith removes her skirt and brushes her teeth; Gregory calmly administers eyedrops and springs a bouquet of brightly-coloured flowers from her bosom.

Spink timed and orchestrated this piece to celebrate the unexpected and the absurd in juxtaposition of events. He also left the work open, posing questions and inciting tension by virtue of what was omitted and what was left ambiguous. Gregory recalls that she was given no clues as to the character she was portraying (typically of Spink), only that all three were like women who live alone in bedsits. She found a way of making sense of her activities for herself, but that sense, she feels, defies straightforward, logical explanation.[16] Reviewers noted both the unsettling qualities and the wit in *26 Solos*. Some noted a certain sadness and emptiness, characters, Jowitt suggested 'widowed of their own bodies and transformed into genteel shells'.[17]

Dead Flight (1980) suggested some influence of Pina Bausch in its passages of repetitive, obsessive behaviour, violent outbursts and under-lying sense of neurosis. The scene is the cross-section of an aeroplane in the thirties, designed by Givens. Five people are brought into this re-stricted environment, fatigued, pressured, clambering with terrible adagio

187

purposefulness over seats, baggage and other bodies, or merely stuck in a groove, fiddling repeatedly with handbags, magazines or other properties. Suddenly, one of them bolts out into space under the impact of some uncontrollable force. Towards the end of the piece, the compartment becomes more like a gas-chamber, there is an air of increased collapse, and an air hostess enters to pick-pocket the passengers' valuables. The statement seems to have broadened into a more general commentary on the precariousness and claustrophobia of human situations. Spink adds weight to his statement by the severity of his restraining devices, the restricted range of movement and controlled, slow-motion timing. Typically, too, he adds humorous touches and draws pathos from them, like the daft placing and replacing of suitcases, and the slightly crazy flailing reactions that spread across the protagonists.

De Gas (1981) uses the slow-motion device again. The odd turnabout here is the transference of female activity to men: Degas' female nudes washing, drying and combing their hair, become three men putting on their evening clothes and abluting in a classy wash- and brush-up room. Again, there is no logical progression between moves. The studied process of dressing can suddenly turn strange: the moment when the trio put on their armbands becomes artificial through the enlargement of perfect unison, a device that Spink often uses in later pieces. An oboist arrives and seats himself with his feet (and later a motorized toy duck) in a bowl of water; Gregory, a Degas ballerina in black, brings him a cup of tea, and there are strange intimations of the dancing men suffocating or blindfolding each other with towels. Pedestrian moves flower unexpectedly into dance.

De Gas introduced to Spink's work the elegance and detail of McDonald's theatre designs, and was Spink's most prop-ridden piece to date. Towel rails, fans, mirrors, bowls, jugs and towels invade the dancing space and even become part of the choreography. Suddenly, out of nowhere, to an angry burst of music, there is a *coup de théâtre* loop of choreography involving towels, a chair, as well as the three dancers. One after another, each man is covered with a towel, brought swiftly down the diagonal, and back to fall centre stage. Then he is up to throw a towel over the next person, over the chair at the back, and the chain continues. Finally, Jeremy Nelson is escorted, skidding on his towel to end up with his feet in a bowl of water downstage.[18] Spink used the loop structure in several later works.

De Gas is an early example of gender subversion in Spink's work. Near the end, there is a brief section of Degas poses forming and reforming, men as women turning to examine their feet or hips or to pat their shoulders gently. Jowitt recalled a series of 'images of female dancers glimpsed through the bodies of men'.[19] Michael Clark, whose androgynous quality interested Spink,[20] was given a solo that alluded to Aurora's movements in

188

The Sleeping Beauty. Distanced from the original gender, we are inclined to see the movement differently, our eyes refocused, and perhaps to reconsider our expectations of female and male movement behaviour. Spink himself has said that *De Gas* was the opportunity for him to explore qualities of vulnerability in men.[21] But *De Gas*, like the other theatrical works discussed, is resonant in a post-modern sense, ambiguous, inviting questions, shifting our imaginations into many different areas.

Two further points arise from these early theatrical essays. Out of the video recordings available of many of Spink's early works, these pieces form an outstanding group, powerful in the economy and distinctiveness of their ideas. They point to Spink's future direction as a choreographer. They also express the recurring theme through Spink's work of isolation and tension between people.

Spink's work since 1981: an introduction

While he turned to a wider range of theatrical resources after 1981 and introduced the possibility of more specific meaning through text and referential sets and props, Spink continued to eschew the straightforward story-line of traditional dance or literary theatre. The traditional theatre situation is the one in which the audience witnesses a 'logical' series of events or narrative (fly-on-the-wall style in the case of naturalistic drama). Thus, earlier, to counter likely expectations about dance with meaning, Spink emphasized in his programme note that *Dead Flight* (1980) was non-narrative. His collaborators are like-minded, working from the anti-illusionist, anti-naturalistic tradition of theatre. Undoubtedly because of this bias, they are interested in working with the stylization of dance. Spink and company also favour a broad frame, often several stories mixing in one work, a multiplicity of reference, and a substantial timespan.

Spink's dance work of the 1980s situates itself rather tenuously within the tradition of dance. *Fugue* (1988) is television drama as much as dance. *Heaven Ablaze in His Breast*, for Second Stride, exists somewhere between dance, theatre and opera. A rich media resource is common across all this work, recalling the work of the much earlier established mixed-media group Moving Being (see pp. 23–25). The lighting designer Peter Mumford provides an interesting bridge: he worked for many years with Moving Being as designer and technical director. Nearly all Spink's Second Stride pieces use text: *New Tactics* (1983), *Further and Further Into Night* (1984), *Bösendorfer Waltzes* (1986), *Dancing and Shouting* (1988) and *Heaven Ablaze*. The exception is *Weighing the Heart* (1987). Production values, design, costume and props, are very high in all these pieces.

This open view towards dance theatre has drawn Spink to work comfortably under the banners of opera and theatre, insomuch as these genres stimulate production compatible with his interests. We are looking here at

189

the director's opera and theatre of highly stylized production. This is also multi-layered opera and theatre, resonant in a post-modern sense and ready to strike out boldly from traditional, single-minded interpretations of the libretti and plays of the past.

Opera choreography

One of the most acclaimed opera productions for which Spink provided dances was *The Trojans* (1986/87). Tim Albery's highly stylized, miniaturized visualization of the Berlioz opera was a co-production between Welsh National Opera, Opera North and Scottish Opera; it has also been staged by the Opéra de Nice. But the new mode of opera production can involve a choreographer in far more than set dances.[22] Throughout Handel's *Orlando* (1985), produced by Christopher Fettes, Spink 'physicalized' the stage for the singers with a movement chorus of nine.[23] Reviewing David Pountney's production of Verdi's *Macbeth* (1990), Nicholas Kenyon remarked that the Second Stride dancers 'give a choreographic air to the whole proceedings, and provide a tautness of gesture which admirably infects the whole production'.[24] Spink's intention was that 'the highly moved sections of Act 3 arise as if from within the [singing] chorus itself'.[25]

In the case of a contemporary opera, Robin Holloway's *Clarissa* (1990), Spink's dancers were pervasive presences. In this story of the repressed desire of the young Clarissa for a libertine, Lovelace, and her eventual rape by him, there are, in Pountney's production, five dancing doppelgängers to Clarissa, and four to Lovelace. In this multi-layered work, Holloway saw dance as 'a realisation ... of hidden depths of pleasure and fulfilment ... far from decorative divertissement; it continues the quest into realms where the conscious characters cannot follow.'[26] Thus a dancer steps out of the sleeping Clarissa's unconscious to dance with Lovelace, a scene that eventually expands to a world of waltzing couples inspired by Busby Berkeley routines.[27]

Directing for theatre

The major thrust towards Spink's later, divergent style undoubtedly came from theatre, from his collaborative experience with Albery and McDonald in two ICA theatre productions.

War Crimes (1981), co-directed by Spink and Albery, an allegory or fantasy about power in business, evolved from the eponymous short story (1980) by Peter Carey. McDonald's open-plan set was used to structure the action of the four 'Andy Warhols of business'.[28] Spink introduced an element of 'unnatural' movement. Significantly, *War Crimes* appeared under the ICA's banner 'Theatre not plays'. *Secret Gardens* (1983), co-directed by Spink, Albery, McDonald and Geraldine Pilgrim, broke into many different areas of meaning from initial ideas generated by Frances Hodgson Burnett's children's book *The Secret Garden* (1911). The production of *A Mouthful of Birds* (1986), a play written by Caryl Churchill and David Lan and directed by Spink and Les Waters, was of the same nature, freely criss-crossing the Bacchus story with an assortment of lives from today. Seven characters slip out of normality into a state of possession; dance is introduced as metaphor for the irrational states of ecstasy and violence.

Secret Gardens, the least straightforward of these pieces in narrative terms, contains perhaps the most dance. In the simplest terms, the piece could be about unlocking the repressed personality of adulthood, and about lonely people trying to forge harmonious connections with others. But it hints at many other ideas. In revealing emotional anxieties, movement can be especially telling. The situation is formal and restrictive, a cast of seven, the men in smart suits, the women in skirts and high heels, within a box set of windowed walls, and at the back something like the façade of a neo-Georgian doll's-house, with a huge, enigmatic reinforced door in the centre. From an array of images and fragmentary utterances, absurd and nightmarish in their disjunction, a family of themes emerges: blindness, ill-ness, relationships forged and then torn apart, isolation, searching, unlock-ing. An assemblage of props supports this: cabinets of medical implements, potions, spectacles, keys. There is only momentary relief in comic outburst or in the nostalgia for liberated childhood – imaginary kite-flying over the heads of the audiences and games of leap-frogging, cartwheels and hand-stands. But, as in much of Spink's work (*Dead Flight*, for instance), humour or lightheartedness are used as a foil for serious comment. A text from Revelations, introduced by Sally Owen and recapitulated at the end, rings hollow: it is a description of the heavenly city with its precious stones and of the river and tree of life. Even the great central door across the 'river of life' opens onto further secret recesses beyond.

Many theatre critics remained baffled by this piece. Some dance critics were enthusiastic and more able to make sense of a collage construction.[29] Steve Goff, during his brief stint as dance critic for *Time Out*, noted *Secret Gardens*' 'sense of narrative and symbolic consistency which develops into an unequivocal, bleak conclusion'.[30]

The main sources for this piece were the Burnett story and Anne Chisholm's *Nancy Cunard* (1981), the biography of the rebellious, doomed heiress who became a symbol of the 1920s. Indeed, fragments of these texts are spoken and expanded upon during the piece. From *The Secret Garden*, 'Might I have a bit of earth?' is Owen's plaintive plea. From *Nancy Cunard* stems the encounter between George Moore and Nancy, 'I do wish you would let me see you naked ... You have a beautiful back' (McDonald to Lucy Burge). However, it was not at all necessary to know this source material in order to find the new work potent. Original material had, in any case, undergone a process of distillation and transformation.

191

The dance theatre of Second Stride

Working methods

The richness of reference in the Second Stride pieces is the result of an exceptional mode of collaboration. The members of Spink's working group enjoy being pushed into a new direction by a colleague, and having other stories added to, or undercutting, their own. They find such a working process challenging and daring. Perhaps McDonald might start by introducing an idea which inspires Spink to read around and introduce another, then Mumford enters the game, the references snowball, the plots thicken. Sometimes, there is a pivotal concept which sparks off several independent enterprises. Often there is a period connection. McDonald drops in a prop or item of furniture which then becomes a part of the choreography. Recently, there has been integration in the live aspects of performance, with musicians appearing on stage since *Bösendorfer Waltzes*, and dancers occasionally doubling as musicians.

The Second Stride dancers have also become creative collaborators. Some time earlier, Spink had encouraged contributions from his dancers: in the section of improvised gestures from a line of chairs in *Some Fugues*, or in the 'armchair choreography'[31] of *Canta*, which was made by the dancers responding to instructions, often in a manner that Spink had not envisaged. At about the same time, Spink began to take the idea of generating material from performers much further into areas of meaning and emotion. For Cycles Dance Company, he directed *Being British* (1981), working from improvisation (to which this group was fully accustomed), exploring personal character, then later incorporating more formal choreographic structure.[32] Later, *War Crimes* and *Secret Gardens* generated verbal material from the performers in rehearsal, a typical procedure in theatre.[33]

Working with Second Stride on *New Tactics*, Spink and Albery asked for the dancers' own memories in gestural movement[34] and words. For *Bösendorfer*, the performers each chose a different surrealist or Dadaist for representation and researched the artist's life and writings for material that would be shaped into the new work. *Bösendorfer*, the programme indicated, was a collaborative theatre piece devised 'together with six members of Second Stride and two pianists'. Childhood memories and personal perceptions of *The Firebird* also found their way into this piece.

Spink can now call upon a range of procedures, including that of setting steps on dancers in the most traditional manner. Spink believes strongly in the input of performers, welcoming ideas that might be more interesting as raw material than his own, and considering that this working method encourages a special commitment between dancer and material and a corresponding intensity in performance. Certainly, the Second Stride enterprise has been notable for developing strong and surprising personalities from its

32. *Goanna* (Ian Spink Group, 1978), choreography by Ian Spink. A 1979 cast is shown here, from left to right: Michele Smith, Tim Lamford, Ian Spink, Siobhan Davies. (Photograph: David Buckland)

33. *26 Solos* (1978), choreography by Ian Spink, design by Craig Givens. Dancers, from left to right: Betsy Gregory, Michele Smith. (Photograph: David Buckland)

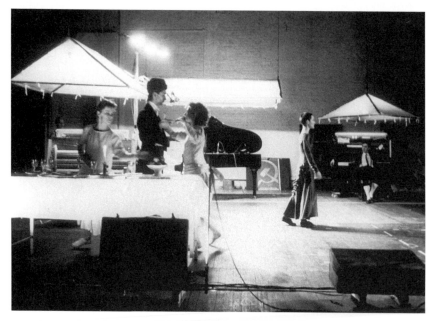

34. LEFT ABOVE: *Canta* (Ian Spink Group, 1981), choreography by Ian Spink. Dancers, from left to right: Betsy Gregory, Jeremy Nelson, Michele Smith. (Photograph: David Buckland)

35. LEFT BELOW: *Bösendorfer Waltzes* (Second Stride, 1986), choreography by Ian Spink, design by Antony McDonald, lighting by Peter Mumford. Performers, from left to right: Michele Smith, Michael Popper, Sally Owen, Cathy Burge, Philippe Giraudeau. (Photograph: David Buckland)

36. ABOVE: *Heaven Ablaze in His Breast* (Second Stride, 1989), choreography by Ian Spink. The photograph captures the dinner scene in the television version of the piece, directed by Peter Mumford, screened by BBC2, 18 May 1991. Dancers, from left to right: Gabrielle McNaughton, Michele Smith, Frances Carty, Stephen Goff, Cathy Burge and, on the floor, Sally Owen. (Photograph: Rosy Sanders) performers as actor-dancers: dancers like Cathy Burge, Philippe Giraudeau, Betsy Gregory and Michele Smith (all founder-members), Lucy Burge, Sally Owen and Michael Popper.

Subjects, sources and structures

New Tactics, Spink's first collaborative dance theatre piece for Second Stride, begins in the style of *Secret Gardens*, with verbal phrases as symbols of social but unheard and unrequited communication. Some utterances are impatient – 'Will you cut that out?' (Gregory). Others are gently pleading – 'Hello! Would you like some tea? Come and see my paintings' (Smith); or funny – 'Someone has put all the jelly babies down the loo and fed Rice Krispies to the potplants' (Juliet Fisher). Physical utterances projecting emotional need are received coldly, even with cruelty. There are tentative references in stage comments to a swimming pool or a seashore, to floating or swimming. Like a swimming pool, the area is cordoned by chrome bars. Possibly the bars represent a place of safety or repose – as in a swimming pool or, for that matter, a dance studio. The designs (here by McDonald and Givens in tandem) show the performers as people in street clothes once again, in off-whites, beiges, greys and browns, evoking the twenties, Siobhan Davies in cloche hat and sheath dress, Owen in straw hat with canvas satchel, various types of outdoor wear for the others. A strict pattern of trios unfolds, each of the six performers at one time in the centre, on two other occasions on the outside. In a second section, now to musical accompaniment (by Gough), shoes are removed and the earlier movement content is expanded. Now we can predict the same system of trios as it unfolds. Then there is an episode in which the stage is strewn with pillows flung on from the perimeter – occasion for some humour – and images of sleep and repose invade the speeches. Suddenly, 'New tactics,' Owen announces, 'don't sleep.' The final section reveals the chrome barriers raised like welcoming frontier posts: the dance builds and takes over entirely from the words, and the dancers seem closer. Davies concludes the proceedings crawling to rest with the comment 'I'm always on the move, but when I need to, I can always put my head down'.

New Tactics seems to demonstrate the power of movement as a force of emotional liberation and bonding after the futility of verbal communication. It also might express the shift from the uncertain state of mind hovering between sleep and wakefulness towards full wakefulness and necessary sleep as desired goals. My reading is that, more broadly, the second theme could be perceived as the theme of decisiveness, the ability to find a balance between facing the world and retreating from it. Yet there is still something unresolved about the ending, still the sudden withdrawals, the moments of rough contact between people as earlier movement ideas are recapitulated, now as material for dances.[35] The audience is left asking questions.

A programme note informed us that the source for this work was the physical and emotional memories of the participants. We were not told, and again it was not necessary for us to know, that another stimulus was the book *Awakenings* (1973) by the psychologist Oliver Sacks.[36] This book discusses the narcolepsy epidemic of 1916–27. It mentions that music could prove therapeutic in the patients' return to consciousness, rather like dance is liberating in *New Tactics*.

McDonald describes the next Second Stride collaboration as 'hermetically sealed' in relation to his other works with Spink. *Further and Further Into Night* is based on Alfred Hitchcock's classic film *Notorious* (1946), with strict monochrome black-and-white decor and costumes. The film's single story-line is referred to, and scenes are selected sufficient to maintain the thread of that story. This is the tale of intrigue and romance, as Alicia (Ingrid Bergman), daughter of a Nazi sympathizer, falls in love with FBI agent Develin (Cary Grant). Most of the movement and the fragments of text in *Further and Further* stem directly from the film. There is therefore a heavy reliance on pedestrian movement, and the same sophistication in dress and social behaviour as in the film. However, this is no mere re-enactment of the plot of the film; again, there is no straightforward narrative, but this time a comment on the film, an attempt 'to create a new landscape.'[37] Spink defuses the traditional forward drive of the story, celebrating detail and the discrete moment by repetition, stranding moments from their narrative and gender context. Thus, he pinpoints the poignancy and particularity of a human gesture or encounter, the erotic gesture of Develin placing his handkerchief around Alicia's bare midriff, the struggle in the car, the kiss, the tortuous exit from the house at the end. Occasionally, Spink allows the action to blossom into larger 'dance' movement (see pp. 202–203 for further discussion of this piece).

Bösendorfer Waltzes was a deliberately crude and anarchic sequel to *Further and Further*, and perhaps the most challenging of all Spink's Second Stride works. As the programme note indicated, it is rooted in Fokine's *The Firebird*, in early twentieth-century surrealism, myth and dream, while also referring to the pianos and evil villagers of the title. Many of the *Firebird* references are obvious: eggs, feathers, apples, entrapments, a wedding, and snatches of the Firebird's movement. And there are textual references: Smith for instance says 'I see a tree containing golden fruit. I see a man struggling with a beautiful bird. I see thirteen girls in their nightgowns, descending, like a procession of angels.' Rather less obvious are the characters, the prince and princess, two Kostchei and two Firebirds. At times, the performers act out, tell stories by, or relate incidents involving certain surrealist and Dadaist figures: Frida Kahlo (Cathy Burge), Tristan Tzara (Philippe Giraudeau), Luis Buñuel (Ikky Maas), Dorothea Tanning (Sally Owen), Salvador Dali (Michael Popper), René Magritte (Michele Smith).[38] The references do not stop here. There are allusions to early Soviet Communism, pictures of Soviet politicians of the 1920s, and the wedding pair, heads swathed Magritte-style in scarves, stand beneath a real hammer and sickle. There are also childhood reminiscences, and a matador dressed by the other performers in his cummerbund, a reference to Rudolf Valentino in *Blood and Sand* (1922). Gough draws for musical source material upon the three Stravinsky ballets *Les Noces*, *The Rite of Spring*, and *The Firebird*, weaving existing threads into his own rhythmically lively, throbbing systems-based texture.[39]

The context that makes sense of the cacophony of imagery in *Bösendorfer* is a Dadaistic event of story-telling, dancing and manipulation of a huge array of props. As well as all those already mentioned, there are the four pianos (of Stravinsky's *Les Noces*), a gynaecological couch-cum-dinner table, screens, projectors, pictures, maps and candles.

What superficially might seem chaotic is in fact very controlled and ordered. Mumford and McDonald have organized a coherence of colour (subtle indications of red and fluorescent blue) and textual reference, presenting Owen at the end, for instance, bare-breasted in a red cardigan as the girl she describes earlier in the piece. Structurally, the piece is a progression from colourful surrealist stories delivered as formal lectures, via dancing passages related to the *Firebird* tale, to passages of dance, text and music overlapping with increasing frequency. Interchange gradually becomes more unruly and more competitive.

One notion that I gained from this piece is its statement about freedom, a plea for artistic freedom, the freedom to dream, to leave your mind untamed, a celebration of divergence – captured and released princesses and birds, Dada/surrealist manifestos and myths become relevant metaphorical content. There are several direct references to this subject matter in texts and appropriately, at the end, when the stage is invaded by the prop paraphernalia of the piece, Owen passionately proclaims, 'In order to live, I shall invent the uninventable.'

McDonald has mentioned the importance of child-like elements to him in the making of this piece. These were indeed a recurring source since *Secret Gardens*. But in *Bösendorfer*, as in *Secret Gardens*, they also seem to represent an alternative to a repressed and dried-up adulthood.

Bösendorfer was a return to large dance movement. It emphasizes this far more than Spink's previous two pieces for Second Stride.

Spink's next work, *Weighing the Heart*, was an attempt to be more straightforward and entertaining, partly because of external pressure, partly his own initiative.[40] There was to be a strong, clear story-line, more spectacular design, inspired by his experience of the larger, grander world of opera, and, this time, no text to break up the continuity of dancing to music. However, the result was by no means as simple as original intentions might have suggested. The theme of religion gave way to a multiplicity of myths from East and West. Part I entwines the tales of Tobias and the Angel from the Apocrypha and Mozart's *Die Zauberflöte*. After an interval, Part II concentrates on various ascetics – John the Baptist, Isis, Mary Magdalen, St Anthony, Simone Weil and Mohammed. There is reference to the Egyptian Book of the Dead, in the title, for instance, describing an ancient religious ceremony where the heart or soul of the dead person is weighed to ascertain the person's worth, and in a danced A-to-Z register of body parts, Tamino's 'confession'. The musical sources for the band, Man Jumping, are correspondingly eclectic: Arab, Oriental, western, vernacular and liturgical.

Certainly, *Weighing the Heart* treats religion with humour and brio, and the theatrical endeavour is seductive, the rapidity of events impressive. In Part I, for instance, we see the Sarah of the Tobias story and her series of doomed husbands juxtaposed with Tamino, encountering the serpent and receiving, with Papageno, the magic flute and bells. Into the picturesque house wherein Pamina is captive rushes the Crocodile with whom Tobias and the Angel tangle. Fluently, the dancers pass in and out of costumes and characters, named and unnamed: nuns, ladies-in-waiting, husbands, angels. However, the material of *Weighing the Heart*, vivid for the eye as it undoubtedly is, remains far less digested than in Spink's earlier Second Stride works, at the level of information, and perhaps when the subject matter would most demand some sort of enquiry. The collaborators agree with this evaluation.[41] McDonald has exposed the problem that Part II, which was supposed to stress illumination in the ascetic state, goes nowhere near far enough in banishing props, in ridding itself of the 'material' clutter of Part I.

A similar problem exists with the next two works *Dancing and Shouting* and *Heaven Ablaze in his Breast*. The first of these shows far less theatrical flair than usual from the Second Stride team and relies heavily on spoken text. The bleak, violent images of contemporary life are in themselves unsettling – the mass murderer Denis Nilsen, the Chernobyl and Piper Alpha disasters, a hospital in Beirut, terrorist activity – amongst dances that display qualities of oppression and assault. But the power of individual images is defused by a litanical manner of delivery.

A single story line, E. T. A. Hoffmann's *The Sandman* (1815), runs through *Heaven Ablaze*, for the first time since *Further and Further Into Night*. Nevertheless, out of Hoffmann's tale of Nathaniel falling in love with the doll Olimpia, his madness and eventual death, the collaborators saw more than a century unfold, from the German romantic movement to Freud and Fascism. The programme indicates the breadth of research and reference, containing Freud's analysis of the story, Kokoschka's instructions for the creation of a life-size doll to replace his absent lover, many photos of dolls and posing women, and an extensive chronology of European

199

events (1749–1939). Judith Weir's score for the electronic voice theatre group Vocem is vibrant and evocative, mixing the nineteenth century of Schubert song and Delibes' *Coppélia* with twentieth-century musical developments. But, as the critic David Hughes has observed, *Heaven Ablaze* exemplifies a 'profligate economy. As soon as an idea is brought out, it's thrown away.'[42] Five singers and five dancers function as doppelgangers to each other, but the psychological potential of the doppelganger concept, introduced 'in the spirit of Hoffmann's fascination with the shattered personality,'[43] is not explored. Surprisingly for the subject matter, the tone is cool, one of icy beauty. The television version of the piece helped to solve several of its problems (see pp. 205–206).

Some stylistic issues

Spink's collaborative works for Second Stride mix imagery from a variety of sources and, by revitalizing ideas in new contexts, demonstrate the fluid relationship between a sign and its meaning, between signifier and signified. In this respect, they are certainly post-modern, according to the second, later meaning of that term for dance (see p. 5). The roots of this aesthetic lay in Spink's earlier theatrical work. The Second Stride pieces draw unashamedly from history or the real world of the present, rather than making supposedly 'original' stories: they borrow from politics, personal history, high and vernacular art. Notably, Second Stride's creative protagonists defend their right not to rationalize or justify every theatrical idea selected, or every formal process used. In interviews, Spink, Albery and McDonald all emphasized their liberation from channelled, logical storytelling into irrational experience, the evocation of an emotional response that cannot be explained. Admitting, too, that the work can stir viewers to take home its puzzles, and there to rationalize their reactions to it, these artists insist on the importance of the spectator's role: each makes his or her own story from the collage. As Spink says, 'there are no single, set answers. Nothing is straightforward.'[44] Or the spectator might trace more than one story, given that this is work that celebrates ambiguity.

It could also be suggested that highly ambiguous, contradictory works like *Bösendorfer* hardly offer anything as firm as 'story'. Perhaps these subscribe more readily to Roland Barthes' post-structuralist notion of a 'writerly', plural text that defies interpretation; writerly because it insists on the active role of the reader as co-author, at the same time answering 'not to an interpretation, even a liberal one, but to an explosion, a dissemination'.[45]

Sometimes, it has been suggested, the Second Stride work has fallen into the traps of its own style and working methods, its abundance of signs constituting a 'heterogeneous soup' of meaning,[46] even though it makes brilliant theatre. It is relevant to refer back to Charles Marowitz's description of some very early work of Moving Being: 'too much can mean too little'. He recommends instead that 'the various ideas [should] collide in interesting smash-ups with each other'.[47] David Hughes, in his review of *Heaven Ablaze*, stresses the rigorous control necessary in work of this style, citing as examples the later work of Moving Being, and the work of the Polish theatre director Tadeusz Kantor.[48] Essential are the careful selection of images to ensure the possibility of rich resonance, and the rooting out of deep connections and oppositions.

The best Second Stride work proves this point. It also proves the value of strong formal argument. The most successful work makes a thread or process visible through its structure. It leads its viewer through its complexities. Thus, *New Tactics* demonstrates a shift of emphasis in medium, from words to dance, with reasons for that shift that stem from the meanings, or half-meanings, of the piece. *Bösendorfer* shifts from blocks of text and dance to an overlapping or integration of the various theatrical media. Theatrical pacing is crucial too, the element of surprise, for instance, as media and threads of reference are brought together in exhilarating and emphatic collision. There are the weddings in *Bösendorfer* and *Weighing the Heart*, which achieve sudden new meanings as hammer and sickle and funeral decorations are added to the respective proceedings. It is the combined effect of stasis after hectic motion and the accumulation of extraordinary design – devices of time, shape, colour, texture, reference, all brought to bear – that make these crowning moments especially powerful.

Another fascinating aspect of the Second Stride work is its manner of play between emotional expressiveness and restraint. Spink and his collaborators often introduce devices that have a highly expressive effect, and at the same time refresh our perceptions: like the subversion of gender, women playing men or *vice versa*, or the catching and repeating of everyday movement, performed in everyday clothes, within the extraordinary circumstances of structured dance. In *Further and Further*, repetition of gesture can draw attention to the humour of a situation, to its poignancy, or tension. In this respect, the critic Alastair Macaulay has singled out the episode where a woman brings a cocktail to a man and watches him drink (Lucy Burge and Ikky Maas, originally Alicia and Develin). The sequence is repeated, with other women, women without men, a man taking the woman's role: 'We are made acutely aware of the behaviour of a woman fascinated by a man. And we watch with mounting unease.'[49] In *New Tactics*, gestural repetition has the different effect of making the characters appear slightly obsessed. Then 'dance movement', when it suddenly springs out of normal, everyday behaviour, acquires a strange, even eccentric tone. But Spink's odd twists and subversions of the expected also have a distancing effect, as reflexive gestures, making us analytically aware of convention as convention. The characteristic role-changing of his performers contributes to this effect.

Of all these pieces, *Further and Further* encourages our analytical response the most strongly. Its opening signals that we are 'outside' the story. The performers comment on the film and the parts that they are just beginning to visualize. The comments were drawn from the performers in rehearsal:

> *Lucy Burge (running through her part):* 'I hear the doorbell. I run across the apartment. I kiss the man.'

> *Smith (commenting on the film):* 'Obviously he cared about her. The fact that he put his scarf around her waist when they went for the drive in the car ... '

> *Giraudeau (also commenting on the film):* 'I still feel that the stairs are very important. And the way people go upstairs is very important as well.'

At one point, the collaborators considered incorporating a taped discussion of the film by the critic Dilys Powell,[50] in which case the signalling of the conceptual issue to the audience would have been even clearer. The intention, Spink has said, was to set up the audience like a voyeur, watching 'people in a goldfish bowl'. He hoped to highlight the conventional male and female role playing in the film by doing this.[51] He also highlights Hitchcock's own voyeuristic tendencies.

In *Further and Further*, there are also reminders of the mechanics of the film medium itself beyond the story-line: the black-and-white retained from *Notorious*; the wind and rewind capacity in the 'Meeting the Germans' episode, when the performers enter and exit to start the introductions all over again. Finally, the telescoped recapitulation of moments from the story at the end of *Further and Further* stands out as an entirely artificial device after the narrative scheme has been followed through.

In *Bösendorfer*, an important device that draws us outside the stories is the presentness of the 'real' performers Popper, Smith, Giraudeau and the others. Such is their resourcefulness and energy in creating the 'real' event, they not only dance, tell stories, shift roles, play pianos, but also activate their own lights (1980s machinery) and props. They function outside the characters that they represent. The lecture format at the beginning immediately signals to us that we are not required to enter naively into the magic of theatre. The verbal allusions to *The Firebird*, some of them the performers' own reminiscences, emphasize the distance between the real performers and the *Firebird* roles that they assume. These collaborations strongly remind us, therefore, of the outside creative hand at work forming and motivating the proceedings – rather than the characters themselves or their 'fate' motivating a logical system of events – and selecting fragments of human experience as if for our laboratory study. In *Bösendorfer*, probably a result of the working process, this seems to be as much the hand of the performers as that of the choreographer.

The effect of detailed patterning from repeated movement sequences in *Further and Further* has been compared to 'a baroque weight of embellishment and elaboration'.[52] But the patterns are also sufficiently short and simple for a spectator to enjoy their structure and subtle variations. Each repetition gives away more information. Repetition, as it did in *Canta*, brings structural processes into the foreground. It is another reflexive gesture. The scarf dance, for instance, which came from the placing of a scarf around Alicia's waist in the film, shows the phrase of capture, return and flourish of the scarf three times. It is like a folk dance, and the pattern is seen across two, then three, couples, the second time less elaborately, the third time with a new swirling ending. We are drawn in to follow how the dance works. Repetition in *Further and Further* is supported by the doubling of beds and Copacabana mountains in McDonald's set. Again, it is as if Hitchcockian artifice, his playful, exaggerated thrust of a crucial image, has been pushed several stages further.

The effect of repetition here and in other works by Spink is much cooler than in the work of Pina Bausch, a choreographer whose name has sometimes been invoked in discussions of Spink's work. Repetition in Spink's work does not create Bauschian extremes of obsession and exhaustion. It encourages a more objective stance. The disintegration or gradual diminution of repeated patterns which characterizes several dances in *Bösendorfer* is sometimes an emotional statement (for example, the gradual tiring of the Firebirds as they repeatedly throw themselves towards the Prince), but it is more often formal in effect. In this piece too, dance phrases looping repeatedly round several performers often generate a dynamic and spatial life of their own, quite distinct from that of any personal dance statement, for instance in the sequence where apples are passed and juggled between performers, or the passage that includes working around a piano and pianist.

The finest Second Stride collaborations encourage the viewers to respond in a 'knowing', analytical state as much as they might be moved by potent images and juxtapositions. Indeed, it could be said that Spink's collaborative works draw their special liveliness from the tension between these two poles, the particular conflict between head and heart that he sets up in the spectators. It is as if Spink echoes Yvonne Rainer's belief that plain emotional involvement is no longer valid in art today, some removal element is now imperative: 'There is no way to go back ... It's like wishing for a lost innocence.'[53]

Television dance

A fascinating recent development in Spink's career is his work for television in association with Dance-lines productions. Spink took naturally to the television medium. The gestural and acting content of his work lent itself readily to the television frame, and he had already used editing, wind and rewind and slow motion techniques in his theatre pieces. Spink made full use of the editing potential of television in the best of his pieces for Dance-lines 1987 (for Channel 4), which he directed himself. An untitled work, it is the piece that darts back and forth restlessly between slices of life in six locations. It was inspired by several paintings by Edward Hopper.[54] We watch, for instance, a woman leaving a bedroom for a journey, taken from *Western Motel* (1957), with a Studebaker arriving outside the window. There is a fight involving two men and an usherette in a cinema, a scene of marital stress, an argument in an office, and women are seen arriving and meeting in a dark room, which is perhaps a refuge (some of the women enter it from other scenes). The atmosphere is fraught, partly because of the rapid editing, partly because of the content, the apparent urgency to escape being a recurring theme.

This is an exceptionally lively piece of television, partly because of its economy, a density of information delivered quickly, also because it invites a host of questions about the time sequence of events, the relationships between the various characters within and across the various scenes, what happens to those who do not end up in the refuge. As usual, these questions are not answered. Spink himself did not have a fixed story in mind as he made the piece, and the audience has to forge its own connections. There is also the familiar distancing. We look at each scene from an unnatural perspective as if observing through a static viewing frame (one stationary camera was used). There are two passages where musical utterances match a series of sharp cuts between locations, thus underlining the artificiality of this editing procedure.

Fugue, the piece that Spink directed and made in collaboration with Caryl Churchill in 1988 (again a Dance-lines production for Channel 4) is more revealing about the content of television. It concerns a man's death, his bereaved family and their process of coming to terms with his death, invoking past wrongs, giving way to aggressive feelings about him. Here is the familiar type of domestic, soap opera situation that is usually guaranteed to mask the forms in which it is presented, but Spink and Churchill again make the audience instantly aware of device as much as content. The family pass on the news: 'He'd just got out of the bath ... Mum says he'd just got out of the bath' – repetitions of fugal proportions. There is a world of unreality surrounding the gossiping and clattering of cups at the post-funeral party: a flash-back to a sandy beach that has somehow strayed into the room of a house, the betowelled father raised heavenwards on a stage wire, and later a scene around a funeral pyre, the family's private, imaginary farewell. Stylization becomes paramount in the final, contrapuntal dance sequence, shot through a wide-angle lens, a self-conscious exaggeration of distance and close-up.

Fugue proves that it is possible to play the game of dramatic intrigue within a formal argument of the strictest kind: entries, subject and counter-subject, resolution and coda. Passages from Bach's *The Art of Fugue*[55] are the fitting accompaniment. Looked at another way, *Fugue* uses a post-modern tactic of audience engagement. 'Unnatural' formal concerns revitalize our attention to a familiar, even hackneyed human predicament. And thus, while a naive response is no longer admissible, we might still be moved.

Heaven Ablaze was conceived as a theatre piece that could be turned into television (screened in 1991 by BBC television). The television version was directed by Dance-lines producer Peter Mumford in close collaboration with Spink and McDonald. Mumford had already lit the theatre piece. More successful than the live event, the television *Heaven Ablaze* pares down source material, adds more cross-referencing of the images that are used, and reinforces the narrative thread. The mode is again highly artificial, with use of black-and-white sequences as well as colour, and people and props racing to camera with unnatural fervour. But the Dance-lines team has also brought out the passion in the content: it reaches our senses. This accomplishment brings out the important tensions in Hoffmann's *The Sandman* between formal bourgeois respectability and a dangerous inner world, and an additional tension between nineteenth-century German romanticism and its distortions under Nazism.

Eyes now become a telling focus throughout the piece, by virtue of television close-up possibilities, a powerful springboard for messages, the gateway to simple, peaceful happiness or to a desire – 'heaven ablaze in his breast' – that brings danger, madness and death. Blindness and the act of blinding signal isolation, imposed or self-willed, a hideous physical violence as well as death of body and spirit. We are not just told or shown these things: we feel them. We experience the evil Coppélius attacking Nathaniel's eyes with scissors (approaching camera) as if he reaches for ours. Nathaniel's delirium after spying on his Father and Coppélius is a nightmare of rapid editing. Huge eyes dominate the screen, both penetrating and vulnerable, burning red and monochrome (shades of the eye in the Buñuel/Dali film *Un chien andalou* (1929)), and they intercut or overlay images of physical brutality, blinding, falling, thudding to the floor again and again, and dying. There is resonance here that reaches deep inside both mind and sensual apparatus.

This new attention to the sensual and emotional helps to create a stronger large form for *Heaven Ablaze*, useful stages of refocusing and renewing our attention as we shift gear from formal situation to tormented inner reality. An example of this is the pacing of events around Nathaniel's spying and delirium. The preparation is an almost painterly scene at the family dinner table, symmetrical, sunny and Biedermeier, interpolated by shots of off-centre dance merriment and close-ups of gluttonous behaviour. This is shattered by an episode when Nathaniel's Mother drags him into his pitch-black bedroom: the door opens to let in a screaming diagonal of light, reminiscent of early expressionist German cinema, and a noisy shower of toy bricks. Thence to the spying episode, nightmare, death of the Father and back to a most proprietous 'choir portrait' which accompanies the reading of Klara's letter to Nathaniel.

Several concerns in Spink's work place him firmly within the post-modern camp of choreographers, referring to the later meaning of that term for dance, the meaning that brings dance in line with the most common notions of post-modernism across the other arts (see p. 5). After building a movement language for himself, in the manner of a modernist, Spink developed a profile as a dance theatre choreographer who works in areas of multi-layered and ambiguous meaning and uses the post-modern technique of radical juxtaposition. Also symptomatic of post-modernism are his penchants for history and nostalgia, and for mixing from a variety of source material.

Collaboration has been a key aspect of Spink's work with Second Stride. His co-authors, most notably Antony McDonald, Associate Director of the group, have eagerly supported his divergent vision, and together they have created a variety of media mixtures. Text, set, costume, props, music and dance: all play their part, the emphasis on one or the other shifting from moment to moment, piece to piece. Spink has remained a distinctive maker of dance steps, but his much broader interests have led him naturally beyond the umbrella of pure dance, and to develop important careers in theatre, opera, and most recently, television.

As an exponent of post-modern dance theatre, Spink belongs to the European tradition of Pina Bausch and Anne Teresa De Keersmaeker, and he is in line with many younger British experimental choreographers who began their careers in the 1980s. He is far more a part of this tradition than Alston, Davies or Butcher. Yet, speaking of the British context, his multi-layered meanings and media ambitions also link him back in time through New Dance to much earlier work that he would never have seen: like the dance theatre experiments at the LSCD in the early 1970s when he was still in Australia and, especially, the work of the British mixed-media group Moving Being. Spink has built for himself an utterly distinctive style, and his brand of post-modernism is attuned to the ethos of today. Yet, as I have tried to show in this book, forerunners of this style can be traced from the early days of contemporary dance in Britain.

APPENDICES

Appendix 1: *The Place as an Arts Centre*

Information from the publicity leaflet (1971)

'BARRIERS BETWEEN THE ARTS ARE DISAPPEARING; THE PLACE IS WHERE THEY MEET ... '

YOU CAN SEE ...

Cinema Clubs
The New Cinema Club presents weekly film shows and the Other Cinema holds special festival-type sessions

Theatre Companies
Wherehouse La Mama; London Theatre Group; TSE Company; Placenta Arts Black Theatre Company; Southdown Theatre; Stratford East Company

Mixed Media
Moving Being (The Place is their headquarters); 'Explorations' (Alan Beatty, Peter Dockley, Peter Logan, Art Bauman, Taller de Montevideo, Meredith Monk, etc); Leopoldo Maler

Music
Fires of London, based at The Place (formerly the Pierrot Players); Music Now; AMM; John Williams; Gerald English; Paco Peña; Mike Westbrook; Jon Hendricks; Bob Downes; pop concerts

Mime and Puppets
Polish Pantomime Theatre; Adam Darius; 'Pinokio' Polish Puppet Theatre

Dance
Northern Dance Theatre; Scottish Theatre Ballet's 'Ploys'; Pauline de Groot Company; Tarveen Mehra; New Swedish Ballet; Won-Kyung Cho (Korean dance); Gerda Geddes (T'ai Chi Chu'an); Noa Eshkol Chamber Dance; Lilian Harmel's dance plays for children; Iris Scaccheri; lectures, discussions, films

The leaflet lists events at The Place between 1969 and 1971. The Royal Shakespeare Company also held a season at The Place Theatre in 1971. Further seasons followed in 1973 and 1974. The note that Meredith Monk took part in *Explorations* is incorrect.

208

Appendix 2: *Strider – the repertory*

Some Strider programmes indicate that a piece is being performed for the first time and clarify premiere dates. Otherwise, the first known date of a completed work (as opposed to a work in progress) is given here, using programmes and publicity as sources.

Title	Choreographer	Composer	Date, place of Strider premiere
Subject to Change	Richard Alston/ Christopher Banner	Subject to change	14 Aug. 1972, The Place Theatre, London
Afar	C. Banner	Michael Finnissy	14 Aug. 1972, The Place Theatre, London
Routine Couple	R. Alston	Taped conversation of George Burns and Gracie Allen	14 Aug. 1972, The Place Theatre, London
Thunder	R. Alston	Three recordings of Harold Arlen's *Stormy Weather*	14 Aug. 1972, The Place Theatre, London
Tiger Balm	R. Alston	Anna Lockwood	14 Aug. 1972, The Place Theatre, London
Solo	Wendy Levett	Michael Finnissy	14 Aug. 1972, The Place Theatre, London (original premiere, 31 Jan. 1972, LSCD).
Fifty Million Robins Can't Be Wrong	Fergus Early, Jacky Lansley	Helen Pope (Lyrics Billy Tracey)	14 Aug. 1972, The Place Theatre, London (original premiere, 16 Jun. 1972, LSCD)
Parable	W. Levett	Michael Finnissy	14 Aug. 1972, The Place Theatre, London (original premiere, 16 Jun. 1972, LSCD)
Event (first of series)		GERM (Groupe d'étude et de realisation musicales)	15 Aug. 1972, The Place Theatre, London
Corridor Falls	C. Banner	J. S. Bach	22 Aug. 1972, Edinburgh Festival (original premiere, 17 Mar. 1972, LSCD)
Corridor Walk	C. Banner	Collage	28 Aug. 1972, Edinburgh Festival (original premiere, 10 May 1972, LSCD)
Traffic	R. Alston	Spoken text *Mobility* by Peter and Alison Smithson	28 Aug. 1972, Edinburgh Festival (original premiere, 20 Dec. 1971, London Festival Ballet Workshop)
Blue	C. Banner		3 Oct. 1972, ICA, London
Counterfoil	Barry Flanagan	T. M. Offredy	3 Oct. 1972, ICA, London
Hundreds and Thousands	Diana Davies, J. Lansley, Sally Potter	Barry Flanagan, Paul du Feu and Ross & Cromarty Orchestra	3 Oct. 1972, ICA, London
Windhover	R. Alston	Anna Lockwood	1 Dec. 1972, ICA, London

209

Striding Out

Title	Choreographer	Composer	Date, place of Strider premiere
Halfway to Paradise	J. Lansley		1 Dec. 1972, ICA, London
Pedestrian	C. Banner	Gordon Mumma – Pedestrian	1 Dec. 1972, ICA, London
Strawberry	C. Banner	George Gershwin	1 Dec. 1972, ICA, London
Nowhere Slowly	R. Alston	Terry Riley Poppy Nogood & the Phantom Band	23 Jan. 1973, Cambridge College Arts Theatre (developed through various versions for Lecture-Demonstration Group of LSCD & LCDT, 1970–71).
Headlong	R. Alston	Anna Lockwood	29 Mar. 1973, White Lion School, Islington, London
Crying in the Rain	J. Lansley	Everly Brothers	18 Apr. 1973, HM Prison Wormwood Scrubs, London
Cathy's Clown, Crying in the Rain	J. Lansley	Everly Brothers	7 May 1973, Oval House, London
Needless Alley	Nanette Hassall	John Cage	21 May 1973, Aston Univ. Centre for the Arts, Birmingham
Wings	S. Potter		21 Jul. 1973, The Place Theatre, London (original premiere, 5 April 1973, LSCD)
The Truth About Me[1]	J. Lansley	Everly Brothers, Elvis Presley	21 Jul. 1973, The Place Theatre, London
The Average Leap Forward	R. Alston	The Majorca Orchestra	21 Jul. 1973, The Place Theatre, London
Dry Dock	D. Davies	Darius Milhaud, John Darling	21 Jul. 1973, The Place Theatre, London
Mingle	R. Alston	Anna Lockwood	6 Sept. 1973, Chapter Arts Centre, Cardiff
Small Brown Shell	Mary Fulkerson	Jim Fulkerson	26 Oct. 1973, Dartington College, Devon
Travelling Companion	C. Banner	Jim Fulkerson	26 Oct. 1973, Dartington College, Devon
Solo . . . for myself	Mirjam Berns		15 Jan. 1974, ICA, London
Common Ground	N. Hassall	Philip Corner Attempts at Whitenesses	15 Jan. 1974, ICA, London
There is and always will be . . .	M. Berns		15 Jan. 1974, ICA, London
Three Romances of an Unobtainable Nature Featuring Air-Hostess Housewife and Call-Girl	D. Davies	Rasputin Compton Collage	15 Jan. 1974, ICA, London
Rainbow Bandit	R. Alston	Charles Amirkhanian Just	15 Jan. 1974, ICA, London
By Pass	C. Banner		16 Jan. 1974, ICA, London

1. Incorporating *Cathy's Clown* and *Crying in the Rain*.

Title	Choreographer	Composer	Date, place of Strider premiere
Dance with Dialogue	W. Levett	Speakers: Kate Gielgud, Stephen Earle. Dialogue: Michael Elster	17 Jan. 1974, ICA, London
Making Light Work	Mary Fulkerson		18 Jan. 1974, ICA, London
Survey (a section from a new work in progress)[2]	R. Alston	Gordon Mumma	20 Feb. 1974, Theatre Ardudwy, Coleg Harlech
Soft Verges (trio)[3]	R. Alston	Jim Fulkerson	25 Apr. 1974, Akademie der Künste, Berlin
Stream Line	N. Hassall	Jim Fulkerson *Tangential Patterns*	6 Jul. 1974, Angers, France
Soft Verges, Hard Shoulder (duet)	R. Alston	Anna Lockwood *Shone* Stephen Montague *Ambush*[4]	24 Sept. 1974, Bingley College of Education, Yorkshire
We Love You, Dennie	Mary Fulkerson		24 Sept. 1974, Bingley College of Education, Yorkshire
Split	R. Alston, Dennis Greenwood	Philip Corner, Stephen Montague	26 Oct. 1974, Musée Galliera, Paris
Event	Richard Johnson	Collage	26 Oct. 1974, Musée Galliera, Paris
Dasan	David Woodberry	Rene Bastian, Eva Karczag & Stephen Montague	26 Oct. 1974, Musée Galliera, Paris
Slow Field[5]	R. Alston	Stephen Montague	7 Nov. 1974, Mappin Art Gallery, Sheffield
Sanction	N. Hassall		16 Nov. 1974, Oval House, London
Bearings	N. Hassall	Robert Schumann	16 Nov. 1974, Oval House, London
Fine Lines	Daniel Press	Stephen Montague	6 Mar. 1975, ICA, London
Swivels	R. Alston	Stephen Montague	6 Mar. 1975, ICA, London
Largo con Moto	Eva Karczag, Stephen Montague	Stephen Montague	6 Mar. 1975, ICA, London
Chinese Notebook	D. Press		6 Mar. 1975, ICA, London
Wheat	S. Potter, D. Greenwood	Igor Stravinsky	14 Mar. 1975, Green Dragon Court, Southwark, London
Souvenir	R. Alston, D. Greenwood	Erik Satie	9 Apr. 1975, Serpentine Gallery, London
Zero through Nine	R. Alston	Stephen Montague	9 Apr. 1975, Serpentine Gallery, London
Two Saints in Three Acts	R. Alston		19 Apr. 1975, Corn Exchange, Cambridge

2. Alston maintains that this is an early version of *Soft Verges*, interview 16 December 1974.
3. *Soft Verges* originated in Autumn 1973 as a duet, became a trio in 1974 and was remade as a duet later in 1974.
4. The last version of this duet was performed to Stephen Montague's *PhaseShiftHeterodyne*, 17 May 1975.
5. Developed through the winter alongside the travelling Jasper Johns exhibition.

Striding Out

Title	Choreographer	Composer	Date, place of Strider premiere
Standard Steps	R. Alston	Voice of Marcel Duchamp, E. Satie	17 May 1975, MOMA, Oxford
Lying Down, Rising	E. Karczag		17 May 1975, MOMA, Oxford
Beside Ourselves	D. Press	Paul Chandler, Miranda Tufnell	17 May 1975, MOMA, Oxford
Compass	R. Alston		25 Jul. 1975, outside Midland Group Gallery, Nottingham
Duet	D. Greenwood, E. Karczag		28 Jul. 1975, St Pauls Portico, Covent Garden, London

Appendix 3: *Strider – the dancers*

Regular dancers

Richard Alston*	1972–75	Jacky Lansley*	1972–73
Christopher Banner*	1972–74	Pietje Law	1973–74
Mirjam Berns*	1974	Wendy Levett*	1972–73
Diana Davies*	1972[1]	John Milne	1974
Russell Dumas	1974	Sally Potter*	1972[2]
Dennis Greenwood*	1972–75	Daniel Press*	1975
Nanette Hassall*	1973–74	Keith Urban	1973
Eva Karczag*	1973–75		

Dancers/performers who appeared with Strider in isolated performances

Ruth Barnes	1975	Tony Gason	1975
Hilary Beckett	1974	Craig Givens	1974, 1975
Terry Berman	1974	John Hilliard (sculptor/	
David Cassidy	1975	photographer)	1972
Raymond Cook	1973	Colette Laffont	1972
Helen Crocker	1974	Timothy Lamford	1975
Maedée Duprès	1973	Cathy Lewis	1973
Fergus Early*	1972	Paula Morell	1974
Nelson Fernandez	1974	Gordon Mumma	
Barry Flanagan		(composer)	1972
(sculptor)	1972	Miranda Tufnell	1975
Mary Fulkerson*	1974		

* Indicates that the dancer also choreographed for Strider.

1. Davies was invited back to Strider to choreograph *Dry Dock* in 1973 and *Three Romances* in 1974.
2. Potter also revived *Wings* from a LSCD workshop in 1973, and performed her *Wheat* under the auspices of Strider in 1974.

Appendix 4: *Strider – performance and residency schedule 1974*

January 15–19	ICA, London
February 4–6	Stopover, Birmingham Arts Lab
February 20	Theatr Ardudwy, Coleg Harlech, Wales
February 21	Bangor Arts Festival
February 23	Gardner Centre, Brighton
March 10–16	Dartington College, Devon, performance March 14
March 18	St Luke's College, Exeter
April 24, 25, 29	Akademie der Künste, Berlin, Germany
May 4	Kulturtäter Biel-Bienne, Switzerland
May 13, 14	Oval House, London
May 28–June 5	Dartington College, performance June 2, 3
June 22–23	Birmingham (in pencil in Chandler's Strider diary)
June 27	Birmingham (in pencil in diary)
July 6	Atelier Chorégraphique d'Angers, France
July 29–August 31	Dartington College (residency with Tropical Fruit Company)
September 24	Bingley College of Education, Yorkshire
September 26	Bretton Hall College, Yorkshire, performance
September 28	Lady Mabel College, Yorkshire
October 23–28	Festival d'Automne, Paris, France
November 1	Royal College of Art, London
November 7–9	Mappin Art Gallery, Sheffield (with Jasper Johns exhibition)[1]
November 14–17	Oval House, London (6 performances)
November 27	Cardiff, lecture-demonstration
November 28	Glynn Vivian Art Gallery, Swansea
November 29–30	Chapter Theatre, Cardiff
December 9–10	Herbert Art Gallery and Museum, Coventry (with Johns' exhibition)
December 12–14	Allardyce Nicholl Studio, Birmingham University

1. The gallery series continued until April 1975, with final performances at the Serpentine Gallery, London.

Sources: programmes, publicity, the diary kept by Strider's administrator Paul Chandler, and Alston's own recollections.

Appendix 5: *Artists in the ADMA Festivals 1977–78*

Listed as in publicity, by title of group, choreographer or solo performer.

1977

Dance

Ailsa Berk
Laurie Booth
Wendy Carter and
  Friends (Giles
  Mitchell, Ailsa Berk,
  Chrissy Sutherland)
Cedars of Lebanon
Emilyn Claid
Helen Crocker
Cycles Dance Company
Helen Dee and Friends
Fergus Early
Arianna Economou

Kate Flatt
Jill Gale
Joanna Gale
Kate Gault
Martin Gerrish
Sarah Green
Betsy Gregory
Raymond Gunn
Linda Hartley
Timothy Lamford and
  Julyen Hamilton
Jacky Lansley

Jayne Lee
Jessica Loeb
Mary Longford
Natural Dance
  Workshop
Martyn Rudin
Roberta Saady and
  Larry Butler
Alpana Sengupta
Janet Smith Dance
  Group
Virginia Taylor and
  Simon Emmerson

Mime

Justin Case

Moving Picture Mime
Show

N.V.C.

1978[1]

Dance

Richard Alston
ARC
Peri Aston
Chris Banner
Melanie Bell
Rosemary Butcher
  Dance Company
Centrestage: Images
Chiswick Dance
Adrianna della Croce,
  Mine Kaylan, Helen
  Crocker, Richard
  Coldman and Martin
  Mayes

Ann Crosset and
  friends (Denmark)
Dance Theatre
  Commune
Dancework
Lyn Dobson
Maedée Duprès
Isabel Eisen
The Explosives
Jill Gale and Martin
  Mayes
Joanna Gale
Craig Givens
Alexandra Graham

Raymond Gunn
Marilyn Halford and
  William Raban
Linda Hartley, Libby
  Dempster and Mikala
  Ritzou
Lilian Harmel Dance
  Theatre Group
Helix
Duncan Holt and Jane
  (Angie) Holloway
INTA
Kickstart
Mary Longford

---

1. Festival calendar listing. For the 1978 festival, I have not been able to find
   an exact, final list of the artists who performed. There were many changes to
   the programmes. The *Time Out* dance critic Jan Murray reported (to the
   Arts Council) that 11 events were definitely cancelled, and often without
   replacements. I have indicated the changes for which I have found records.

Bonnie Meekums
Natural Dance Theatre
Krystyna Nowak
Shelagh O'Brien
Martha Partridge
Polyglot
Martyn Rudin and
  Mary Copple
Roberta Saady

Janet Smith Dance Group
Ian Spink
Spur of the moment
Thyrsus Dance Combine
  (dance and mime)
Miranda Tufnell,
  Martha Grogan and
  Dennis Greenwood

Paul Versteeg
Judy Webb, Sally
  Mason and Rosanne
  Donahoe
Workshop No. 7
X6 Collective

Mime

Almost Mime Theatre
  Company
Anglo-Italiano Teatro
  d'Azione (Italy)
Harry Jones, Norma
  Lee and Crawford
  Marshall

Evelyn Langlands and
  André Lorrain
  (France)
Marita Phillips

N.V.C.
The Silents
Teatro Chileno de
  Mimos (Chile)

Cancellations

Dance

Miranda Tufnell,
  Martha Grogan and
  Dennis Greenwood
  (replaced by Maedée
  Duprès)

Rosemary Butcher
  Dance Company

Additional and substitute artists

Dance
Penny Ward

Mime
Eclipse Theatre

Mimeteater Termiek (Holland)

Sources: ADMA Festival calendars, Arts Council reports, reviews and *Time Out* listings.

Appendix 6: *Artists in the Dance at Dartington Festivals 1978–80*

1978
Richard Alston
Rosemary Butcher
Dancemakers – Arianna
 Economou, Sarah
 Willis, Laurie Booth
 (Dartington College
 Students)

Maedée Duprès
Fergus Early
Mary Fulkerson (USA)
Katherine Litz (USA)
Susan Motycka (USA)
Marsha Paludan (USA)
Steve Paxton (USA)

Janet Smith
Ian Spink
Nancy Topf (USA)
Miranda Tufnell
Nancy Udow (USA)

1979
Richard Alston
Patricia Bardi (USA)
Laurie Booth (UK) and
 Steve Paxton (USA)
Rosemary Butcher
Emilyn Claid

Barbara Dilley (USA)
Mary Fulkerson (USA)
Pauline de Groot
 (Holland)
Lisa Kraus (USA)

Marsha Paludan (USA)
Steve Paxton (USA)
Miranda Tufnell
Nancy and Mike Udow
 (USA)

1980
Richard Alston
Laurie Booth
Mia Borgetta
Susan Buirge (France)
Rosemary Butcher
Dartington College
 student group
Sarah Carter, Tricia
 Durdey and Sue
 Robinson
Maedée Duprès
Adrianna Economou
 (Cyprus)

Anne Eriksen and Leif
 Heines (Norway)
Kate Flatt and Tim
 Lamford
Mary Fulkerson (USA)
Pauline De Groot
 (Holland)
Sue MacLennan
Oslo dance school
 group – Sidsel
 Byhring, Lisa Ferner
 and Regni Kierulf
 (Norway)

Steve Paxton (USA)
Mary Prestidge and
 Carol DeVaughn
Kirstie Simson
Albert Reid (USA)
John Rolland (USA)
Janet Smith
Wind Witches (Sweden)

Sources: Dance at Dartington archive material at Dartington College of Arts (programmes, lists of participants and correspondence) and reviews.

Appendix 7: *Artists in the Dance Umbrella Festivals 1978, 1980*

1978
From Britain
Richard Alston and Dancers
Basic Space Dance Theatre
Rosemary Butcher Dance Company
Cycles Dance Company
Maedée Duprès
Fergus Early
EMMA Dance Company
Extemporary Dance Company
Junction Dance Company
MAAS Movers
Tamara McLorg
Janet Smith and Robert North
Leigh Warren and Yair Vardi

ICA Dance Platform: Ian Spink, Chris Bannerman, Sally Estep
For schools:
East Anglian Dance Theatre
Ludus

From the USA
Remy Charlip
Douglas Dunn
John Jones (guest teacher and choreographer[1])
Brooke Myers
Sara Rudner

1980
From Britain
Richard Alston and Dancers
Choreographers from Ballet Rambert
Rosemary Butcher Dance Company
Choreographers from LCDT
Choreographers from The Royal Ballet
Cycles Dance Company
Dancework
Maedée Duprès
Fergus Early and Jacky Lansley
EMMA Dance Company
Extemporary Dance Company
Ingegerd Lonnroth (choreographer[1])
MAAS Movers
Janet Smith (as soloist and with Robert North and Dancers)
Tim Head, Miranda Tufnell and Dennis Greenwood

From Canada
Danny Grossman Dance Company

From Holland
Pauline de Groot, Dancers and Musicians
Springplank

From the USA
Simone Forti and Peter Van Riper
David Gordon and Valda Setterfield
Elisa Monte and David Brown
Rosalind Newman and Dancers
Steve Paxton (with David Moss or Lisa Nelson)
Kathryn Posin[2] and Michael Kane
Naomi Sorkin

1. Indicates a choreographer in the Festival who did not perform.
2. Through illness, Posin had to cancel as a performer, but some of her choreography was still shown.

Sources: Jan Murray, *Dance Umbrella: A Short History* (London: Dance Umbrella, 1985), publicity and reviews.

Appendix 8: *Richard Alston – works*

Richard Alston, b. 30 October 1948.

Compiled by Angela Kane.

Abbreviations: C. costume, D. design, L. lighting, S. set.

Title	Composer	Designer	Dancers	Date, place of premiere
Transit	Ronald Lopresti	C. Jenny Henry L. Brian Benn	LSCD workshop	18 Feb. 1968, LAMDA Theatre
Matrix	Bahutu chant		Student workshop	5 Jul. 1968, Acland Burghley School
Something to Do[1]	Gertrude Stein (text)		LSCD workshop	Summer 1969, Studio 3, The Place
Still Moving Still	Shakuhachi		LSCD workshop	16 Dec. 1969, The Place Theatre
Cycladic Figure[2]	John Cage		LSCD workshop	1969, The Place
Winter Music[3]	John Cage		LSCD workshop	7 Feb. 1970, Studio 3, The Place
Departing in Yellow[4]	Michael Finnissy		LSCD workshop	1970, Studio 3, The Place
Pace	G. F. Handel		LSCD workshop	12 Jul. 1970, The Place Theatre
Nowhere Slowly[5]	K. Stockhausen		LSCD lecture- demonstra- tion	Aug. 1970, St Mary's College, Twickenham

1. The work was taken into the repertory of LCDT in 1970. The first performance was at Highbury Technical College on 29 April 1970. The first public performance was on 3 June 1970 at The Place Theatre.
2. Originally for five women. Alston re-worked this for the LSCD Demonstration Group in 1970. The work was re-titled *Fall* and it was danced by three women. The first performance was at the International Drama Festival, Birmingham University on 24 February 1970. The following year, the work was taught to second-year students and was extended to include seven women and one man.
3. Originally created for three women. In 1971, performances by the London Contemporary Dance Experimental Group were by two women and one man. A programme note dated 7 July 1971 for a performance at The Place Theatre lists the dancers as Celeste Dandeker, Christopher Banner and Eva Lundqvist.
4. The work was re-titled *Broadwhite* and re-worked for two women. The premiere was on 12 July 1970.
5. Version 1 was to Stockhausen's *Red Sails in the Sunset*. Subsequent versions used different music:
   Version 2 – Terry Riley's *Keyboard Studies* – LSCD lecture demonstration, Sunday Brunch Concert at The Place on 1 November 1970. This version included the solo *Departing in Yellow*. The solo and some of the new duet material were included in Alston's *UnAmerican Activities* in New York in 1976.
   Version 3 – Terry Riley's *In C*.
   Version 4 – Stockhausen's *Plus Minus* – LCDT premiere on 6 January 1971 at The Place Theatre. L. Nora Stapleton.
   Version 5 – Terry Riley's *Poppy Nogood and the Phantom Band* – LCDT at The Place Theatre on 12 May 1971. This version was also performed by graduating students of the LSCD at the Jeanetta Cochrane Theatre, London in 1974. In 1978, it was included in Alston's 'Doublework and Other Dances' programme at Riverside Studios; premiere on 30 May 1978.

Title	Composer	Designer	Dancers	Date, place of premiere
Goldrush[6]	Neil Young		LSCD workshop	7 Dec. 1970, The Place Theatre
End, which is never more than this instant, than you on this instant, figuring it out and acting so. If there is any absolute, it is never more than this one, you, this instant, in action, which ought to get us on	Michael Finnissy		LSCD workshop	28 Mar. 1971, The Place Theatre
Shiftwork	G. Rossini		LSCD workshop	16 Jul. 1971, Studio 3, The Place
Cold[7]	A. Adam		LSCD workshop	29 Jul. 1971, The Place Theatre
After Follows Before[8]	R. Wagner		LSCD	13 Oct. 1971, London University College Union
Who is Twyla Tharp?[9]	Spoken text by Peter and Alison Smithson		London Festival Ballet Workshop	20 Dec. 1971, Collegiate Theatre, London
Combines[10]	F. Schubert, J. S. Bach and F. Chopin. Songs by Ella Fitzgerald, Connie Boswell, Frances Langford and Mildred Bailey	Film by Sally Potter L. Michael Alston	LCDT	30 May 1972, The Place Theatre
Balkan Sobranie	Jean Françaix, I. Stravinsky and Japanese flute music (Fukushimo)	D. Myra Visser	Scottish Ballet	28 Jun. 1972, 'Tangents' programme The Close Theatre, Glasgow

6. Originally created for three women. A press release for a performance by the LSCD group at the Everyman Theatre, Liverpool on 13 March 1971 lists the cast as one male, two females.
7. The programme for the premiere indicates that this performance also included Schubert's 'Am Meer' from his *Six Heine Songs*. The work was taken into the repertory of LCDT the following year; premiere on 1 February 1972 at The Place Theatre, L. John B. Read.
8. Originally a solo, the work was danced by Jacky Lansley and Christopher Banner at The Place Theatre on 31 January 1972. The solo was included in the newly-formed Strider company's debut at the International Carnival of Experimental Sound (ICES). Then, it was danced to Gordon Mumma's music *Ambivex* and, together with a solo *Blue*, choreographed by Banner, it formed the work *Subject to Change*. (See also *Windhover*.)
9. The title was mis-spelt in the programme for the first performance. Then, it was given as *Who is Twyla Pharp?* The following year, the work was re-titled *Traffic* and was included in Strider's season at the Edinburgh Festival Fringe, at Moreton House on 28 August 1972.
10. See also *Lay-Out*.

Title	Composer	Designer	Dancers	Date, place of premiere
Routine Couple	Taped conversation of George Burns and Gracie Allen		Strider	14 Aug. 1972, The Place Theatre
Thunder	Three recordings of Harold Arlen's *Stormy Weather*		Strider	14 Aug. 1972, The Place Theatre
Tiger Balm[11]	Anna Lockwood	L. Charles Paton	Strider	14 Aug. 1972, The Place Theatre
Windhover[12]	Anna Lockwood		Strider	1 Dec. 1972, ICA Theatre, London
Headlong[13]	Anna Lockwood	L. Charles Paton	Strider	29 Mar. 1973, White Lion School, Islington, London
Interior[14]	Scott Joplin, Bulgarian folk music		LSCD workshop	18 Jun. 1973, The Place Theatre
The Average Leap Forward	Majorca Orchestra		Strider	21 Jul. 1973, The Place Theatre
Lay-Out[15]	Anna Lockwood	L. Michael Alston	LCDT	28 Aug. 1973, The Place Theatre
Rainbow Bandit[16]	Charles Amirkhanian		Strider	15 Jan. 1974, ICA Theatre, London
Blue Schubert Fragments[17]	F. Schubert	L. Michael Alston	LCDT	26 Feb. 1974, The Shaw Theatre, London

11. The work was premiered during the 1972 ICES season. It was also performed during the same season by LCDT – 22 August 1972.
12. The work begins with the solo *After Follows Before*. *Windhover* was first presented as a work in progress during Strider's season at the ICA Theatre in October 1972. Then, it was danced in silence. The completed work was premiered on 1 December and was danced to Anna Lockwood's tape of the same title. Two later productions were danced in silence – as part of *UnAmerican Activities* and as part of Alston's 'Behind the Piano and Other Dances' programme at Riverside Studios in April 1979.
13. *Headlong* was first performed as *Trailer*, i.e. as a work in progress. The London premiere of the completed work was at the Oval House on 10 May 1973. A new production by LCDT received its premiere on 15 November 1975 at Sadler's Wells Theatre. Some of the dance material was later included in *UnAmerican Activities*.
14. This was a joint collaboration. Other choreographers were Terry Berman, Diana Davies and Sally Potter.
15. This incorporated material re-worked from *Combines*. The solo, *Interior*, was later re-set as part of *Lay-Out*. (See also *Blue Schubert Fragments*.)
16. Some material was included in *UnAmerican Activities*. After returning from New York in 1977, Alston created an entirely new version of *Rainbow Bandit* for LCDT, premiere on 8 December 1977 at Sadler's Wells Theatre, C. Anne Guyon, L. Charter. The new version retained the original Amirkhanian sound tape, 'Just' but in this later version, the tape is preceded by a long section danced in silence. (See also *Rainbow Ripples*.)
17. Prior to its 1973 premiere, *Lay-Out* had been announced as *Blue Schubert Fragments*. Alston's intention had been to use sections from his earlier work, *Combines*, particularly one section – a sextet to the theme from Schubert's 'Death and the Maiden'. Due to time pressures, Alston abandoned his intention of working closely with the Schubert music and, instead, assembled a tape of sections from Anna Lockwood's *Glass Music*. In 1974, he returned to his original idea and, thus, the choreography of *Blue Schubert Fragments*. Some material was included in *UnAmerican Activities*.

Striding Out

Title	Composer	Designer	Dancers	Date, place of premiere
Soft Verges/Hard Shoulder[18]	Anna Lockwood Stephen Montague		Strider	24 Sep. 1974, Bingley College of Education, Yorkshire
Split[19]	Philip Corner (after Chopin)		Strider	26 Oct. 1974, Festival d'Automne, Musée Galliéra, Paris
Slow Field[20]	Stephen Montague		Strider	7 Nov. 1974, Mappin Gallery, Sheffield
Souvenir	E. Satie		Strider	9 Apr. 1975, Serpentine Gallery, London
Zero Through Nine	Stephen Montague		Strider	9 Apr. 1975, Serpentine Gallery
Two Saints in Three Acts			Strider	19 Apr. 1975, The Corn Exchange, Sheffield
Standard Steps	Voice of Marcel Duchamp, E. Satie		Strider	17 May 1975, Museum of Modern Art, Oxford
Compass			Strider	25 Jun. 1975, outside the Midland Group Gallery, Nottingham
Slight Adventure[21]			Mirjam Berns, Albert Reid	Autumn 1975, Studio 505, New York
Solo Soft Verges[22]			Eva Karczag	May 1976, Studio 505, New York
Edge			Christopher Banner, Siobhan Davies and Sally Hess	8 May 1976, Cunningham Studio, New York
UnAmerican Activities			Richard Alston, Christopher Banner, Siobhan Davies and Eva Karczag	8 May 1976, Cunningham Studio

18. The work became known as Soft Verges. In 1974, Alston re-worked the original duet and added an improvised first section. The work developed over several performances and the completed version was first performed at the Museum of Modern Art, Oxford on 17 May 1975. (See also Solo Soft Verges.)
19. This was a work created jointly by Alston and Strider dancer Dennis Greenwood. It was danced in two rooms with set phrases performed whenever the two dancers came together in the same space. At other times, their movements were improvised.
20. Slow Field, Zero Through Nine and Souvenir were works created in relation to an exhibition of drawings by Jasper Johns. In Slow Field, the dancers were given choices as to which movement phrases to perform.
21. This was never presented as a live performance. A film of the dance was shown at Studio 505 in the autumn of 1975.
22. This work evolved from the solo material in Soft Verges, Slow Field and Zero Through Nine. Solo Soft Verges was included in UnAmerican Activities.

Title	Composer	Designer	Dancers	Date, place of premiere
Connecting Passages[23]			Richard Alston, Ruth Barnes	20 May 1977, Cunningham Studio
Blueprint[24]		C. Jenny Henry	Extemporary Dance Company	1977–78, Hornchurch
Home Ground[25]	H. Purcell		Maedée Duprès	23 Mar. 1978, *Dance and Slide* X6 Dance Space, London
Breaking Ground[26]	H. Purcell		Richard Alston and Dancers	30 May 1978, Riverside Studios, London
Doublework[27]		C. Jenny Henry	Richard Alston and Dancers	30 May 1978, Riverside Studios
The Seven Deadly Sins	K. Weill/ B. Brecht	D. Ralph Koltai and Nadine Baylis L. David Hersey	English National Opera	22 Aug. 1978, The Coliseum, London
Distant Rebound[28]	Gordon Mumma		Richard Alston and Dancers	7 Nov. 1978, Riverside Studios
Unknown Banker Buys Atlantic	Cole Porter		Richard Alston and Dancers	7 Nov. 1978, Riverside Studios
Behind the Piano	E. Satie	C. Jenny Henry	Richard Alston and Dancers	3 Apr. 1979, Riverside Studios

23. Alston created three subsequent versions:
    Version 2 – a solo danced by Ruth Barnes in New York.
    Version 3 – a solo by Eva Karczag danced in London.
    Version 4 – a video performance of Karczag dancing in Version 3 was shown during a live performance of the same material by Julyen Hamilton. This was first performed at the Hayward Annual Exhibition in 1978 and then in Alston's 'Single Dances' programme at Riverside Studios in November 1978.
24. For a performance at the Oval House by Extemporary dancer Abigail Ben-Ari in February 1978, music by Charles Ruggles was added.
25. The solo was included in Alston's 'Doublework and Other Dances' programme at Riverside Studios in May 1978. It was also danced by Duprès at the 1983 Dance Umbrella Festival Finale.
26. Danced to Purcell's *Fantasia on a Ground*, this was created as a companion piece to *Home Ground* (which was danced to Purcell's *Musicke's Handmaid*). When danced together, the collective title was *Grounds for Dancing*. *Breaking Ground* was created as a trio for three men but at the premiere, Duprès replaced Alston due to injury.
27. A revised version, to a commissioned score by James Fulkerson, was created for the newly-formed Second Stride in 1982. The first London performance was on 8 June 1982. During a tour of America in 1982, a film of the work was made at the Dance Theatre Workshop, Bessie Schoenberg Theatre. A new production of the Second Stride version was danced by LCDT in 1984; premiere on 27 November at Sadler's Wells Theatre.
28. The music was originally created by Mumma for Christopher Banner's *Pedestrian*.

223

Title	Composer	Designer	Dancers	Date, place of premiere
Elegiac Blues[29]	Constant Lambert		Richard Alston and Dancers	3 Apr. 1979, Riverside Studios
Dumka	A. Dvořák	C. Sarah Green and Jenny Henry, L. Peter Mumford	LSCD workshop	9 Jul. 1979, The Place Theatre
Bell High[30]	Peter Maxwell Davies	D. Peter Mumford	Ballet Rambert	24 Jan. 1980, Royal Northern College of Music, Manchester
Schubert Dances[31]	F. Schubert	D. Craig Givens	Maedée Duprés (Richard Alston and Dancers)	22 Feb. 1980, Arnolfini Theatre, Bristol
The Field of Mustard[32]	R. Vaughan Williams	L. Peter Mumford	Siobhan Davies and Juliet Fisher	28 Feb. 1980, The Place Theatre
Landscape[33]	R. Vaughan Williams	S./L. Peter Mumford, C. Jenny Henry	Ballet Rambert	11 Jul. 1980, Theatre Royal, Bristol
Rainbow Ripples[34]	Charles Amirkhanian	D. David Buckland L. Sid Ellen	Ballet Rambert	21 Oct. 1980, New Theatre, Oxford
Sugar	Fats Waller		Belinda Neave	1981, Derby Playhouse
The Rite of Spring[35]	I. Stravinsky	S./L. Peter Mumford C. Anne Guyon	Ballet Rambert	6 Mar. 1981, Sadler's Wells Theatre , London

29. This was danced by the choreographer. At later performances, it was danced by Siobhan Davies.
30. See also *Hymnos*.
31. The solo was included in Duprès' 1980 solo programme.
32. A subsequent production featured the same two dancers – for a programme by Siobhan Davies and Dancers at Riverside Studios in April 1981. The duet was later performed by Fisher and Lenny Westerdijk during a Second Stride programme at the Playhouse Theatre, Oxford in April 1982.
33. In 1982, Alston reduced the number of dancers from seven to five. The date given is that of the official premiere. However, due to injury, *Landscape* replaced *Bell High* in a performance at the Everyman Theatre, Cheltenham on 9 July 1980.
34. The work incorporated material from the 1977 version of *Rainbow Bandit*. The original 'Just' tape by Amirkhanian was supplemented by a second, 'Heavy Aspirations' and the work ends with a rag-time composition by George Hamilton Green. *Rainbow Ripples* was taken into the repertory of Aterballetto in 1982.
35. Alston later reduced the number of dancers from nineteen to sixteen. Also, he created new choreography for the Chosen Maiden and, to a lesser extent, for the Elder. Both were re-costumed. A new ending in which the dance concludes after the Stravinsky music ends was also introduced at this time.

Title	Composer	Designer	Dancers	Date, place of premiere
Soda Lake[36]		Sculpture by Nigel Hall. L. Sid Ellen	Michael Clark	15 Apr. 1981, Riverside Studios
Swedish Dances	Swedish folk music		Richard Alston and Mary Fulkerson	1981 Dartington Festival
Berceuse	F. Chopin		Lucy Burge	7 Jun. 1981, Derby Playhouse (EMMA Dance Company fund-raising gala)
Night Music[37]	W. A. Mozart	D. Howard Hodgkin	Ballet Rambert	9 Oct. 1981, Theatre Royal, Newcastle
Bellezza Flash[38]	C. Monteverdi	C. Jenny Henry	Michael Clark, Siobhan Davies and Tom Jobe	14 Mar. 1982, 'The South Bank Show', London Weekend Television
Danse fra Pagodernes Rige	B. Britten	D. Antony McDonald L. Peter Mumford	Royal Danish Ballet	2 Apr. 1982, Royal Theatre, Copenhagen
Dutiful Ducks[39]	Charles Amirkhanian		Michael Clark	25 Apr. 1982, Riverside Studios
Crown Diamonds	D. Auber		Rambert Academy	5 Jul. 1982, West London Institute of Higher Education

36. Alston created the solo after seeing Nigel Hall's sculpture *Soda Lake* in the Whitechapel Gallery, London. The sculpture is hung in the dance space and the dancer relates to it throughout the solo. In 1986, the work was taken into the repertory of the Rambert company. It was first danced by Mark Baldwin on 2 February 1986 at the Royal Northern College of Music, Manchester. During a tour of Spain and Portugal in 1989, the solo was performed for the first time by a female dancer – Cathrine Price; the first performance was on 5 February 1989 at the Teatro Municipal di São Luiz, Lisbon. Subsequently, Price danced the solo in performances on tour in England. In June 1990, a video recording was made of two Rambert company dancers performing the solo – Baldwin and Amanda Britton.
37. The work was taught to Ballet Rambert School students and presented at an end-of-term performance in March 1986.
38. The work was commissioned by 'The South Bank Show'. Although Alston had worked with each of the dancers previously, this was the first time he had worked with all three together. (See also *Voices and Light Footsteps*.)
39. Alston extended the work for the Rambert company. In this version, first performed on 10 October 1986 at the Marlowe Theatre, Canterbury, the Amirkhanian tape is played twice. The original solo is succeeded by new material for three women. They enter in silence, dance briefly together then exit. They return to perform overlapping solos to successive verses of the repeated tape. In the fourth verse, they are joined by the male dancer and all four perform a repetition of the final chorus from the original solo. During the company's 1987 spring tour, the work was performed minus the male solo. At Sadler's Wells Theatre in June 1988, the fourth verse of the repeat was performed without the male dancer.

Title	Composer	Designer	Dancers	Date, place of premiere
Apollo Distraught	Nigel Osborne	S./L. Peter Mumford, C. Candida Cook	Ballet Rambert	27 Jul. 1982, Big Top, Battersea Park, London
Fantasie	W. A. Mozart	C. Anne Guyon L. Sid Ellen	Ballet Rambert	27 Jul. 1982, Big Top, Battersea Park
Chicago Brass	P. Hindemith	D. Richard Alston L. Peter Mumford	Ballet Rambert	3 Feb. 1983, Birmingham Repertory Theatre
Facing Out[40]	Lindsay Cooper	D. Peter Mumford (assisted by Candida Cook)	Maedée Duprès	15 Feb. 1983, Logan Hall, London
Java[41]	The Inkspots	C. Jenny Henry L. Peter Mumford	Second Stride	22 Jun. 1983, Leeds Playhouse
The Brilliant and the Dark	B. Britten	C. Richard Alston L. Peter Mumford	Second Stride	22 Jun. 1983, Leeds Playhouse
Midsummer	M. Tippett	S. John Hubbard C. John Hubbard and Richard Alston L. John B. Read	Royal Ballet	7 Dec. 1983, Royal Opera House, Covent Garden
Voices and Light Footsteps[42]	C. Monteverdi	S./L. Peter Mumford C. Candida Cook	Ballet Rambert	27 Mar. 1984, Sadler's Wells Theatre, London
Wildlife	Nigel Osborne	D. Richard Smith (assisted by Candida Cook) L. Peter Mumford	Ballet Rambert	17 May 1984, Theatre Royal, Brighton
Coursing	Oliver Knussen		Ashley Page, Bruce Sansom	13 Nov. 1984, Riverside Studios
Mythologies[43]	Nigel Osborne	S./L. Peter Mumford C. Candida Cook	Ballet Rambert	13 Mar. 1985, Sadler's Wells Theatre
Dangerous Liaisons	Simon Waters	C. Richard Smith (assisted by Candida Cook) L. Peter Mumford	Ballet Rambert	30 Apr. 1985, Gaumont Theatre, Southampton

40. The solo was created by Alston for Duprès' solo programme 'Face On'.
41. Alston extended the work for the Rambert company. He retained three songs from the Second Stride version – 'We Three', 'Java Jive' and 'Whispering Grass' and, to six additional songs, also by the Inkspots, he created new choreography. The original version was for six women; the Rambert version is for five men and seven women. The premiere of the version for the Rambert company was on 26 June 1985 at the Big Top, Battersea Park, London.
42. Alston extended the original trio *Bellezza Flash*. After five performances at Sadler's Wells Theatre in 1984, the trio was omitted. The work now begins with the trio 'Damigella tutta bella'. A new production of the Rambert version was danced by the Royal Danish Ballet in 1986.
43. Retaining the Osborne score and Mumford designs, Alston re-choreographed the work in 1989; the premiere was on 21 June at Sadler's Wells Theatre.

Title	Composer	Designer	Dancers	Date, place of premiere
Cutter[44]	John Marc Gowans	C. Ashley Martin-Davis L. Mike Seignior	Extemporary Dance Theatre	26 Sept. 1985, Epsom Playhouse
Zansa	Nigel Osborne	D. John Hoyland (assisted by Candida Cook) L. Peter Mumford	Ballet Rambert	30 May 1986, Alhambra Theatre, Bradford
Pulcinella[45]	I. Stravinsky	D. Howard Hodgkin L. Peter Mumford	Ballet Rambert	13 Jan. 1987, Grand Theatre, Leeds
Strong Language[46]	John Marc Gowans	C. Katharine Hamnett L. Peter Mumford	Ballet Rambert	6 Aug. 1987, Big Top, Battersea Park
Rhapsody in Blue[47]	G. Gershwin	C. Victor Edelstein L. John B. Read	Rambert Dance Company	3 Mar. 1988, Birmingham Repertory Theatre
Hymnos[48]	Peter Maxwell Davies	L. Malcolm Glanville	Rambert Dance Company	21 Oct. 1988, Marlowe Theatre, Canterbury
Cinema	E. Satie	D. Allen Jones	Rambert Dance Company	2 Mar. 1989, Birmingham Repertory Theatre
Pulau Dewata	Claude Vivier	D. Antony McDonald	Rambert Dance Company	21 Jun. 1989, Sadler's Wells Theatre
Dealing With Shadows	W. A. Mozart	C. English Eccentrics L. Malcolm Glanville	Rambert Dance Company	14 Mar. 1990, Sadler's Wells Theatre
Roughcut	Steve Reich	D. Tim Hatley	Rambert Dance Company	7 Dec. 1990, Theatre Royal, Newcastle

44. The costumes were later abandoned and the work performed in practice clothes. (See also *Strong Language*.)
45. The work was first performed as part of a double bill with Opera North's production of *Oedipus Rex*. For a season at the Big Top, Battersea Park in August 1987, Alston revised the dance material in the Gavotte and two variations. Originally, reconciliation duets for each of the three pairs of lovers, the section is now an extended duet for the two principals, Pulcinella and Pimpinella. In the second variation, they are joined by the lovers and the section concludes as before. During the 1988 Sadler's Wells season, the original four pairs of townspeople were reduced to three.
46. Alston re-worked material from *Cutter*. Sections were re-organized and the central duet from *Cutter* now opens the work. New material was created for another duet later in the work. In January 1988, Alston collaborated with Peter Mumford to create a video version of the work. Using special camera effects and editing techniques, this version is distinctly different from that performed on stage. The video version was televised on 15 May 1988 as part of Channel 4's 'Dance-lines' series.
47. The work was created for three couples and a trio. The male dancer in the trio has the only solo in the work. During the Rambert company's 1988 Spring tour, this solo was danced by a woman – Cathrine Price. For the company's 1988 season at Sadler's Wells Theatre, Edelstein re-costumed the two trio women.
48. The score for *Hymnos* is the same as that used by Alston for the first half of *Bell High*. 'Hymnos' is the title of Maxwell Davies' score. 'Bell High' is an instruction to the clarinetist indicated in the score.

Appendix 9: *Siobhan Davies – works*

Siobhan Davies, b. 18 September 1950.

Abbreviations: C. costume, D. design, L. lighting, S. set.

Title	Composer	Designer	Dancers	Date, place of premiere
Duet in *People – a work in progress* (initiated by Robert Cohan)	Shakuhachi		LCDT (Siobhan Davies and Namron)	22 May 1972, The Place Theatre, London
Relay	Colin Wood/ Bernard Watson	L. Michael Alston	LCDT	29 Aug. 1972, The Place Theatre, London
Pilot	Igg Welthy/ Stephen Barker	L. Charter	LCDT	7 Feb. 1974, Nuffield Theatre, Southampton
The Calm	Geoffrey Burgon	L. Charter	LCDT	26 Sept. 1974, Royal Northern College of Music, Manchester
Diary	Gregory Rose (new score by Morris Pert, 1976)	L. Charter	LCDT	6 Oct. 1975, Royal Court Theatre, Liverpool
Step at a Time	Geoffrey Burgon	L. Charter Photography: Michael Creevy	LCDT	4 Nov. 1976, Royal Northern College of Music, Manchester
Nightwatch (with Micha Bergese, Robert Cohan and Robert North)	Bob Downes	D. Norberto Chiesa L. Charter	LCDT	5 Apr. 1977, Sadler's Wells Theatre, London
Sphinx	Barrington Pheloung	L. Charter	LCDT	18 Oct. 1977, Royal Northern College of Music, Manchester
Then You Can Only Sing	Judyth Knight	D. Jenny Henry L. Charter and Adrian Dightam	LCDT	24 Oct. 1978, Royal Northern College of Music, Manchester
Celebration	10th and 15th century Organa and Motets arr. Nicholas Carr	D. Caroline Fey L. John B. Read	Ballet Rambert	29 Jun. 1979, Arts Centre, Christ's Hospital, Horsham
Ley Line	Vincent Brown	D. Craig Givens	LCDT	2 Oct. 1979, The Roundhouse, London
Something to Tell	Benjamin Britten	D. Antony McDonald L. Peter Mumford	LCDT	9 Oct. 1980, Theatre Clwyd, Mold
Recall	Vincent Brown	L. Peter Mumford	Siobhan Davies	27 Feb. 1980, The Place Theatre, London
If My Complaints Could Passions Move	Benjamin Britten		LSCD	18 Nov. 1980, Sadler's Wells Theatre, London
Plain Song	Erik Satie	D. David Buckland L. Peter Mumford	Siobhan Davies and Dancers	1 Mar. 1981, Theatre Royal, Stratford East, London

Title	Composer	Designer	Dancers	Date, place of premiere
Standing Waves	Stuart Dempster	D. David Buckland L. Peter Mumford	Siobhan Davies and Dancers	1 Mar. 1981, Theatre Royal, Stratford East, London
Free Setting	Michael Finnissy	D. David Buckland L. Peter Mumford	LCDT	15 Oct. 1981, Arts Centre, University of Warwick
Mazurka Elegiaca	Benjamin Britten		Linda Gibbs	Jan. 1982, King's Lynn
Rushes[1]	Michael Finnissy	D. David Buckland L. Peter Mumford	Second Stride	4 May 1982, Oxford Playhouse
Carnival[2]	Camille Saint-Saëns	D. David Buckland, Antony McDonald. L. Peter Mumford	Second Stride	13 May 1982, Arts Centre, University of Warwick
The Dancing Department	J. S. Bach	D. David Buckland L. Peter Mumford	LCDT	10 Feb. 1983, Apollo Theatre, Oxford
Minor Characters	Text by Barbara McLauren	D. Antony McDonald L. Peter Mumford	Second Stride	6 Sept. 1983, Assembly Rooms, Edinburgh
New Galileo	John Adams	D. and L. David Buckland and Peter Mumford	LCDT	14 Feb. 1984, Grand Theatre, Leeds
Silent Partners	Silence; Final section – Orlando Gough	D. David Buckland L. Peter Mumford	Second Stride	10 Oct. 1984, Gardner Centre, Brighton
Bridge the Distance	Benjamin Britten	D. David Buckland L. Peter Mumford	LCDT	7 Feb. 1985, Apollo Theatre, Oxford
The School for Lovers Danced	W. A. Mozart	L. Peter Mumford	Second Stride	15 Sept. 1985, Queen's Hall Arts Centre, Hexham
The Run to Earth	Brian Eno	D. David Buckland, Russell Mills L. Peter Mumford	LCDT	12 Feb. 1986, Congress Theatre, Eastbourne
and do they do	Michael Nyman	D. David Buckland L. Peter Mumford	LCDT	25 Nov. 1986, Sadler's Wells Theatre, London
Red Steps	John Adams	D. Hugh O'Donnell L. Charter	LCDT	19 Feb. 1987, Marlowe Theatre, Canterbury
(3 untitled pieces for TV)	David Owen (and text by Susan Sontag)	Dir.: Terry Braun D. Peter Mumford	Assembled group for Dance-lines	26 Apr. 1987, Channel 4 Television
(Play within play scene in Ron Daniels' production of *Hamlet*)			Royal Shakespeare Company	22 Sept. 1988, Wimbledon Theatre, London
Embarque	Steve Reich	D. David Buckland L. Peter Mumford	Rambert Dance Company	27 Oct. 1988, Royal Northern College of Music, Manchester
White Man Sleeps	Kevin Volans	D. David Buckland L. Peter Mumford	Siobhan Davies Company	9 Nov. 1988, Riverside Studios, London
Wyoming	John Marc Gowans	D. David Buckland L. Peter Mumford	Siobhan Davies Company	9 Nov. 1988, Riverside Studios, London

1. Taken into the repertory of Ballet Rambert, first performance, 8 May 1987, Royal Northern College of Music, Manchester.
2. Taken into the repertory of LCDT, first performance, 6 December 1983, Sadler's Wells Theatre, London.

Striding Out

Title	Composer	Designer	Dancers	Date, place of premiere
Sounding	Giacinto Scelsi	L. Peter Mumford	Rambert Dance Company	12 May 1989, Nottingham Playhouse
Cover Him with Grass	Kevin Volans	S./C. David Buckland Floorcloth: Patrick Jeffs. L. Peter Mumford	Siobhan Davies Company	8 Nov. 1989, Riverside Studios, London
Drawn Breath	Andrew Poppy	D. Hugh O'Donnell L. Peter Mumford	Siobhan Davies Company	8 Nov. 1989, Riverside Studios, London
Signature	Kevin Volans	D. Kate Whiteford L. Peter Mumford	Rambert Dance Company	24 May 1990, Theatre Royal, Brighton
Dancing Ledge	John Adams	D. David Buckland L. Peter Mumford	English National Ballet	18 July 1990, London Coliseum
Different Trains	Steve Reich	D. David Buckland L. Peter Mumford	Siobhan Davies Company	8 Nov. 1990, Sadler's Wells Theatre, London

Appendix 10: *Rosemary Butcher – works*

Rosemary Butcher, b. 4 February 1947.

Abbreviations: RBDC, Rosemary Butcher Dance Company, C. costume, D. design,
      L. lighting, S. set.

Title	Composer	Designer	Dancers	Date, place of premiere
Uneven Time			Scottish Ballet's Moveable Workshop	Feb. 1974, Edinburgh College of Art
Multiple Event			Dance Theatre Commune	Nov. 1974, Stanhope Institute, London
Pause and Loss[1]	Alan Lamb		RBDC	27 Mar. 1976, Serpentine Gallery, London
Landings	Alan Lamb		RBDC (Maedée Duprès and Julyen Hamilton)	27 Mar. 1976, Serpentine Gallery, London
Ground Line			Maedée Duprès	20 Jun. 1976, Bermondsey Docklands, London
Passage North East			RBDC	27 Aug. 1976, Arnolfini Gallery, Bristol
Multiple Event			RBDC	28 Aug. 1976, Arnolfini Gallery, Bristol
Space Between[2]			RBDC (Duprès and Hamilton)	5 Feb. 1977, Riverside Studios, London
White Field[3]	Colin Wood		RBDC	5 Feb. 1977, Riverside Studios, London
Empty Signals[4]	Colin Wood		RBDC (Dennis Greenwood)	25 Jun. 1977, Serpentine Gallery, London
Anchor Relay[5]			RBDC (Duprès and Hamilton)	14 Feb. 1978, Riverside Studios, London
Theme		Darryl Williams (photography)	RBDC	14 Feb. 1978, Riverside Studios, London
Suggestion and Action	Verbal instructions, R. Butcher		Duprès and Hamilton	28 Feb. 1978, Acme Gallery, London
Uneven Time			Duprès	23 Mar. 1978, X6 Dance Space, London

1. Later, in 1978, the duet section alone was performed, as *First Step*, first accompanied by Lamb, then by Schubert's String Quintet.
2. Later, in 1979, reworked as a duet *Space Between No. 2* for two women.
3. Later performed in silence.
4. Later performed in silence and, in 1978, reworked as a duet with Miranda Tufnell, accompanied by Bach's 1st Cello Suite.
5. Later, in 1979, reworked as a duet *Anchor Relay No. 2* for two women.

Title	Composer	Designer	Dancers	Date, place of premiere
Touch and Go			RBDC	28 Jul. 1978, Middlesex Polytechnic
Catch 5, Catch 6[6]			RBDC	25 Oct. 1978, Battersea Arts Centre, London
Dances for Different Spaces	Jane Wells		RBDC	28 Feb. 1979, Riverside Studios, London
Solo/Duo[7]			RBDC (Butcher and Sue MacLennan)	28 Feb. 1979, Riverside Studios, London
Landscape	George Crumb		Laurie Booth and MacLennan	Apr. 1979, Atlantic College, Glamorgan
Five-Sided Figure	Mark Turner, Jane Wells, Peter Wiegold	Jon Groom	RBDC	19 Feb. 1980, Riverside Studios, London
Six Tracks			RBDC (Hamilton and MacLennan)	25 Apr. 1980, Dartington College, Devon
Solo Dance for Different Spaces			RBDC (Butcher)	Summer, 1980
Solo from Instructions			RBDC (Hamilton)	Summer, 1980
Shell: Force Fields and Spaces	Jim Fulkerson	Jon Groom	RBDC	1 Apr. 1981, Riverside Studios, London
Spaces 4		Heinz-Dieter Pietsch	RBDC	27 Oct. 1981, ICA, London
Traces	Tom Dolby	Heinz-Dieter Pietsch	RBDC	27 Oct. 1982, Riverside Studios, London
Field Beyond the Maps	Jim Fulkerson		MacLennan	Aug. 1982, Edinburgh Festival
The Site	Malcolm Clarke	Heinz-Dieter Pietsch	RBDC	30 Mar. 1983, Riverside Studios, London
Imprints	Malcolm Clarke	Heinz-Dieter Pietsch	RBDC (Gaby Agis and Dennis Greenwood)	30 Mar. 1983, Riverside Studios, London
Night Mooring Stones	Max Easterly	Film: Jane Rigby Flags: D. Berridge	RBDC	13 Nov. 1984, Riverside Studios, London
Flying Lines	Michael Nyman	S. Peter Noble C. Spyros Coscinas	RBDC	26 Nov. 1985, Riverside Studios, London
Touch the Earth	Michael Nyman	D. Heinz-Dieter Pietsch L. David Richardson	RBDC	29 Apr. 1987, Whitechapel Art Gallery, London
After the Crying and the Shouting	Wim Mertens	D. Ron Haselden L. David Richardson	RBDC	24 Jan. 1989, ICA, London
d1	Jim Fulkerson	Zaha Hadid	RBDC	10 Sept. 1989, Royal Festival Hall, London
d2	Jim Fulkerson	John Lyall	RBDC	29 May 1990, Christ Church, Spitalfields, London
3d	Jim Fulkerson	John Lyall	RBDC	14 Sept. 1990, Tramway Theatre, Glasgow

6. Later, in 1979, reworked for dancers as *Catch 3, Catch 4*.
7. Listed as *Untitled* at first performance.

Appendix 11: *Ian Spink – works*

Ian Spink, b. 8 October 1947.

Abbreviations: C. costume, D. design, L. lighting.

DANCE

Title	Composer	Designer	Dancers	Date, place of premiere
Starship	MC5		Australian Ballet Workshop	8 Jul. 1971, Princess Theatre, Melbourne
Waltzes	J. Brahms		Australian Ballet Workshop	19 Jun. 1972, Princess Theatre, Melbourne
Four Explorations	S. Prokofiev		Australian Ballet Workshop	23 Mar. 1973, AMP Theatre, Melbourne
Landscape	Peter Sculthorpe		Assembled for Australian National Choreographic Competion	1973, Sydney
Game	I. Stravinsky		Dance Company of New South Wales	1974, Sydney Opera House
Aspects	H. W. Henze		Queensland Ballet	1974
Couple	H. W. Henze		Australian Ballet Workshop	29 Jul. 1974, Canberra Theatre, Canberra
Players	Romano Crevicki	Gary Johns	State Dance Theatre of Victoria	Nov. 1976, Castlemaine
New Work I	Elhay		Dance Company of New South Wales	1976, New South Wales
New Work II	I. Xenakis		Dance Company of New South Wales	1976, Sydney
Cut Lunge	Carl Vine/ Fontana		Dance Company of New South Wales	1976, Sydney Town Hall
Slow Turn	Cameron Allan		Assembled for Australian National Choreographic Competition	1977, Sydney
Two Numbers	Cameron Allan/ McMahon		Dance Company of New South Wales	1977, Sydney Opera House
Work in Progress			Tim Lamford, Michele Smith and Ian Spink	25 Nov. 1977, ICA, London
Low Budget Dances	Tim Lamford and Keith Wilson		Betsy Gregory, Smith and Spink	16 Dec. 1977, St Saviour's Church, Chalk Farm, London
Conspectus I	Stephen Srawley	Julia Peyton Jones	Gregory, Stephanie St Clair, Smith and Spink	9 Mar. 1978, Royal College of Arts, London
Duet			Basic Space Dance Theatre (Smith and Spink)	22 Mar. 1978, Dunfermline College, Scotland

Striding Out

Title	Composer	Designer	Dancers	Date, place of premiere
Trio	L. Beethoven		Basic Space Dance Theatre	22 Apr. 1978, Aberdeen Art Gallery
Elly's Arm			Ian Spink Group (Eleanor Brickhill and Smith)	16 Jul. 1978, X6 Dance Space, London
Goanna	Julian Spink (recorded radio)		Ian Spink Group	16 Jul. 1978, X6 Dance Space, London
26 Solos		Craig Givens	Brickhill, Gregory and Smith	6 Oct. 1978, Battersea Arts Centre, London
Autumn Walk	BBC sound effects		Dancers Dances	5 Nov. 1978, Tolworth Recreation Centre, Surrey
Nude Banana	Improvised text		Craig Givens	17 Feb. 1979, X6 Dance Space, London
Low Budget Dances II		Craig Givens	Ian Spink Group	28 Feb. 1979, Riverside Studios, London
Standing Swing		Craig Givens	Maedée Duprès	2 Jun. 1979, X6 Dance Space, London
Tropical Flashes	Carl Vine	Craig Givens	Basic Space Dance Theatre	Sept. 1979, Theatre Workshop, Edinburgh
Three Dances[1]	John Cage	Craig Givens	Ian Spink Group	16 Oct. 1979, Aldershot
Cloud Cover	Brian Eno	Craig Givens	Werkcentrum Dans	12 Dec. 1979, Holland
Elly's Arm II			Spink Inc.	3 Jan. 1980, Sydney Town Hall
Return	Carl Vine	Michele Smith	Australian Dance Theatre	8 May 1980, National Theatre, Melbourne
Solo	Bernd Zimmerman		Smith	12 Jun. 1980, Balcony Theatre, Adelaide
Solo with Sheep	Yuji Takahashi		Spink Inc.	19 Aug. 1980, Cell Block Theatre, Sydney
Scene Shift	Carl Vine		Spink Inc.	19 Aug. 1980, Cell Block Theatre, Sydney
Three Poems	Yuji Takahashi		Spink Inc.	19 Aug. 1980, Cell Block Theatre, Sydney
When Soft Voices Die	Alan Holley		Spink Inc.	19 Aug. 1980, Cell Block Theatre, Sydney
Dead Flight	Brian Eno	Craig Givens	Ian Spink Group	26 Nov. 1980, Riverside Studios, London
Ice Cube	Carl Vine	Craig Givens	Ian Spink Group	26 Nov. 1980, Riverside Studios, London
Kondalilla	Carl Vine and Simone de Haan	Craig Givens	Ian Spink Group	26 Nov. 1980, Riverside Studios, London
(Two untitled solos)	Michael Nyman/ The Flying Lizards		Belinda Neave	4 Feb. 1981, Aberystwyth

1. Restaged for Extempory Dance Theatre in 1982.

Title	Composer	Designer	Dancers	Date, place of premiere
Madrigal for Donna	Carl Vine	Craig Givens	Ian Spink Group	3 Mar. 1981, University of Warwick
Some Fugues	J. S. Bach	Antony McDonald	Ian Spink Group	19 Mar. 1981, Roehampton Institute, London
Blue Table	Jane Wells	Craig Givens	Ian Spink Group	23 Apr. 1981, Battersea Arts Centre, London
Being British	Mixed British music (16th century to present)	Craig Givens	Cycles Dance Company	18 Jul. 1981, Loft Theatre, Leamington Spa
Coolhaven	J. S. Bach	Antony McDonald	Werkcentrum Dans	16 Sept. 1981, Rotterdam
De Gas²	Jane Wells	Antony McDonald	Ian Spink Group	15 Oct. 1981, York Arts Centre
Canta	David Cunningham	Craig Givens	Ian Spink Group	15 Oct. 1981, York Arts Centre
Canta II	David Cunningham	Craig Givens	Ian Spink Group	6 Dec. 1981, Riverside Studios, London
Vesalii Icones	Peter Maxwell Davies		Mark Wraith	7 Mar. 1982, The Round-house, London
There is No Other Woman	I. Stravinsky	D. Antony McDonald L. Peter Mumford	Second Stride	7 May 1982, Oxford Playhouse
Threeway	Michael Birch (text) and Jane Wells	Carmel Collins	Intermedia	4 May 1983, Battersea Arts Centre, London
New Tactics (with director Tim Albery)	Orlando Gough	D. Craig Givens and Antony McDonald L. Peter Mumford	Second Stride	22 Jun. 1983, Leeds Playhouse
Lean, Don't Lean, Jasper	David Owen		P6	Mar. 1984, Bristol Dance Centre
Work in Progress	Improvised text		P6	30 May 1984, The Arnolfini, Bristol
Coco Loco	David Owen	D./L. Pamela Marre and Kate Owen	Extemporary Dance Theatre	25 Sept. 1984, Towngate Theatre, Basildon
Further and Further into Night	Orlando Gough	D. Antony McDonald L. Peter Mumford	Second Stride	10 Oct. 1984, Gardner Centre, Brighton
Slow Down	Man Jumping	C. Beatrice Berry L. Ross Cameron	Transitions Dance Company	21 Feb. 1985, Laban Centre, London
Solo			Simon Limbrick³	8 Jul. 1985, Almeida Theatre, London

2. Restaged for Basic Space Dance Theatre in 1985.
3. Limbrick, a percussionist, created the piece with Spink, making movement to initiate sound devices attached to his body.

235

Title	Composer	Designer	Dancers	Date, place of premiere
Bösendorfer Waltzes	Orlando Gough	D. Antony McDonald L. Peter Mumford	Second Stride	30 Jan. 1986, The Arnolfini, Bristol
Mercure	E. Satie arr. Harrison Birtwistle	D. Catherine Felstead and Antony McDonald L. Paul Pyant	Ballet Rambert	11 Jun. 1986, Sadler's Wells Theatre, London
Weighing the Heart	Orlando Gough	D. Antony McDonald L. Peter Mumford	Second Stride	21 May 1987, Gardner Centre, Brighton
Left-handed Woman	John Thorne	D. John Thorne	Belinda Neave	16 Mar. 1988, Chapter Arts Centre, Cardiff
Dancing and Shouting	Evelyn Ficarra	D. Antony McDonald L. Tina MacHugh	Second Stride	6 Oct. 1988, Towngate Theatre, Basildon
Heaven Ablaze in his Breast	Judith Weir	D. Antony McDonald L. Peter Mumford	Second Stride	5 Oct. 1989, Towngate Theatre Basildon
Lives of the Great Poisoners	Writer: Caryl Churchill. Composer: Orlando Gough. Co-Director: James McDonald	D. Antony McDonald L. Peter Mumford	Second Stride	13 Feb. 1991, The Arnolfini, Bristol

THEATRE

Title	Author	Director(s)	Company*	Date, place of premiere
War Crimes	(based on Peter Carey novel)	Tim Albery		18 Nov. 1981, ICA, London
Secret Gardens	(based on Frances Hodgson Burnett story and other sources)	Tim Albery, Antony McDonald,[4] Geraldine Pilgrim and Ian Spink		21 Jan. 1983, ICA, London
Under Western Eyes	(based on Joseph Conrad novel)	Tim Albery	Ro Theatre Company	10 Dec. 1983, Ro Theatre, Rotterdam
The Winter's Tale	Shakespeare	Adrian Noble	Royal Shakespeare Company	28 Aug. 1984, Scunthorpe
The Crucible	Arthur Miller	Barry Kyle and Nick Hamm	Royal Shakespeare Company	31 Aug. 1984, Scunthorpe

*If not specially assembled group.

4. McDonald, Spink's regular designer, collaborator and eventually Associate Director of Second Stride, has also designed frequently for theatre and opera productions with which he has been involved: apart from *Secret Gardens*, the theatre pieces *War Crimes* and *Under Western Eyes* and the operas *Orlando, The Midsummer Marriage* and *The Trojans* (the latter two operas co-designed with Tom Cairns).

Title	Author	Director(s)	Company*	Date, place of premiere
A Mouthful of Birds	Caryl Churchill and David Lan	Ian Spink and Les Waters	Joint Stock Theatre Group	2 Sept. 1986, Birmingham Repertory Theatre
The Winter's Tale	Shakespeare	Tom Cairns and Stephen Pimlot	Crucible Theatre Company	16 Nov. 1987, Crucible Theatre, Sheffield
For the Love of the Nightingale	Timberlake Wertenbaker	Gary Hines	Royal Shakespeare Company	27 Oct. 1988, The Other Place, Stratford

OPERA

Title	Composer	Director	Company	Date, place of premiere
Death in Venice[5]	B. Britten	Jim Sharman	South Australian State Opera	6 Mar. 1980, Festival Theatre, Adelaide
Mazeppa	P. I. Tchaikovsky	David Alden	English National Opera	21 Dec. 1984, The London Coliseum
Orlando	G. F. Handel	Christopher Fettes	Scottish Opera	8 May 1985, Theatre Royal, Glasgow
The Midsummer Marriage	Michael Tippett	Tim Albery	Opera North	30 Sept. 1985, Grand Theatre, Leeds
The Marriage of Figaro	W. A. Mozart	John Cox	Scottish Opera	30 Apr. 1986, Theatre Royal, Glasgow
The Trojans (Fall of Troy)	H. Berlioz	Tim Albery	Opera North	27 Sept. 1986, Grand Theatre, Leeds
The Trojans (Trojans in Carthage)	H. Berlioz	Tim Albery	Welsh National Opera	28 Feb. 1987, New Theatre, Cardiff
Tannhäuser	R. Wagner	Elijah Moshinsky	Royal Opera House	19 Dec. 1987, Royal Opera House, Covent Garden
Carmen	G. Bizet	Richard Jones	Opera North	19 Dec. 1987, Grand Theatre, Leeds
Macbeth	G. Verdi	David Pountney	English National Opera	5 Apr. 1990, The London Coliseum
Clarissa	Robin Holloway	David Pountney	English National Opera	18 May 1990, The London Coliseum
Vanishing Bridegroom	Judith Weir	Ian Spink	Scottish Opera	17 Oct. 1990, Theatre Royal, Glasgow

DANCE FOR TELEVISION (all Dance-lines Productions)

Title	Director	Music	Performers	Broadcast details
(3 untitled pieces)	Terry Braun (Designer Peter Mumford)	David Owen	Assembled group for Dance-lines	26 Apr. 1987, Channel 4
Fugue	Ian Spink (Writer Caryl Churchill)	J. S. Bach	Assembled group for Dance-lines	26 Jun. 1988, Channel 4
Heaven Ablaze in His Breast	Peter Mumford	Judith Weir	Second Stride and Vocem	18 May 1991, BBC2

*If not specially assembled group.

5. Another production of this opera, with new choreography by Spink, was filmed by Tony Palmer in 1981.

OTHER

Title	*Performers*	*Date, place of first performance*
Much ado about knitting (fashion show)	Assembled group of professional dancers	3 Apr. 1981, ICA, London

Selected general and background bibliography

BANES, SALLY. *Democracy's Body: Judson Dance Theater 1962–1964.*
Ann Arbor, Michigan: UMI Research Press, 1983.

BANES, SALLY. *Terpsichore in Sneakers: Post-Modern Dance.*
Middletown, Conn.: Wesleyan University Press, 1987.

BRINSON, PETER. *Dance as Education: Towards a National Dance
Culture.* Basingstoke: Falmer Press, 1991.

CLARKE, MARY AND CLEMENT CRISP. *London Contemporary Dance
Theatre: the First 21 Years.* London: Dance Books, 1989.

CRISP, CLEMENT, ANYA SAINSBURY AND PETER WILLIAMS (EDS). *Ballet
Rambert: 50 Years and On.* 2nd edn. Scolar Press, 1981.

MURRAY, JAN. *Dance Now: A Closer Look at the Art of Movement.*
Harmondsworth, Middlesex: Penguin Books, 1979.

ROBERTSON, ALLEN AND DONALD HUTERA. *The Dance Handbook.*
Harlow, Middlesex: Longman Group UK, 1988.

TUFNELL, MIRANDA AND CHRIS CRICKMAY. *Body, Space, Image: Notes
Towards Improvisation and Performance.* London: Virago Press,
1990.

WHITE, JOAN (ED). *Twentieth Century Dance in Britain: A History of
Five Dance Companies.* London: Dance Books, 1985.

Periodicals

Dance and Dancers
Dance Theatre Journal
The Dancing Times
New Dance

Notes to the chapters

Unless otherwise indicated, all interviews and conversations referenced have been conducted by the author.

Abbreviations: n.d. not dated.

Introduction

1. Conversations with Robert Cohan (1 March 1990) and Janet Eager (12 March 1990) informed me that the new term was coined to distinguish the Graham-based dance form from European modern dance (notes for a talk by Robin Howard in Eager's archive, n.d.) and from modern jazz and ballroom. Both terms seem to be in currency today.
2. Twyla Tharp's visit was promoted by the philanthropist Robin Howard.
3. Interview with Diana Davies, 20 July 1987.
4. Richard Alston in a panel discussion at the LSCD, 1979.
5. Fergus Early, 'Liberation notes, etc.' *New Dance* 40 (April–June 1987) p. 11.
6. Davies, Gulbenkian Dance Award application, 1973.
7. I am thinking particularly of the choreographers Miranda Tufnell and Janet Smith.
8. With hindsight, I feel that the work of Geoff Moore for the mixed-media group Moving Being presses for more attention than I have given it here.
9. Deborah Jowitt, 'Sinking into green fields' *Village Voice* (3 August 1982). Dale Harris also noted the independent identity: 'A big step for dance' *The Guardian* (24 August 1982). At that time, the only British contemporary dance company that had visited the USA was LCDT, which had performed at the American Dance Festival, New London, in 1977.
10. Note, for instance, the differences in opinion between Sally Banes and Susan Manning. Banes' application of the term is much more limited than that of Manning. She reserves it for post-expressionist styles of dance. See Susan Manning, 'Modernist dogma and post-modern rhetoric: a response to Sally Banes' *Terpsichore in Sneakers' The Drama Review*, T-120 (Winter 1988) pp. 32–39. This article was succeeded by the debate 'Terpsichore in combat boots' between the two writers in *The Drama Review*, T-121 (Spring 1989) pp. 13–16, and T-122 (Winter 1989) pp. 17–18.
11. Clement Greenberg, *Art and Culture* (Boston: Beacon Press, 1961) p. 6.
12. Sally Banes, *Terpsichore in Sneakers: Post-Modern Dance* (Middletown, Conn.: Wesleyan University Press, 2nd edn 1987) p. xiii.
13. *Ibid.* Refer also to Banes' *Democracy's Body: Judson Dance Theater 1962–1964* (Ann Arbor, Michigan: UMI Research Press, 1983).
14. Banes, 'Terpsichore in combat boots' *The Drama Review*, T-121 (Spring 1989) p. 13.
15. Banes, *Terpsichore in Sneakers*, p. xv, xx.
16. Roger Copeland, 'Merce Cunningham and the politics of perception'

in Roger Copeland and Marshall Cohen (eds), *What is Dance? Readings in Theory and Criticism* (Oxford: Oxford University Press, 1983) pp. 320, 323.

17. Banes, *Terpsichore in Sneakers*, p. xvi.
18. There is considerable disagreement about this. Charles Jencks, the architecture critic, for instance, cites several writers who call Post-Modern what he calls Late Modern, in his book *What is Post-modernism?* (London: Academy Editions, 1986) p. 38.
19. Roger Copeland, 'Postmodern dance: postmodern architecture: postmodernism' *Performing Arts Journal*, 19 (1983) pp. 28, 39.
20. Banes, 'Terpsichore in combat boots' *The Drama Review*, T-121 (Spring 1989) p. 14.
21. Banes, *Terpsichore in Sneakers*, p. xxiv, after the branch of metaphoric postmodern dance of the 1970s, pp. xxii–xxiv.
22. *Ibid.* p. xxiii. The term 'radical juxtaposition' has been used since the 1960s; for example, Susan Sontag used it in 'Happenings: an art of radical juxtaposition' in *Against Interpretation* (New York: Farrar, Straus & Giroux, 1966) pp. 263–74.
23. Banes, *Terpsichore in Sneakers*, p. xxxv.
24. David Michael Levin, 'Postmodernism in dance: dance, discourse, democracy' in Hugh J. Silverman (ed.), *Postmodernism – Philosophy and the Arts* (New York & London: Routledge, 1990) p. 221.
25. Susan Foster, 'The signifying body: reaction and resistance to postmodern dance' *Theatre Journal*, 37/1 (March 1985) p. 46.
26. Umberto Eco, *Reflections on 'The Name of the Rose'* (London: Secker & Warburg, 1989), pp. 67–68.
27. Jencks, *What is Post-modernism?*, pp. 14-30.
28. *Ibid.* p. 27.
29. Susan Manning, 'Modernist dogma and post-modern rhetoric: a response to Sally Banes' *Terpsichore in Sneakers*' pp. 35–36.

Chapter 1: The Contemporary Dance Trust
1. Note by Robin Howard in the LCDT programme, May/June 1970.
2. Interview with Howard, 13 April 1987.
3. Former LSCD students interviewed for this chapter, between 1987 and 1989, include Richard Alston, Alan Beattie, Primavera Boman, Sally Cranfield, Diana Davies, Dennis Greenwood, Betsy Gregory, Henrietta Lyons, Jacky Lansley and Sally Potter.
4. Robert Hewison makes the point that 'the Sixties did not really begin until about 1963, and that they do not fade away until 1975', in *Too Much: Art and Society in the Sixties 1960–75* (London: Methuen, 1986) p. xiii.
5. Interview with Lansley, 1 May 1987.
6. In British sculpture, this was the period of reaction against the modernist New Generation school of Anthony Caro, Phillip King and associated sculptors. See Richard Cork, 'The emancipation of modern British sculpture' in Susan Compton (ed.), *British Art in the Twentieth Century* (London: Royal Academy of Arts, 1985) pp. 46–51.
7. 'The Contemporary Ballet Trust' *The Dancing Times* (September 1969) p. 634.
8. Interview with Michael Finnissy, 15 April 1987.
9. Interview with Alston, 8 April 1987.
10. Information from: programmes and publicity; the Newsletter of The Place Society; Jane Nicholas' report on Early's work at the LSCD for the Arts Council of Great Britain.
11. Interview with Diana Davies, 20 July 1987.
12. Interview with Dick Matchett, 6 April 1988.
13. Alston in a panel discussion at the LSCD, 1979.
14. Alston admits that, given a free rein, the demonstration turned into a very free version of the Graham class technique. His publicity for his group was deliberately written to sound like Cunningham himself speaking, although its content has remained relevant to

241

Alston's thinking ever since: 'A choreographer's work is of no consequence, he provides the dancer with something to do – how they develop this with their particular equipment is the happening of a dance.' Interview with Alston, 8 April 1987.

15. Interview with Pat Hutchinson, 20 July 1987.

16. *Ibid.*

17. Gray Watson's biography of Barry Flanagan in Susan Compton (ed.), *British Art in the Twentieth Century*, p. 427.

18. For a discussion of work that encourages the spectator's objective stance, see Roger Copeland, 'Merce Cunningham and the politics of perception' in Roger Copeland and Marshall Cohen (eds), *What is Dance? Readings in Theory and Criticism* (Oxford: Oxford University Press, 1983) pp. 307–324; Copeland, 'Postmodern dance and the repudiaton of primitivism' *Partisan Review*, 50/1 (1983) pp. 101–121.

19. Susan Sontag, 'One culture and the new sensibility' in *Against Interpretation* (New York: Farrar, Straus & Giroux, 1966) p. 303.

20. The title of an article by the Pop Art theorist Lawrence Alloway in the journal *Cambridge Opinion* (1959). The 'long front' image is used frequently by Hewison in his book *Too Much* (see n. 4).

21. Primavera Boman was also a film-maker.

22. 8, 10, 12 July 1968.

23. The programme also contained a musical composition by Ronald Lloyd, and a dance by Clover Roope.

24. Peter Dockley, 'Into space' *Dance and Dancers* (July 1968) p. 30.

25. *Ibid.*, and Boman and Dockley, 'Dance in mixed-media' *Dance and Dancers* (March 1969) p. 39.

26. Interviews with Alan Beattie, 1 October 1987; Peter Logan, 11 December 1987; and Barry Flanagan, 25 February 1988. See also S. Jordan, 'British modern dance: early radicalism' *Dance Research*, 7/2 (Autumn 1989) pp. 3–15, in which

the cultural context of this thinking is more fully explained.

27. Interview with Boman, 22 August 1987.

28. Boman, 'Dance in mixed-media', p. 38.

29. Dockley, 'Into space,' p. 31. This piece was premiered at the International Student House, London, 5 May 1968.

30. Information from Beattie's notes on this piece and the author's interview with Beattie, 1 October 1987.

31. John Percival, 'Five situations at the Mermaid Theatre' *Dance and Dancers* (October 1968) p. 41.

32. Interview with Boman, 22 August 1987.

33. Dockley, 'Into space', pp. 30–32. Dockley's later work tended to introduce more semantic content, while juxtaposing diverse imagery.

34. Meanwhile, Boman had gone to the USA on a Churchill Fellowship.

35. Descriptions of the events have been taken from reviews by Lucy Venable, *The Dancing Times* (September 1969), p. 635, and by Peter Williams, *Dance and Dancers* (October 1969) pp. 25–26.

36. Programme note for *Explorations*, 24–26 July 1969.

37. Conversation with Peter Logan, 6 January 1990.

38. Geoff Moore borrowed the term 'mixed-media' from painting, where it was applied to work that used anything other than oils or ink: Moore, *Moving Being: Two Decades of a Theatre of Ideas* (Cardiff: Moving Being, 1988) p. 13.

39. Conversation with Moore, 22 June 1990.

40. Geoff Moore, 'A very moving being' *Dance and Dancers* (July 1969) p. 38.

41. John Percival, 'Moving Being at Liverpool University' *Dance and Dancers* (May 1969) p. 43.

42. Charles Marowitz, 'Moving Being: anti-dance' *The Village Voice* (27 August 1970).

43. Geoff Moore, 'A very moving being', p. 37.

44. Unless otherwise indicated, the descriptions of Moore's work are derived from the author's interviews and conversations with Moore, 20 April and 30 May 1988, and 22 June 1990.

45. Marowitz, 'Moving Being: anti-dance'.
46. The Largo from Bach's *Concerto in A minor* for four harpsichords.
47. Interview with Pamela Moore, the woman in *Trio*, 14 June 1990.
48. Percival, 'Moving Being at Liverpool University', pp. 43–44.
49. These include Peter Mumford, the Moving Being lighting designer, interviewed 9 May 1990.
50. Several details of this piece came from Bill Harpe, 'A visual LP' (unpublished review, September 1971).
51. John Ashford, Director of The Place Theatre, first drew my attention to this in interview, 26 June 1987.
52. Interview with Henrietta Lyons, 2 July 1987, upon which this discussion of her work is based.
53. This is Alston's estimation; photographs confirm his observation.
54. Interview with Alston, 8 April 1987. This account of Alston's work is based on information from this interview.
55. Selma Jeanne Cohen (ed.), 'Time to walk in space' *Dance Perspectives*, 34 (Summer 1968).
56. John Cage, 'Grace and clarity' *Dance Observer*, 11/11 (November 1944) pp. 108–109.
57. Alston has spoken of his visits to the Kasmin Gallery, London to seek solace in work by artists like Kenneth Noland, Anthony Caro and Jules Olitski.
58. Merce Cunningham, 'The impermanent art' (1955) in Richard Kostelanetz (ed.), *Esthetics Contemporary* (New York: Prometheus Books, 1978) p. 310.
59. Quoted in Peter Williams, 'Placed' *Dance and Dancers* (July 1970) p. 35.
60. *Tulane Drama Review*, 10/2 (Winter 1965).
61. Don McDonagh, *The Rise and Fall and Rise of Modern Dance* (New York: Outerbridge & Dienstfrey, 1970); (2nd edn, London: Dance Books, 1990).
62. This is discussed by Jill Johnston, 'Rainer's *Muscle*' *Village Voice* (18 April 1968).
63. Interviews with Diana Davies, 20 July 1987; Jacky Lansley, 24 April 1987; and Sally Potter, 6 April 1987. Unless otherwise indicated, the descriptions of their work that follow are based on these interviews.
64. Jill Johnston, *Marmalade Me* (New York: E.P. Dutton, 1971).
65. For further information on structural/materialist film, see Peter Gidal (ed.), *Structural Film Anthology* (London: BFI, 1976).
66. Interview with Sally Potter in *Time Out* (17–23 March 1972).
67. Clement Crisp, 'Choreographic workshop' *The Financial Times* (15 July 1974).
68. Interview with Betsy Gregory, 4 December 1989.
69. Davies' choreographic notes on *Band 7*.
70. Interview with Matchett, 6 April 1988.
71. Of course, some students undoubtedly would have realized after a while that they were not the right material for LCDT, and would have modified their aims accordingly.
72. Howard agreed with this observation in interview, 13 April 1987.

Chapter 2: Strider

1. Interview with Richard Alston, 8 April 1987.
2. The festival, 'based on a theme of myth, magic, madness and mysticism' was organized and produced by an American, Harvey Matusow, and took place at various London venues.
3. In December 1972, as part of a symposium called 'The Body as a Medium of Expression'.
4. Interview with Alston, 8 April 1987. Unless otherwise stated, information on Strider as an organization and descriptions of Alston's work stem from this interview, supported by numerous other interviews and conversations with Alston between 1984 and 1990.
5. Alston recalled in interview.
6. Information from Strider's grant application to the Arts Council, 14 January 1974.
7. Interview with Mary Fulkerson, 3 August 1987. This is the basis of my

account of Fulkerson's history in relation to Strider.

8. Information on Strider's schedule was taken from the Strider diary kept by its administrator Paul Chandler. The 1974 grant application to the Arts Council also indicates a plan to hold a dance festival directed by Strider at Dartington College in June 1974, but this did not materialize.

9. Comments by Alston and Hassall in Strider's grant application to the Gulbenkian Foundation, 14 April 1974.

10. 'Enormous tensions within the group' in the early days are also noted in the minutes of the Arts Council meeting with Strider, 2 December 1974.

11. Richard Alston, 'Movement and people first' *Dance and Dancers* (June 1978) p. 23.

12. Strider's grant application to the Arts Council, 14 January 1974.

13. However, this kind of circuit (apart from the galleries) had already been carried out, since 1964, by The Royal Ballet's educational group Ballet for All.

14. The problems of regional touring are raised in Jane Nicholas' notes on Strider's Second General Meeting, 11 February 1975, and her note on the Arts Council meeting with Strider, 2 December 1974. Nicholas joined the Council as an Officer specializing in dance in 1970. She became Director of Dance there, 1979–1989.

15. Peter Brinson, letter to the author, 10 October 1990.

16. Researching the funding of Strider, I am indebted to Jane Nicholas for her advice and expertise, also to Susan Davies, author of 'Shifts in patterns of funding for small-scale dance companies 1976-1981', unpublished MA dissertation, The City University, London, (1985). Gulbenkian Foundation and Arts Council annual reports have also been consulted.

17. This is corroborated by Jan Murray, who was an Arts Council advisor in the late 1970s, in 'Transatlantic passage' *Time Out* (25 November–1 December

1977). Murray writes: 'Again and again, when the subject of revenue grants comes up, Strider is cited as justification for not assisting new companies on a yearly basis.'

18. This is the view frequently stated by Fergus Early as he struggled to improve the funding of experimental dance in the late 1970s. For instance, in 'The funding of new work in dance' *New Dance*, 1 (New Year 1977) pp. 20–21.

19. Interview with Nicholas, 4 August 1977.

20. Alston's letter to the Gulbenkian Foundation, 10 May 1973.

21. Minutes of a meeting of the then Ballet Sub-Committee, 22 July 1968, report Peter Williams' feeling that there was no room at that time for a new company, and de Valois' concern that too much was being attempted too soon.

22. Minutes of the Dance Theatre Sub-Committee, 19 February 1973.

23. Robert Hewison, *Too Much: Art and Society in the Sixties 1960–75* (London: Methuen, 1986) p. xvii, 57–58, 221–223.

24. Interview with Nicholas, 4 August 1977.

25. Minutes of the Dance Theatre Sub-Committee meeting, 16 January 1974.

26. Report from John Drummond to the Arts Council, n.d., on Strider's performance at Oval House, 17 November 1974.

27. The meeting on 2 December 1974. Notes on this meeting were prepared for the Dance Theatre Sub-Committee of the Arts Council.

28. Conversation with Paul Chandler, 12 August 1987.

29. Alston, 'Movement and people first', p. 24.

30. Brinson believes that 'it may be significant that community arts were accepted for funding by the Arts Council in 1974 (The Baldry Report), just when Strider began to wind down. Letter to the author, 10 October 1990.

31. Minutes of Strider's First General Meeting, 12 November 1974.

32. Gulbenkian Foundation annual report, 1972.

33. The group modified the spacing of its work to fit the star-shaped Sonja Henie Centre.

34. *Traffic* was first performed at a London Festival Ballet workshop as *Who is Twyla Tharp?* (1971), a teasing, 'found' title that had nothing whatsoever to do with the work.

35. LCDT programme note for *Tiger Balm*, 1972.

36. Andrew Porter, 'Strider' *The Financial Times* (15 August 1972).

37. LCDT programme note for *Headlong*, 1975.

38. Information taken from the LCDT video of *Headlong*, 1975.

39. Information on Christopher Banner's work comes from programme notes and from the choreographer's comments, generously recorded in a letter from Alastair Macaulay in New York, 25 March 1988.

40. Fergus Early, 'Liberation notes, etc.' *New Dance*, 40 (April–June 1987) pp. 11–12.

41. Interview with Jacky Lansley, 24 April 1987.

42. John Percival, 'Strider at The Place' *Dance and Dancers* (October 1973) p. 48.

43. Interview with Diana Davies, 20 July 1987.

44. Interview with Sally Potter, 6 April 1987, and Dennis Greenwood, 7 April 1987.

45. Press release for the January 1974 ICA season.

46. Alston recalled in interview.

47. This discussion of Mary Fulkerson's contribution to Strider stems from my interview with her, 3 August 1987. For a more detailed assessment of Fulkerson's work, see my article, 'Mary Fulkerson' *Dance Theatre Journal*, 5/3b (1987) pp. 4–6. Mirjam Berns' *Solo ... for Myself* (1974) also introduced the process of making a dance; it was accompanied by a recording of her thoughts on the problems of devising a solo for herself. See Percival, 'Strider ICA' *The Times* (16 January 1974).

48. Percival, 'Strider at the Institute of Contemporary Arts, London' *Dance and Dancers* (March 1974) p. 40.

49. Mabel Todd, *The Thinking Body* (1937: reprint Brooklyn: Dance Horizons, 1972).

50. Noted by Eva Karczag in a letter to me, 9 July 1990. I also interviewed Karczag, 26 March 1988.

51. The title *Slow Field* comes from a 1962 painting by Jasper Johns.

52. The source of the programme note is biographical. In the 1960s, Johns had a home at Edisto Beach and visited Tokyo.

53. Harold Arlen's song *Stormy Weather* sung by Frances Langford, Lee Wiley and Connie Boswell.

Chapter 3: X6

1. Susan Davies, 'Shifts in patterns of funding for small-scale dance companies 1976–1981' (unpublished MA dissertation), The City University, London, (1985) Table 1.1, p. 22.

2. ADMA was dissolved in 1984.

3. Robert Hewison, *Too Much: Art and Society in the Sixties 1960–75* (London: Methuen, 1986) pp. 221–2.

4. Peter Williams, 'The way ahead' *Dance and Dancers* (November 1976) p. 15.

5. Committee status meant that dance had direct representation at Council level. Dance achieved full panel status in 1980. In relation to the total dance budget, funding for New Dance remained small from the late 1970s through into the 1980s. Short term project grants remained the means of funding for nearly all experimental artists, however much their experience, offering no promise of continuity.

6. Another Many Ways of Moving Congress was held at Theatre Clwyd in 1978, organized by the Welsh Dance Association.

7. Fergus Early, 'Liberation notes, etc.' *New Dance* 40 (April–June 1987) p. 12. This is the paper given at the May 1986 Chisenhale/NODM weekend.

8. Interview with Early, 6 April 1989. Unless otherwise indicated, all Early's

comments stem from this interview. The same noting procedure has been used for all other interviews with artists in this chapter.

9. A 1975 application to the Arts Council stated the intention to make X6 a centre for radical research and experiment.

10. Arts Council minutes suggest that Early's interests were unsupported.

11. Interview with Mary Prestidge, 17 February 1989.

12. Early, 'Liberation notes, etc.', p. 12.

13. Early, 'A good year' *New Dance*, 5 (New Year 1978) p. 3.

14. Early, 'Naples' *New Dance*, 9 (New Year 1979) p. 11.

15. Dance Organisation publicity leaflet, 1975.

16. Dance Organisation press release, April 1975.

17. Interview with Jacky Lansley, 22 July 1989.

18. The Collective's taped response as a group to an early draft of this chapter, 28 November 1989.

19. Early, 'Liberation notes, etc.', p. 10.

20. Emilyn Claid, 'New Dance' *New Dance*, 3 (Summer 1977) p. 2.

21. Ramsay Burt and Michael Huxley continue this argument in 'La nouvelle danse: comment ne pas jouer le jeu de l'establishment' in Michèle Febvre (ed.), *La danse au défi* (Montréal: Parachute, 1987) pp. 149–76. They examine New Dance of both the 1970s and 1980s as an essentially oppositional form that uses as points of resistance the structures through which dance is produced and reported, attitudes towards the body, male and female imagery. The article is underpinned by Marxist theory, and it argues how, by being oppositional, New Dance has been kept 'invisible' in Britain.

22. Other dance collectives preceded X6 in Britain: Strider (established 1972); and Cycles, Another Dance Group and the Cambridge Contemporary Dance Group (all established 1974).

23. Interview with Paul Burwell of the London Musicians Collective, 23 February 1989.

24. Interview with Claid, 20 March 1989.

25. Interview with Anna Furse, 27 April 1989.

26. Confirmed by Jane Nicholas, then Director of Dance at the Arts Council, in interview, 22 March 1989.

27. This remark needs qualification. X6 Collective members had work, outside as well as within X6.

28. The information on teaching at X6 comes from interviews with all the Collective members. See also Claid, 'Teaching practice' *New Dance*, 1 (New Year 1977) p. 11.

29. Programme note on contact improvisation for performances of Steve Paxton and Company, Riverside Studios, 24–29 March 1981. Paxton originated the contact improvisation form in 1972.

30. Patricia Bardi publicity leaflet 'Dancing in the Body', 1979; Peter Hulton's interview with Bardi, 'The presence of the organs in dancing' *Theatre Papers* (Dartington College), 5 (1979).

31. Early's description.

32. Maedée Duprès' taped response to the author, 11 April 1989.

33. Lists of performers and teachers at X6 have been drawn from programmes housed in the Chisenhale Dance Space archive, and in a variety of personal archives.

34. The following account of the work produced at X6 is based on articles in *New Dance*, also on interviews/conversations with the Collective and regular core community at X6, as well as Sue MacLennan and Rose English.

35. Conversation with Snaith, 4 April 1989.

36. The Collective's taped response as a group to an early draft of this chapter.

37. Interview with Sue MacLennan, *Dance Theatre Journal*, 7/2 (Autumn 1989) p. 9.

38. Kit Gerould, 'Nocturne' *New Dance*, 13 (New Year 1980) p. 14.

39. Description based on my own viewing of the dance in Dance Umbrella and Riverside dance seasons.

40. Early, 'Dances for small spaces: a diary' *New Dance*, 2 (Spring 1977) p. 9.

41. *Ibid.*
42. My own observations, based on Early's performance of the *Gymnopédies* at the Study of Dance Conference, University of Surrey, April 1983.
43. Press release on *Two Man, One Man*.
44. Manley is a district of Sydney, Australia.
45. Early, 'Naples', p. 11.
46. Description based on Jane Nicholas' report on *Naples* for the Arts Council.
47. The last major production with which X6 members had been involved was *Oceanflight* (1977), Brecht's cantata about Lindbergh. This was a collaboration between Duprès, Early, Givens and Prestidge with Central School design students and singers from the Guildhall School of Music. It was performed at the Jeannetta Cochrane Theatre.
48. Early, 'Liberation notes, etc.', p. 12.
49. See Nadine Meisner, 'Jacky Lansley and Rose English at the X6 Dance Space' *New Dance*, 11 (Summer 1979) p. 20.
50. This notion had already been discussed by the feminist film writer Laura Mulvey in her influential article about the controlling male gaze (and the female gaze styled according to male fantasy), 'Visual pleasure and narrative cinema' *Screen*, 16/3 (Autumn 1975) pp. 6–18. It had also been discussed by John Berger, *Ways of Seeing* (London: BBC and Penguin, 1972) p. 46. Yvonne Rainer had drawn parallels between the theatrical relationship of performer/audience and man/woman social relationships in the film *This is the Story of A Woman Who ...* (1974); at one point, for instance, a projected title reads 'his very gaze seems to transform her into a performer'.
51. This description of *Dance Object* is based on my unpublished review of the piece and interview with Lansley.
52. Lansley, 'Women Dancing' *New Dance* 6 (Spring 1978) p. 11.
53. *Ibid.*, p. 10.
54. See Stefan Szczelkun, 'Going back' *New Dance*, 2 (Spring 1977) pp. 14–15; Prestidge, 'Sarah Green *Family Background*' *New Dance*, 3 (Summer 1977) p. 15; Szczelkun, 'X6 performances' [including a review of Prestidge's Film Event], *New Dance*, 1 (New Year 1977) p. 12; Julia Blackburn, 'Choice and presence' *New Dance*, 2 (Spring 1977) p. 13; Will Milne, 'Maedée at X6 Butler's Wharf' *Readings*, 2 (1977) p. 3.
55. Sarah Green, '*Making a Baby*: Emilyn Claid' *New Dance*, 11 (Summer 1979) p. 6.
56. Recorded in Stuart Hopps' report on Claid's performance at X6 (7 May 1977), for the Arts Council.
57. Duprès' taped response to the author, 11 April 1989, and a later live interview, 21 July 1989.
58. As a result of Duprès' experience dancing with Rosemary Butcher's company, but also, she recalls, as a result of study with Bob Solomons, an American guest teacher at the LSCD.
59. Milne, 'Maedée at X6', p. 3.
60. Programme instructions for *Overall White*.
61. Duprès, 'A dance score' *New Dance*, 9 (New Year 1979) p. 11.
62. Prestidge's notes to the author, 7 January 1990.
63. The creator's notes on *Around Rolling*, 1978.
64. Interview with Craig Givens, 23 March 1989.
65. Lansley, 'Writing' *New Dance*, 1 (New Year 1977) p. 3.
66. Advertisement, *New Dance*, 10 (Spring 1979) p. 20.
67. Early, '*New Dance*: how the magazine is made' *New Dance*, 4 (Autumn 1977) III.
68. *New Dance* had more in common with the American magazine *Contact Quarterly* started in 1975, an outcome of the contact improvisation movement.
69. For instance, Jane McDermott's letter to *New Dance*, 6 (Spring 1978) pp. 20–21; Furse in 'Speakout' *New Dance*, 10 (Spring 1979) p. 3, and *New Dance*, 11 (Summer, 1979), p. 3.
70. Lansley, 'Women dancing', pp. 10–11.
71. Furse, 'Body politics: 2. From outside in to inside out' *New Dance*, 17 (New Year 1981) pp. 9–11.

72. Rose English, 'Alas alack: the representation of the ballerina' *New Dance*, 15 (Summer 1980) pp. 18–19.

73. Jan Murray, for instance, refers to the debt to Judson and 'release' in her report on Lansley's *Dance Object* (1977) for the Arts Council, and Geoff Moore mentions the precedents of Cunningham/Cage and the Judson generation in his letter to *New Dance*, 7 (Summer 1978) p. 10.

74. Roger Copeland, 'Postmodern dance and the repudiation of primitivism' *Partisan Review*, 50/1 (1983) p. 109; and his 'Postmodern dance: postmodern architecture: postmodernism' *Performing Arts Journal*, 19 (1983) pp. 32–3.

75. Szczelkun, 'A commentary' *New Dance*, 3 (Summer 1977) p. 20.

76. The Collective's taped response to the author.

77. Minutes of the New Dance and Mime Sub-Committee meetings, 6 December 1979, and 2 June 1980.

78. The Collective's taped response to the author.

79. Interview with Betsy Gregory, 23 March 1989.

80. Conversation with Rosemary Butcher, 22 May 1989.

81. Kate Flatt's taped response to the author, 18 June 1989.

82. Lansley in interview with Andy Solway, *New Dance*, 39 (January–March 1987) p. 18.

83. Lansley in 'X6 leaves the Wharf' *New Dance*, 16 (Autumn 1980) p. 14.

84. The name was changed from English Dance Theatre to English New Dance Theatre in 1989.

85. Interview with Green, 28 March 1989.

86. Although some groups, and DV8 Physical Theatre is the most prominent example, still make politics explicit in their work.

Chapter 4: Sharings and Showcases

1. Indicated in ADMA's 1978 grant application to the Arts Council.

2. Jym MacRitchie (Natural Dance Workshop) and Bob Carlisle, 'Natural dance – an interview' *New Dance*, 7 (Summer 1978) p. 19.

3. 'Digs' *New Dance*, 7 (Summer 1978) p. 2.

4. Sarah Rubidge, 'Dance Umbrella and New Dance' *Dance Theatre Journal*, 6/3 (Autumn 1988) p. 8.

5. Fergus Early, 'Cycles Dance Company' *New Dance*, 3 (Summer 1977) p. 12.

6. C. G. Jung, *Memories, Dreams, Reflections*, recorded and edited by Aniela Jaffe, trans. Richard and Clara Winston (London: Collins, 1963) p. 205.

7. The description stems from Jan Murray, 'ADMA Festival at Action Space Drill Hall' *Dance and Dancers* (August 1977) p. 34; Vincent Meehan, 'Timothy Lamford and Julyen Hamilton' *New Dance*, 3 (Summer 1977) p. 12; conversation with Lamford, 9 July 1990.

8. Emilyn Claid, 'Fergus Early and Craig Givens, Dance of the Hours from The Ballet of the Night' *New Dance*, 3 (Summer 1977) p. 13.

9. Murray's Arts Council report on the 1978 ADMA Festival.

10. 'Helen Crocker at the ADMA Festival' *New Dance*, 7 (Summer 1978) pp. 4–5.

11. 'Digs' *New Dance*, 8 (Autumn 1978) p. 2.

12. Minutes of the New Dance and Mime Sub-Committee meeting, 13 September 1978.

13. Mary Malecka, '2nd ADMA Festival' *New Dance*, 7 (Autumn 1978) pp. 3–4; 'Digs', *New Dance*, 8 (Autumn 1978) p. 2.

14. 'Mary Fulkerson, an interview' *New Dance*, 7 (Summer 1978) p. 14; Mary Fulkerson, 'Regarding the Festival' *New Dance*, 32 (Spring 1985) p. 17.

15. Publicity for the 1978 Dance at Dartington Festival.

16. 'Regarding the Festival', p. 17.

17. Murray, 'Dance at Dartington' *Dance and Dancers* (August 1978) pp. 34–5; Murray, 'Dance Weekend at Dartington College of Arts, Devon' *Dance and Dancers* (July 1979) p. 38.

18. Claire Hayes, 'Dance at Dartington' *New Dance*, 7 (Summer 1978) p. 15.

19. Interview with Fulkerson, 30 April 1983.
20. Murray, 'Dance at Dartington' *Dance and Dancers* (August 1978) p. 34.
21. Fulkerson left Dartington to become Head of the School for New Dance Development at the Amsterdam Theatre School.
22. Robin Howard gave a talk at the 1979 Dance at Dartington Festival.
23. Murray, 'Dance at Dartington', p. 35.
24. Interview with Fulkerson, 30 April 1983.
25. Murray, 'Dance Weekend at Dartington College of Arts, Devon', p. 38.
26. In 1979, Paxton performed a solo version of his *Pa . . . rt* (1978) (see p. 74).
27. Barbara Dilley originally performed under the name Barbara Lloyd.
28. Programme for Dance Umbrella '80, quoting from Miranda Tufnell and her collaborator Dennis Greenwood.
29. During the 1978 festival, Peter Curtis, an ex-Rambert dancer and tutor at Dartington College 1972–74, taught a Graham-influenced class.
30. Stephanie Jordan, 'Natural philosophy' *The New Statesman* (2 May 1986).
31. 'Dance at Dartington' *New Dance*, 11 (Summer 1978) p. 9.
32. See, for instance, Mary Prestidge, 'Dartington – the dance festival 1978–1987' *New Dance*, 40 (Easter 1987) p. 19.
33. Murray, *Dance Umbrella: A Short History* (London: Dance Umbrella, 1985) p. 3.
34. Interview with Early, 6 April 1989.
35. On Umbrella books for the first year, 1980, were Janet Smith and Dancers, the Ian Spink Group, Maedée Duprès, Tara Rajkumar, Siobhan Davies and Dancers, and Ingegerd Lonnroth.
36. Fiona Dick, 'Ten years of development and change' *Dance Theatre Journal*, 6/3 (Autumn 1988) p. 29.
37. Murray, 'Everybody's brolly' *Time Out*, (3–9 November 1978); Ruth Glick interviewed by Sarah Green in 'Dance Umbrella: trying to comprehend' *New Dance*, 13 (New Year 1980) p. 10. This justification for selection conflicts with Fiona Dick's later statement in 'Ten years of development and change', p. 29: 'It is hard now to believe that the first Dance Umbrella Festival was able to include virtually every British artist or company then in existence. There were a few dancers unavailable at the right time, but otherwise the groups selected themselves.'
   In *Dance Umbrella: A Short History*, p. 8, Murray refers to an open-door policy for every one working 'professionally'.
38. Dance Umbrella's report on its 1978 festival.
39. Dance Umbrella's report on its 1980 festival.
40. Paper presented for discussion at the meeting of the Arts Council's Dance Theatre Sub-Committee, 9 November 1977.
41. Glick, 'Dance Umbrella: trying to comprehend', pp. 10–11.
42. Paper presented by Val Bourne for discussion at the meeting of the Directors of Dance Umbrella, 22 July 1980.
43. Umbrella's 1978 report.
44. For instance, Mary Clarke, 'Dance Umbrella 80' *The Dancing Times* (March 1980) p. 387; John Percival, 'Too much of a good thing?' *Dance and Dancers* (February 1980) pp. 24, 27.
   At one point, Pina Bausch was scheduled to perform at the 1980 festival, but this never materialized.
45. Umbrella's 1980 report.
46. This organization superseded ADMA (dissolved 1984) as an information-sharing body and pressure group for dance.
47. Minutes of the meeting of the Directors of Dance Umbrella, 22 July 1980.
48. This is also Sarah Rubidge's opinion, 'Dance Umbrella and New Dance' p. 7.
49. Some American performers were not so innovatory, for example, the Elisa Monte and David Brown duo (both Graham dancers) and Naomi Sorkin.
50. Percival, 'Too much of a good thing?', p. 27.

51. Murray, 'Trans-Atlantic impetus' *Dance and Dancers* (January 1979) p. 22.

52. 'Digs' *New Dance*, 8 (Autumn 1978) p. 2.

53. Interview with Val Bourne, 29 March 1989. Bourne's other comments quoted in this chapter stem from this interview.

54. Rubidge, 'Dance Umbrella and New Dance', p. 8.

55. Interview with Early, 6 April 1989.

56. Publicity for the 1989 Dance Umbrella Festival.

57. As Administrator of The Place Theatre in the early 1980s, Caroline Peacock re-opened the programme of dance and theatre there after a dark period. The programme was considerably enlarged after John Ashford was appointed Director of the Theatre in 1986.

Chapter 5: Richard Alston

1. Public interview with Richard Alston for the Society for Dance Research Study Day on Richard Alston, The Haymarket Theatre, Leicester, 11 March 1989.

2. *Ibid.*

3. Interview with Alston, 9 April 1987. Unless otherwise indicated, all Alston's comments and opinions cited stem from my numerous interviews and conversations with him between 1984 and 1990.

4. The *Combines* film was shown to the author by Potter. This is the earliest existing filmed record of Alston's work. Information on the content of this piece has been taken from interviews with Alston, and with Sally Potter, 21 January 1988. It has also been taken from reviews by Peter Williams, John Percival and Noel Goodwin in *Dance and Dancers* (July 1972) pp. 31–35; James Monahan in *The Dancing Times* (July 1972) p. 535.

5. For my biographical material, I am indebted to Angela Kane, 'Richard Alston: a discussion of his dances and choreographic style' (unpublished MA dissertation), The Laban Centre for Movement and Dance (1988), and her 'Richard Alston: twenty-one years of choreography' *Dance Research, 7/2*

(Autumn 1989) pp. 16–54. Other key sources are Richard Alston, 'Movement and people first' *Dance and Dancers* (June 1978) pp. 22–25; John Percival, 'How Richard Alston came to be a pioneer' *The Times* (27 March 1980); Tom Sutcliffe, 'Steps in the right direction' *The Guardian* (21 August 1978).

6. Sutcliffe, 'Steps in the right direction'.

7. Alston also performed in her *Dance Score* at the 1978 ADMA Festival.

8. Alston in interview with Richard Davies, 'Ringing the changes' *Classical Music* (12 April 1980).

9. Stephen Goff, 'Classical gas' *Time Out* (18 March 1983).

10. Stephanie Jordan, 'Step by step' *The New Statesman* (2 April 1982); Alastair Macaulay, 'Alston and Ashton' *Performance* (June 1982) pp. 36–38; Macaulay, 'Processes, connections, bloodlines: Ballet Rambert' *Dance Theatre Journal*, 1/3 (August 1983) p. 36; Bryan Robertson, 'Ballet' *Harpers & Queen* (March 1982) p. 178; David Vaughan, 'The evolution of ballet Rambert' *Dance Magazine* (October 1982) p. 77.

11. Alston, 'Working with bodies – Richard Alston' The South Bank Show, London Weekend Television (14 March 1982).

12. Alston, 'Movement and people first', p. 23, and quoted by Mary Clarke and Clement Crisp in *Making a Ballet* (London: Studio Vista, 1974) pp. 81–82. Alston was edging towards using musical structure in two earlier pieces, *Pace* (to Handel, 1970) and *Blue Schubert Fragments* (1974).

13. Interview with Alston in *Labanews*, 2/3 (August 1982) p. 7, which was a version of an open discussion at the Laban Centre Summer School, 1981; Alston in public discussion at the Laban Centre, 16 December 1986.

14. Nigel Osborne's programme note about the music.

15. Barbara Newman, 'Richard Alston' *The Dancing Times* (January 1987) p. 316.

16. Alston explained the differences between the two versions of *Mythologies* in a

lecture-demonstration with Nigel Osborne at Sadler's Wells Theatre, part of the Almeida Festival, 23 June 1989.

17. Alston explained this in a public discussion at the Laban Centre, 30 July 1985.

18. Alston's reference to popular culture also derives from the influence of Twyla Tharp.

19. Crisp, 'New ballets/Covent Garden' *The Financial Times* (8 December 1983).

20. Alston alludes here to a Renaissance literary type.

21. Alston quoted by Alexander Bland in 'Creating a new Rite' *The Observer* (1 March 1981).

22. This has been noted by Kane in 'Richard Alston: a discussion of his dances and choreographic style', pp. 116–7.

23. See Sophie Constanti, 'Richard Alston – the humanistic approach' *Dance Theatre Journal*, 7/2 (Autumn 1989) p. 15.

24. Alston in interview with Judith Mackrell, 'Step by step approach' *The Independent* (30 March 1989).

25. See, for instance, Alston, 'Movement and people first' p. 23; Alston in interview with Macaulay, 'Java ready to erupt' *The Guardian* (26 July 1985); Newman, 'Richard Alston' p. 316. Alston has responded with versatility and sensitivity to dancers of various styles and trainings.

26. Alston quoted by Goff in 'Classical gas', and by Richard Davies in 'Two dance premieres at the Garden' *Classical Music* (10 December 1983).

27. Arlene Croce, 'Dancing: artists and models' *The New Yorker* (1 November 1982).

28. This principle was first theorized by the American modern dance pioneer Doris Humphrey. Alston has used the principle in a more subdued and less emotionally intense manner than Humphrey.

29. For a comparison between Alston and Cunningham styles and technique classes, see Howard Friend and Stephanie Jordan, 'Britain and Cunningham' *Dance Theatre Journal*, 3/2 (Summer 1985) p. 14. It is interesting that characteristics of Alston's move-

ment style have been shared by many teachers of 'Cunningham-based' technique in Britain. Indeed, these characteristics became the root of a technique class that has sometimes borne little relation to Cunningham.

30. The notion of ease also stemmed from Alston's T'ai Chi experience at the LSCD, interview with Alston, 23 March 1985. Alston told Kane that he was impressed by Astaire's combination of ease and speed, (Kane, p. 132).

31. Alston's technique classes began to incorporate these balletic elements at about this time.

32. Macaulay notes this in 'Processes, connections, bloodlines', p. 38, although I propose an alternative to his characterization of *épaulement* here.

33. Although I cannot comment on *The Prince of the Pagodas*, which I was unable to see.

34. And the antecedent to *Voices and Light Footsteps*, for television, *Bellezza Flash* (1982), in 'Working with bodies – Richard Alston.'

35. Alston, 'Wildlife' *Dancemakers*, BBC2, 13 July 1986.

36. This became very clear when *Nowhere Slowly* (1970) was revived for the Study of Dance Conference, University of Surrey, 11 April 1983.

37. The video recording of this piece was made in Australia in 1977.

38. Alston, 'Two recent dances' *Artscribe*, 16 (February 1979) p. 44.

39. The description of *Soda Lake* is based on my viewing of the piece, and on the description by Sarah Rubidge and Alston in their *Soda Lake* teaching notes.

40. John Cage, 'Grace and clarity' *Dance Observer*, 11/11 (November 1944) pp. 108–9.

41. Crisp, 'Ballet Rambert/Battersea' *The Financial Times* (23 July 1985).

42. Alston recollected the motto from the title of a BBC 'Kaleidoscope' programme broadcast shortly after Balanchine's death, 'See the music, hear the dancing' Radio 4, (29 August 1983).

43. Macaulay, 'Rambert's Alston' *Dance Theatre Journal*, 5/3 (Summer 1987) pp. 5-6; 'Richard Alston's Rambert' *The Dancing Times* (May 1989) p. 741.
44. See note 11.
45. Interview with Alston in *Labanews* (August 1982) p. 7.
46. Croce, 'Dancing: artists and models'.
47. Interview with Alston in *Labanews* (August 1982) p. 7.
48. Alston's lecture-demonstration during the Society for Dance Research Study Day, Leicester, 11 March 1989.
49. Osborne, lecture-demonstration with Alston, 23 June 1989.
50. Alston, 'Two recent dances' p. 44.
51. *Ibid.*, p. 45.
52. Interview with Alston accompanying the video recording of *Doublework* (London: Dance Umbrella, 1983).
53. Alston used the score earlier for his *Bell High* (1980).
54. This is the letter analysis in the teaching notes by Rubidge and Alston on *Dangerous Liaisons*.
55. Certainly, this was implied by Alston's use of the word in interview, 23 September 1988.
56. I am indebted to Rubidge for her draft teaching notes on *Zansa*, which prompted this analysis.
57. Interview with Osborne, 23 September 1988.
58. Alston in interview with Richard Davies, 'Ringing the changes'; interview with Alston in *Labanews* (August 1982) p. 4. Alston had begun to use devices of simplification in *Rainbow Bandit*.
59. Kane has also referred to Alston's growing use of block formations, after his visit to New York, in 'Richard Alston: a discussion of his dances and choreographic style', pp. 114-5.
60. The Rambert policy under Alston puts the company in a unique and fascinating international position. There are no other repertory modern dance companies featuring this kind of work.
61. Macaulay, 'Notes on dance classicism' *Dance Theatre Journal*, 5/2 (Summer 1987) p. 39.
62. Interview with Osborne.
63. David Vaughan, 'Postmodern prototype' *The Village Voice* (22 September 1987).
64. Interview with Alston, 16 December 1989.

Chapter 6: Siobhan Davies

1. The trade union Equity required that Davies adopt a new forename name (Siobhan) in order to distinguish her from another Equity member called Sue Davies.
2. Davies also performed with Ballet for All in 1971, contributing to the contemporary part of its programme.
3. Interview with Davies, 17 August 1984. Unless otherwise indicated, all Davies' comments and opinions cited stem from my numerous interviews and conversations with her between 1983 and 1990.
4. Before *Relay*, Davies had made a duet for herself and Namron within *People – a work in progress* (1972), a larger piece initiated by Robert Cohan.
5. Peter Williams, 'Contemporary maturity' *Dance and Dancers* (January 1975) p. 21; Williams, 'Defying the auguries: Graham for a British temperament' *Dance and Dancers* (January 1976) p. 19.
6. Clement Crisp, 'Sphinx', *The Financial Times* (18 November 1977).
7. Davies danced in a programme of Ian Spink's work in 1979.
8. Indicated in a letter from Richard Alston to Jane Nicholas at the Arts Council, 19 February 1973.
9. This group is discussed further in Stephanie Jordan, 'Second Stride: the first six years' *Dance Theatre Journal*, 6/3 (Autumn 1988) pp. 12–14.
10. Davies' problems with the LCDT dancing style are discussed in Judith Mackrell, 'Conversation pieces' *The Independent* (8 November 1989).
11. For instance, Clement Crisp, Mary Clarke and Alastair Macaulay.
12. Early in her career, Davies indulged her interest in narrative in short-story writing rather than in choreography. While a student, she had several short stories published.

13. Allen Robertson, 'Meaning on the move' *Time Out* (17–23 May 1984).
14. Interview with Davies, 17 August 1984.
15. Interview with Davies on 'Kaleidoscope' (BBC Radio 4), 6 June 1985.
16. Davies' programme note on *Something to Tell*.
17. See Colin Nears, 'Bridging a distance' *Dance Research*, 5/2 (Autumn 1987) pp. 46, 48. This article, which discusses the televising of *Bridge the Distance*, indicates that Davies 'had undertaken to the publishers of Britten's work not to create a narrative work' (p. 48).
18. Davies, The South Bank Show, London Weekend Television, 17 March 1985.
19. Davies explained these sources in a public discussion after the first performance of *Wyoming*, 9 November 1988.
20. Davies in Digital Dance Interview (video) (Reading: Digital, 1989).
21. This choreographic technique she also uses for abstract purposes.
22. Generally, critics found more problems with Davies' 'narrative' works than they did with her abstract works. The restraint was not seen as the 'compelling simplicity' that Mary Clarke had once praised, 'London Contemporary Dance Theatre at Sadler's Wells' *The Dancing Times* (January 1978) p. 204.
23. Alston, The South Bank Show on Davies.
24. Davies in interview with Julie Kavanagh, 'Dual purposes' *Harpers & Queen* (May 1984) p. 208.
25. Davies supplied the background to these two pieces in interview.
26. Both *Wyoming* and *White Man Sleeps* were made with the possibility of television close-up in mind.
27. Davies in Digital Dance Interview.
28. Interview with Davies, 28 November 1986.
29. Davies, The South Bank Show on Davies.
30. The programme for the Oxford season of Rambert, February 1989, includes the following comment on *Embarque*: 'the patterns of movement and grouping of the dancers subtly shift and change, rather like the topography of the vast plains and deserts Davies travelled through across America'.
31. Noel Goodwin, 'Spiritual uplift' *Dance and Dancers* (January 1975) p. 25.
32. Davies, The South Bank Show on Davies.
33. Interview with Davies, 26 July 1988.
34. Interview with Antony McDonald, 30 June 1984.
35. McDonald became Spink's regular collaborator, and in 1988 Associate Director of Second Stride.
36. Interview with Davies accompanying the video recording of *Rushes* (London: Dance Umbrella, 1983).
37. Robertson, 'Meaning on the move'.
38. We see the same double or multiple layering of reference in some of Buckland's photographic work.
39. The Degas String Quartet.
40. However, in a very simple manner, an earlier piece in the Dance-lines 1987 programme mixes two 'characters' in streetclothes, Sally Owen and Lucy Burge, with more abstract dancing personalities. Again, Buckland indicates process on a screen covered with notes such as 'enclosed space, corner, trapped edges of TV'.
41. Davies and Spink in interview with Jann Parry, *Dance and Dancers* (January 1983) p. 18.

Chapter 7: Rosemary Butcher

1. Interview with Miranda Tufnell, 7 February 1986.
2. Interview with Butcher, 29 January 1990. Unless otherwise indicated, all Butcher's comments and opinions cited and all information related to the making of her pieces stem from my numerous interviews and conversations with her between 1984 and 1990. Descriptions of Butcher's early works have been based on video recordings (as indicated) and her own memories. Except where referenced otherwise, I have used my own observations of live performance and video when discussing the work from 1978 to 1990.

This chapter is an expansion of my essay 'Rosemary Butcher' *Dance Theatre Journal*, 4/2 (Summer 1986) pp. 6–8, 24. Other articles specifically on Butcher's career are Chris Crickmay, 'Dialogues with Rosemary Butcher' *New Dance*, 36 (Spring 1986) pp. 10–15; Nadine Meisner, 'An English pioneer' *Dance and Dancers* (February 1987) pp. 17–19, 23.

3. Maureen Hanscombe and Norma Pitfield, 'The Rosemary Butcher Dance Company' *Spare Rib* (April 1978) p. 39.

4. 'New Dance . . . What is it?' *New Dance*, 3 (Summer 1977) pp. 16–18.

5. Elaine Summers performed with her group at the Place Theatre during the 1972 ICES Festival (see p. 35).

6. Description taken from a video recording of *Uneven Time*.

7. The Butcher Company was at one point publicized to perform in the ADMA '78 Festival (on 31 May), but no performance took place.

8. Information on funding has been taken from the Arts Council file (1976–79) on Butcher and from Arts Council annual reports.

9. Edward Thorpe, *The Evening Standard* (7 March 1977).

10. Clement Crisp, 'Rosemary Butcher: ICA Gallery' *The Financial Times* (25 January 1989).

11. John Percival, 'Hard knocks' *The Times* (22 May 1986).

12. Later, the company performed in Utrecht (1980) and Rome (1981).

13. This video recording was made at Middlesex Polytechnic in 1978, when the duet, performed by itself, was called *First Step*.

14. Information on *Suggestion and Action* has been taken from Jane Nicholas' Arts Council report on the event.

15. Andrea Hill, 'Stephen Cripps, Maedée Duprès, William Henderson' *Artscribe* 12 (June 1978) p. 56.

16. Andrea Hill, 'Noticing dance' *Artscribe*, 16 (February 1979) p. 18.

17. Butcher followed the lead of Cunningham and American post-modern choreographers who have also given rule structures to their dancers.

18. Butcher, 'Fragments of a diary' *New Dance*, 1 (New Year 1977) p. 19.

19. Dancers interviewed for this chapter, in 1986, include Gaby Agis, Laurie Booth, Maedée Duprès, Sue MacLennan and Miranda Tufnell.

20. Yvonne Rainer, *Work: 1961–73* (Press of the Nova Scotia College of Art and Design, Halifax and New York University Press, 1974) p. 47.

21. *Arnolfini Dance Diary*, March 1987.

22. This perhaps betrays the influence of Lucinda Childs on Butcher.

23. Note contained in a 1978 press release.

24. *Arnolfini Dance Diary*, March 1987.

25. An experimental film of episodes from *Passage North East* (at the Arnolfini Gallery) was made by an American Colin Pahow.

26. The experience with Butcher renewed Pietsch's interest in three-dimensional work. See Hetty Einzig in *Heinz-Dieter Pietsch* (Karlsruhe: Sudwest Galerie, 1984).

27. See Butcher's 'Fragments of a diary', p. 19.

28. Allen Robertson in 'Double score' *Time Out* (3–10 February 1988).

29. Judith Mackrell, 'Kitsch and courtship at the Umbrella' *Dance Theatre Journal*, 4/1 (Spring 1986) p. 29.

30. Butcher supports this interpretation.

31. *After the Crying and the Shouting* had started out as a collaboration with a film-maker, at this stage entitled *Silent Spring*. This collaboration fell through.

32. Noted by Simon Usher in *Heinz-Dieter Pietsch*.

33. This has also been noted by Crickmay, 'Dialogues with Rosemary Butcher', p. 11.

34. See Geoff Andrew in 'Double score' *Time Out* (3–10 February 1988), in which Nyman explains the sources of his score and his performance process.

35. *Touch the Earth: A Self-Portrait of Indian Existence*, compiled by T.C. McLuhan (London: Abacus, 1973).

36. Programme note on *Touch the Earth*.

37. Caroline Pegg, 'Dancing on worn carpets: the spring tour of the Rosemary Butcher Dance Company' *New Dance*, 44 (Summer 1988) p. 14.

38. Butcher quoted by Nadine Meisner in 'Stepping out gracefully' *The Sunday Correspondent* (4 February 1990).

39. This was the venue where I first saw *d1*.

40. Significantly, Butcher turned to the ideas of the modernist architect Le Corbusier when working on *d1*. She derived ideas from his Modulor principles of proportion.

41. Peter Blake, *Mies van der Rohe: Architecture and Structure* (Harmondsworth, Middlesex: Penguin Books, 1963) p. 28.

42. Robert Venturi, *Complexity and Contradiction in Architecture* (New York: The Museum of Modern Art, 1966) pp. 16–17.

Chapter 8: Ian Spink

1. For biographical material, I am indebted to two seminal articles on Spink by Sarah Rubidge, 'Ian Spink' *Dance Theatre Journal*, 3/3 (Autumn 1985) pp. 8–11; 'Weighing Spink's heart' *Dance Theatre Journal*, 5/2 (Summer 1987) pp. 10–13. Rubidge also generously lent me her notes from her interviews with Spink, May 1985, and 13 March 1987.

2. Interview with Spink, 30 July 1988.

3. Later, Spink conceived *Blue Table* (1981) as a criticism of funding institutions, amongst other aspects of establishment dance. The title was derived from Kurt Jooss' *The Green Table* (1932), another attack upon the establishment. Several members of the Arts Council dance panel were slyly represented in the piece.

4. Interview with Antony McDonald, 4 August 1988.

5. Spink quoted by Jan Murray in 'Political movements' *Time Out* (21–27 November 1980).

6. Interview with Betsy Gregory, 30 September 1988.

7. Stephen Goff, 'Ian Spink and Dancers' *Labaneye* (1981) p. 5.

8. Programme note on *Some Fugues*.

9. Interview with Spink, 30 July 1988.

10. Deborah Jowitt, 'London notebook' *The Village Voice* (October 1981).

11. Clement Crisp, 'Extemporary Dance' *The Financial Times* (12 January 1982).

12. Programme note on *Kondalilla*.

13. Spink quoted by Jan Murray in 'Political movements'.

14. Description and quotation taken from Brian Hoad, 'Young company turns Coppelia on her head' *The Bulletin*, n.d. (cutting in Dance Umbrella archive).

15. *Dark Coming* was the fourth in a series of eight solos by Mary Fulkerson expressing a woman's journey to understanding. This dance explores the dark areas of the mind, the descent into madness. Interview with Fulkerson, 16 October 1988.

16. Interview with Gregory, 30 September 1988.

17. Jowitt, 'Sinking into green fields' *The Village Voice* (3 August 1982).

18. The loop was a late development in the piece, appearing when Second Stride performed *De Gas* in 1982.

19. Jowitt, 'London Notebook'.

20. Spink in interview with Rubidge, May 1985.

21. Rubidge, 'New criteria – alternative evaluations' *Dance Theatre Journal*, 2/4 (Winter 1984) p. 38.

22. Jann Parry discusses the new wave of contemporary dance choreographers working in opera in 'Opera dances' *Opera Now* (April 1990) pp. 67–70.

23. *Ibid.*, p. 67.

24. Nicholas Kenyon, 'Even the blood runs green' *The Observer* (8 April 1990).

25. Spink quoted by Mark Pappenheim in 'The spell of the dance' *The Independent* (29 March 1990).

26. Holloway quoted by Antony Bye in 'Introducing *Clarissa*' *Music and Musicians* (May 1990) p. 14.

27. Holloway, '*Clarissa* – someone who needs to sing' *Opera* (May 1990) p. 530.

28. Description taken from the ICA publicity leaflet.

29. For instance, Ann Nugent, 'Secret Gardens: ICA' *Dance and Dancers* (May 1983) p. 48; Alastair Macaulay, 'Secret Gardens of dance theatre' *The Dancing Times* (April 1983) p. 537.

30. Goff, 'Cross-fertilisation' *Time Out* (4–10 February 1983).

31. Spink quoted by Rubidge in 'Weighing Spink's heart', p. 12.

32. Programme note on *Being British*.

33. Information related to the making of Spink's work from 1981 stems from Rubidge's articles and interviews, from discussions before and after performances, and from my interviews with Spink (30 July 1988), McDonald (4 August 1988), and Tim Albery (4 August 1988).

34. Gregory recalled in interview that the Second Stride dancers were asked not to produce abstract movement.

35. Macaulay, who has written with great insight about *New Tactics*, prefers to emphasize the cathartic, trusting nature of this final section, 'Second Stride second year' *Dance Theatre Journal*, 1/4 (Autumn 1983) pp. 11–12.

36. Oliver Sacks, *Awakenings* (London: Duckworth, 1973).

37. Programme note on *Further and Further Into Night*.

38. In the case of *Bösendorfer Waltzes*, more programme information would have been useful to audience appreciation, perhaps a collage of information in the spirit of the piece itself. It would have been especially useful to know the identities of the Surrealist and Dadaist figures represented.

39. The scores of the three ballets are referred to in their reversed chronological order. The 'systems' structure is based on the repetition of blocks of material.

40. Spink's intentions for *Weighing the Heart* are quoted by Rubidge in 'Weighing Spink's heart', p. 13.

41. Interviews with Spink (30 July 1988), and McDonald (4 August 1988).

42. David Hughes, 'Heaven Ablaze in His Breast' *Dance Theatre Journal*, 7/4 (February 1990) p. 15.

43. Spink's programme note on *Heaven Ablaze*.

44. Interview with Spink, 30 July 1988.

45. Roland Barthes, 'From work to text' in his *Image – Music – Text*, trans. Stephen Heath (New York: Hill and Wang, 1977) p. 159.

46. John Roberts' vivid term in 'Postmodernism, television and the visual arts' in Philip Hayward (ed.), *Picture This* (London: John Libbey, 1988) p. 61.

47. Charles Marowitz, 'Moving Being: anti-dance' *The Village Voice* (27 August 1970).

48. Hughes, 'Heaven Ablaze in His Breast', p. 15.

49. Macaulay, 'Umbrellitis' *The Dancing Times* (January 1985) p. 324.

50. Interview with McDonald, 4 August 1988.

51. Spink in Digital Dance Interview (video) (Reading: Digital, 1989).

52. Judith Mackrell, 'Words words words' *Dance Theatre Journal*, 3/1 (Spring 1985) p. 34.

53. Rainer quoted by Lucy Lippard, 'Yvonne Rainer on feminism and her film' in *From the Center* (New York: Dutton, 1976) p. 279.

54. The paintings were *Western Motel* (1957), *Office at Night* (1940), *New York Movie* (1939), *Summer in the City* (1949) and *Excursion into Philosophy* (1959).

55. Spink returned to this music after having used it earlier in *Some Fugues* (1981).

Index

Pages including illustrations are shown in *italic*.

263